W9-AVO-969

Brian:

May God Bless you as you begin the Next phase of your life. Our prayer is that you will "Stand Firm" in all that is important. "Be on your guard; stand firm in the faith; be 'a man' of courage; be strong. Do everything in Love."

1 Cor. 16: 13

Congratulations on your graduation!

Tom ♥ Rhoda

INTRODUCTION

THE BOOK OF ROMANS—A CLARION CALL TO CHRISTIANS

Down through the ages, men and women of God have stood firm for their faith, even in the face of death. The Book of Romans—the Apostle Paul's letter to the church in Rome—builds an unshakable doctrinal foundation for the faith and addresses issues central to the life of all believers. Paul also shares lessons learned in his own life laid down in the service of the Gospel. For these reasons, we have interwoven passages from this pivotal letter throughout *Standing Firm* for clarity and to help ground the reader in the faith. In Romans, the righteousness of God is proclaimed and God is exalted.

As you read the passages from this profound book of the Bible, intermingled with the marvelous and deeply moving quotes of men and women of faith, allow the Holy Spirit to teach you the need for a Savior, the debt of His love, the marvel of His grace, the wonder of His peace, the glory of His presence, the purpose of the law, the act of justification, the reality of faith, the acceptance of hope in the living Christ, God's eternal plans for His children, and the joy of the Lord. Let us commune in sweet relationship with God who inspired Paul to write the church at Rome a letter destined to preach the Gospel of Jesus Christ to the world!

As a memorial to all the great saints of the past and present, willing to STAND FIRM for the truth of God's Word, we dedicate this book.

~The Publisher

STANDING FIRM

*365 Devotionals to
Strengthen Your Faith*

Compiled by Patti M. Hummel
ISBN # 1404185453

Copyrights for translations:

Scripture quotations marked (KJV) are taken from the Holy Bible, King James Version, Cambridge, 1769.

Scripture quotations marked (NKJV) are taken from The Holy Bible: New King James Version (NKJV). Copyright © 1979, 1980, 1982 by Thomas Nelson, Inc. Used by permission. All rights reserved.

Cover and interior design by Greg Jackson, Jackson Design Co, llc

PARABLE

STANDING

365 DEVOTIONS TO STRENGTHEN YOUR FAITH

FIRM

*Paul, a bondservant of Jesus Christ, called to be an apostle,
separated to the gospel of God which He promised before through
His prophets in the Holy Scriptures, concerning
His Son Jesus Christ our Lord, who was born of the seed
of David according to the flesh, and declared to be the
Son of God with power according to the Spirit of holiness,
by the resurrection from the dead. Through Him we have received
grace and apostleship for obedience to the faith
among all nations for His name, among whom you also
are the called of Jesus Christ; To all who are in Rome,
beloved of God, called to be saints: Grace to you and
peace from God our Father and the Lord Jesus Christ.*

ROMANS 1:1-7 NKJV

STANDING FIRM

STANDING FIRM

Put on the whole armor of God, that you may be able to stand against the wiles of the devil. For we do not wrestle against flesh and blood, but against principalities, against powers, against the rulers of the darkness of this age, against spiritual hosts of wickedness in the heavenly places.

Therefore take up the whole armor of God, that you may be able to withstand in the evil day, and having done all, to stand. Stand therefore, having girded your waist with truth, having put on the breastplate of righteousness, and having shod your feet with the preparation of the gospel of peace; above all, taking the shield of faith with which you will be able to quench all the fiery darts of the wicked one.

And take the helmet of salvation, and the sword of the Spirit, which is the word of God; praying always with all prayer and supplication in the Spirit, being watchful to this end with all perseverance and supplication for all the saints—Peace to the brethren, and love with faith, from God the Father and the Lord Jesus Christ. Grace be with all those who love our Lord Jesus Christ in sincerity. Amen.

EPHESIANS 6:11-18, 23, 24 NKJV

IT'S ALL ABOUT LOVE

And above all things have fervent love for one another,
for "love will cover a multitude of sins."

——— I PETER 4:8 NKJV ———

The longer I live, the more I understand that the Christian life is "all about love." In all the contexts of our lives, we are tested again and again to see if we will let love prevail. Whether in our marriages, families or work, the Lord tests our love forbearance to see if we will choose to love when the other person disagrees with us. Even when persecution finally rears its head and the evil of another heart comes close to slaying us, we must choose love. It is in those moments that we become like Him. There isn't another way that takes us closer to the cross than this, that we love when we are misunderstood and betrayed. All too often, even in ministry with other Christians, we find ourselves at cross-purposes with another. Hot words can fly into the atmosphere, never to be retrieved. It is then that love, if it is truly in our hearts, can rise up to save the moment, to prevent the sin. And, it is then that we tread victorious on the ground Satan sought to control with his strategy to destroy relationships. The Christian life is not about getting the right doctrine correct and convincing everyone else about it. No, the Christian life is all above love. ~ Jacquelyn Sheppard (1943 –)

PEACE WITH GOD

Lord, thou wilt ordain peace for us:
for thou hast wrought all our works in us.
———— ISAIAH 26:12 KJV ————

There is Peace that comes from submission; tranquility of spirit, which is the crown and reward of obedience; repose, which is the very smile upon the face of faith, and all these things are given unto us along with the Grace and Mercy of our God. And the man that possesses these is at Peace with God, and at Peace with himself, so he may bear in his heart that singular blessing of a perfect tranquility and quiet amidst the distractions of duty, of sorrows, of losses, and of cares. "In everything by prayer and supplication with thanksgiving let your requests be known unto God; and the Peace of God which passeth all understanding shall keep your hearts and minds in Christ Jesus." And he who is thus at friendship with God, and in harmony with himself, and at rest from sorrows and cares, will surely find no enemies amongst men with whom he must needs be at war, but will be a son of Peace, and walk the world, meeting in them all a friend and a brother. So all discords may be quieted; even though still we have to fight the good fight of faith, we may do, like Gideon of old, build an altar to "Jehovah Shalom," the God of Peace. ~ Alexander Maclaren (1826-1910)

SACRILEGE

I beseech you therefore, brethren, by the mercies of God,
that you present your bodies a living sacrifice, holy,
acceptable to God, which is your reasonable service.

——————— ROMANS 12:1 NKJV ———————

Sacrilege we have always thought was the breaking into a church and stealing there from. That is not so; it is going into Church and putting something on the plate. Do not forget that. Sacrilege is centered in offering God something which costs nothing, because you think God is worth nothing. God looks for the giving at His alter of a gift that costs something. Men are perpetually bringing into the Christian church the things they do not need themselves. I know there is much sacrificial giving, thank God, but there is also an enormous amount of sacrilegious giving abroad in the world today, giving devoid of sacrifice. We offer to God in the Church, things which we would never offer to our governors. This is sacrilege. If the giving in the Church of God today was of the type and the pattern of the gift of the widow to the treasury in the days long since passed away, the work of God would never have to go begging to men and women outside the Church.

~ G. Campbell Morgan (1898-1945)

THE HEART OF JESUS

. . . do this in remembrance of Me.

LUKE 22:19 NKJV

The Best Preparation is — to look into the heart of Jesus. When you understand what He that sits on the throne desires for you, how He longs after you, what He has prepared for you, this will more than aught else set your desires and longings in motion, and impart to you the right preparation. That word of Jesus at the Paschal table enables me to look into His heart. He knew that he must go from that feast to the cross. He knew that His body must be broken, and His blood shed, in order that He might really be your Passover. He knew how in that night they should grieve and betray Him, and yet He says: "With desire have I desired to eat this Passover with you." What a love this is! And Jesus is still the same. Even with you, poor sinner, He earnestly desires to eat the Passover. Yea, on the throne of heaven, He looks forward with longing to the day of the Supper, to eat with you, and to quicken you. O man, let your sluggishness put you to shame: Jesus earnestly desires — Jesus greatly longs — to observe the Supper with you; He would not enjoy the food of heavenly life alone; He would fain eat of it along with you.

~ Andrew Murray (1828-1917)

ANOINTED VESSELS

. . .that they all may be one, as You, Father, are in Me, and I in You; that they also may be one in Us, that the world may believe that You sent Me.

JOHN 17:21 NKJV

In the task of world evangelization that faces the church today, we must have believers who are anointed with Holy Spirit power, not just filled with enthusiasm and equipped with better methods. It is time for us to pray for God's power to anoint His people and for His Glory to fill His Church. Just as Christ said He could do nothing of Himself and lived in unbroken union with the Father, so must we if we are to accomplish the task we've been given. We cannot complete the Great Commission unless we have a deeper work of union with our Lord that empowers us for the evangelization of the world.

Christ prayed that we would be one in Him and in the Father so that the world would believe and be convinced that He was sent from God. We may never completely agree on doctrine until we are in Heaven but while we are still here on earth, our unity and common purpose in Christ constrains us to work together and love one another. We can be One in Him, even though there may be small differences in doctrine and practices. Let us live out the words of John 17 so that He may pour out anointing upon us and glorify Himself in His blood-bought believers to reach the world. ~ Glenn Sheppard (1943-)

First, I thank my God through Jesus Christ for you all, that your faith is spoken of throughout the whole world. For God is my witness, whom I serve with my spirit in the gospel of His Son, that without ceasing I make mention of you always in my prayers, making request if, by some means, now at last I may find a way in the will of God to come to you. For I long to see you, that I may impart to you some spiritual gift, so that you may be established—that is, that I may be encouraged together with you by the mutual faith both of you and me. Now I do not want you to be unaware, brethren, that I often planned to come to you (but was hindered until now), that I might have some fruit among you also, just as among the other Gentiles. I am a debtor both to Greeks and to barbarians, both to wise and to unwise. So, as much as is in me, I am ready to preach the gospel to you who are in Rome also.

ROMANS 1:8-15 NKJV

THE UNSURPASSED INTIMACY
OF TESTED FAITH

Jesus saith unto her, Said I not unto thee, that,
if thou wouldest believe, thou shouldest see the glory of God?

JOHN 11:40 KJV

Every time you venture out in your life of faith, you will find something in your circumstances that, from a commonsense standpoint, will flatly contradict your faith. But common sense is not faith, and faith is not common sense. In fact, they are as different as the natural life and the spiritual. Can you trust Jesus Christ where your common sense cannot trust Him? Can you venture out with courage on the words of Jesus Christ, while the realities of your commonsense life continue to shout, "It's all a lie?" When you are on the mountaintop, it's easy to say, "Oh yes, I believe God can do it," but you have to come down from the mountain to the demon-possessed valley and face the realities that scoff at your Mount-of-Transfiguration belief (Luke 9:28-42). Every time my theology becomes clear to my own mind, I encounter something that contradicts it. As soon as I say, "I believe God shall supply all [my] need," the testing of my faith begins (Philippians 4:19). When my strength runs dry and my vision is blinded, will I endure this trial of my faith victoriously or will I turn back in defeat?
~ Oswald Chambers (1874-1917)

PARADISE

I wait for the Lord, my soul doth wait, and in his word do I hope.
———— PSALM 130:5 KJV ————

What is Paradise? All things that are. For all things are good and pleasant, and may therefore fitly be called Paradise. It is also said, that Paradise is an outer court of heaven. In the same way, this world is truly an outer court of the eternal, or of eternity; and this is specially true of any temporal things or creatures which manifest the Eternal or remind us of eternity; for the creatures are a guide and path to God and eternity. Thus the world is an outer court of eternity, and therefore it may well be called a Paradise, for so indeed it is. And in this Paradise all things are lawful except one tree and its fruit. That is to say, of all things that exist, nothing is forbidden or contrary to God, except one thing only. That one thing is self-will, or to will otherwise than as the eternal Will would have it. Not that everything which is so done is in itself contrary to the eternal Will, but in so far as it is done from a different will, or otherwise than from the Eternal and Divine Will.
~ Johannes Eckhart (1260-1327)

ASSURANCE

Now faith is the substance of things hoped for,
the evidence of things not seen.

HEBREWS 11:1 NKJV

Assurance will make us active and lively in God's service; it will excite prayer, and quicken obedience. As diligence begets assurance, so assurance begets diligence. Assurance will not breed self-security in the soul, but industry. Doubting discourages us in God's service, but the assurance of His favour breeds joy. "The joy of the Lord is our strength." Assurance makes us mount up to heaven, as eagles, in holy duties; it is like the Spirit in Ezekiel's wheels, that moved them, and lifted them up. Faith will make us walk, but assurance will make us run: we shall never think we can do enough for God. Assurance will be as wings to the birds, as weights to the clock, to set all the wheels of obedience running. ~ Thomas Watson (1620-1686)

A CALL TO CHRIST

And let the peace of God rule in your hearts,
to which also you were called in one body; and be thankful.

COLOSSIANS 3:15 NKJV

Abraham Lincoln, the great emancipator, is reported to have said: "Those who deny freedom to others deserve it not for themselves, and, under a just God, cannot long retain it." On more than one occasion Jesus laid down this principle concerning the use and abuse of gospel gifts and privileges: "For whosoever hath (made gain), to him shall be given (still more to invest), and he shall have more abundance; but whosoever hath not (made gain), from him shall be taken away even that he hath." It is as though He had said, Make gain with your spiritual gifts, your earthly riches, your gospel freedoms — pass then on to others. Use them, or lose them — it is divine law.

~ Abraham Lincoln (1809-1865)

THE UPLIFT OF THE CROSS

"And I, if I be lifted up from the earth, will draw all men unto me."
—— JOHN 12:32 KJV ——

Speaking of it He said, "I, if I be lifted up from the earth." To Him it brought no sense of degradation or failure, but only a sense of glory and honor and victory. As He spoke of it to His disciples in advance it was always only as a stepping stone to the resurrection which was to follow. On the Mount of Transfiguration His heavenly visitors conversed of nothing else, but they spoke of it as "his decease which he should accomplish at Jerusalem," and the word decease expresses not so much the idea of death as of departure. It was but the beginning of a glorious ascension which was to lift Him up to higher honors and loftier ministries through the ages to come. The Apostle Paul, speaking of the cross, can only express himself in terms of the loftiest exultation, "God forbid that I should glory, save in the cross of our Lord Jesus Christ." In the visions of the Apocalypse we find it occupying the place of highest honor in the heavenly world. It is the continual theme of the songs, both of the angels and the ransomed, and the highest distinction of Him who shares the Father's throne is the mark of the cross. He is described as the "Lamb that was slain." *He died for all, that they which live should not henceforth live unto themselves, but unto him that died for them, and rose again!* ~ A. B. Simpson (1844-1919)

CHRIST THE COMFORTER

But the Comforter, which is the Holy Ghost, whom the Father will send in my name, he shall teach you all things, and bring all things to your remembrance, whatsoever I have said unto you.

JOHN 14:26 KJV

Job had comforters, and I think he spoke the truth when he said, "Miserable comforters are ye all." But I dare say they esteemed themselves wise; and when the young man Elihu rose to speak, they thought he had a world of impudence. Were they not "grave and reverend seigniors?" Did not they comprehend his grief and sorrow? . . . But they did not find out the cause ... It is a bad case when the doctor mistakes a disease and gives a wrong prescription, and so perhaps kills the patient. Sometimes, when we go and visit people, we mistake their disease; we want to comfort them on this point, whereas they do not require any such comfort at all, and they would be better left alone, than spoiled by such unwise comforters as we are. But oh, how wise the Holy Spirit is! He takes the soul, lays it on the table, and dissects it in a moment; He finds out the root of the matter, He sees where the complaint is, and then He applies the knife where something is required to be taken away, or puts a plaster where the sore is; and He never mistakes. O how wise is the blessed Holy Ghost; from every comforter I turn, and leave them all, for thou art He who alone givest the wisest consolation. ~ Charles H. Spurgeon (1834-1892)

For I am not ashamed of the gospel of Christ, for it is the power of God to salvation for everyone who believes, for the Jew first and also for the Greek. For in it the righteousness of God is revealed from faith to faith; as it is written, "The just shall live by faith." For the wrath of God is revealed from heaven against all ungodliness and unrighteousness of men, who suppress the truth in unrighteousness, because what may be known of God is manifest in them, for God has shown it to them.

ROMANS 1:16-19 NKJV

STANDING FIRM

BELIEVER'S EXPERIENCES

So then with the mind I myself serve the law of God,
but with the flesh the law of sin.

ROMANS 7:25 KJV

A BELIEVER is to be known not only by his peace and joy, but by his warfare and distress. His peace is peculiar: it flows from Christ; it is heavenly, it is holy peace. His warfare is as peculiar: it is deep-seated, agonising, and ceases not till death. If the Lord will, many of us have the prospect of sitting down next Sabbath at the Lord's table. Coming to Christ takes away your fear of the law; but it is the Holy Spirit coming into your heart that makes you love the law. The Holy Spirit is no more frightened away from that heart; He comes and softens it; He takes out the stony heart and puts in a heart of flesh; and there He writes the holy, holy, holy law of God. . .The law of God is sweet to that soul. . .Oh that all the world but knew that holiness and happiness are one! Oh that all the world were one holy family, joyfully coming under the pure rules of the gospel! Try yourselves by this. Can you say, "I delight," etc.? Do you remember when you hated the law of God? Do you love it now? Do you long for the time when you shall live fully under it — holy as God is holy, pure as Christ is pure?

~ Robert Murray McCheyne (1813-1843)

WHAT IS GOD'S WILL?

. . . The God of our fathers hath chosen thee,
that thou shouldest know His will . . .
—————— ACTS 22:14 KJV ——————

When God puts down His great will beside me telling me to do it, He puts down just beside it as great a thing, His Love. And as my soul trembles at the fearfulness of will, Love comes with its calm omnipotence, and draws it to Himself; then takes my timid will and twines it around His, till mine is fierce with passion to serve, and strong to do His will. Just as if some mighty task were laid to an infant's hand, and the engine-grasp of a giant strengthened it with his own. Where God's law is, is God's love. Look at Law — it withers your very soul with its stern inexorable face. But look at Love, or look at God's will, which means look at Love's will, and you are re-assured, and your heart grows strong. No martyr dies for abstract truth. For a person, for God, he will die a triple death. So no man will die for God's law. But for God he will do it. Where God's will, then, seems strong to command, God's love is strong to obey. Hence the profound texts, "Love is the fulfilling of the law." "And this is the love of God that we keep His commandments, and His commandments are not grievous."

~ Henry Drummond (1851-1897)

ZION STANDS BY HILLS SURROUNDED

Zion stands by hills surrounded,
Zion, kept by power divine;
All her foes shall be confounded
Though the world in arms combine.
Happy Zion, What a favored lot is thine!
Every human tie may perish,
Friend to friend unfaithful prove,
Mothers cease their own to cherish,
Heaven and earth at last remove;
But no changes can attend Jehovah's love.
In the furnace God may prove thee,
Thence to bring thee forth more bright,
But can never cease to love thee;
Thou art precious in His sight.
God is with thee,
God, thine everlasting Light.
~ Thomas Kelly (1769-1854)

CHRIST THE DELIVERER

. . .but he that doth the will of God abideth for ever.
——— I JOHN 2:17 KJV ———

Christ is God's Deliverer for the world: This is God's method of deliverance. He gives us in Christ a new center, and the wheel of life runs truly and smoothly because it is truly centered. But because Christ is the center of the whole kingdom of God, in heaven and on earth, the life that is centered in Him is thereby in harmony with God and all His kingdom, the world of order, harmony, peace, and joy, the world where one will alone prevails, the will of God — and being such, is therefore eternal but for the same reason which a life is eccentric, out of center, with that portion of the universe, heavenly and earthly, which is not centered in Christ. If two sets of powerful machinery were at work in the same space, there would arise friction, clash, damage. In this age, this situation induces conflict of spirit and practical trouble for the Christ-centered man. But he can endure with patience and confidence, seeing that he knows that Christ has conquered this world, and that His world, the heavenly, will prevail finally. Christ is God's Savior for the individual and for the world: association with Him, by faith and obedience, is God's method of salvation. There is no other, nor can there be (John 3:35, 36). ~ G.H. Lang (1874-1958)

GOD, OUR PROVISION

But my God shall supply all your need
according to His riches in glory by Christ Jesus.
PHILIPPIANS 4:19 KJV

What can we possibly need that we do not find provided in Him? Do we hopelessly groan under the curse of the broken law, hanging menacingly over us? Christ has "redeemed us from the curse of the law, having been made a curse for us" (Gal. 3:13). Do we know that only he that worketh righteousness is acceptable to God, and despair of attaining life on so unachievable a condition? Christ Jesus "hath of God been made unto us righteousness" (I Cor. 1:30). Do we loathe ourselves in the pollution of our sins, and know that God is greater than we, and that we must be an offence in His holy sight? The blood of Christ cleanseth us from all sin (I John 1:7). But do we not need faith, that we may be made one with Him and so secure these benefits? Faith, too, is the gift of God: and that we believe on Him is granted by God in the behalf of Christ (Phil. 1:29). Nothing has been forgotten, nothing neglected, nothing left unprovided. In the person of Jesus Christ, the great God, in His perfect wisdom and unfailing power, has taken our place before the outraged justice of God and under His perfect law, and has wrought out a complete salvation. ~ B.B. Warfield (1851-1921)

THE WORKING CHRIST

Is not this the carpenter. . .?

MARK 6:3 KJV

There are few places where human nature can be better studied than in a country village; for there one sees the whole of each individual life and knows all one's neighbors thoroughly. In a city far more people are seen, but far fewer known; it is only the outside of life that is visible. In a village it is the view outwards of life that is visible. In a village the view outwards is circumscribed; but the view downwards is deep, and the view upwards unimpeded. Nazareth was a notoriously wicked town, as we learn from the proverbial question, Can any good thing come out of Nazareth? Jesus had no acquaintance with sin in His own soul, but in the town He had a full exhibition of the awful problem with which it was to be His life-work to deal. He was still further brought into contact with human nature by His trade. That He worked as a carpenter in Joseph's shop there can be no doubt. Who could know better than His own townsmen, who asked, in their astonishment at His preaching, Is not this the carpenter? It would be difficult to exhaust the significance of the fact that God chose for His Son, when He dwelt among men, out of all the possible positions in which He might have placed Him, the lot of a working man. It stamped men's common toils with everlasting honor. It acquainted Jesus with the feelings of the multitude, and helped Him to know what was in man. It was afterwards said that He knew this so well that He needed not that any man should teach Him. ~ James Stalker (1848-1927)

For since the creation of the world His invisible attributes are clearly seen, being understood by the things that are made, even His eternal power and Godhead, so that they are without excuse, because, although they knew God, they did not glorify Him as God, nor were thankful, but became futile in their thoughts, and their foolish hearts were darkened. Professing to be wise, they became fools, and changed the glory of the incorruptible God into an image made like corruptible man—and birds and four-footed animals and creeping things. Therefore God also gave them up to uncleanness, in the lusts of their hearts, to dishonor their bodies among themselves, who exchanged the truth of God for the lie, and worshiped and served the creature rather than the Creator, who is blessed forever. Amen.

—— ROMANS 1:20-25 NKJV ——

STANDING FIRM

REDEEMED

Therefore doth my Father love me, because I lay down my life,
that I might take it again. No man taketh it from me, but I lay it
down of myself. I have power to lay it down, and I have power to
take it again. This commandment have I received of my Father.

JOHN 10:17, 18 KJV

The death of Christ is, my friends, the most wonderful event past, present, or future in the whole universe. It is so in the eye of God. "Therefore doth my Father love me, because I lay down my life." There is nothing in the whole world so lovely as his Son. It is not only for his Godhead, but on account of his manhood, through which he laid down his life. "Therefore doth my Father love me, because I laid down my life." These words of Christ, "I lay down my life," are dearer to God than a thousand worlds. It is the same in the eyes of the redeemed. All the redeemed love Christ, because he laid down his life. John says, "I beheld, and lo, in the midst of the throne, and of the four beasts, and in the midst of the elders, stood a lamb as it had been slain. And when he had taken the book, the four beasts, and four and twenty elders fell down before the Lamb, having every one of them harps, and golden vials full of odours, which are the prayers of saints. And they sang a new song, saying, Thou art worthy to take the book, and to open the seals thereof; for thou was slain, and hast redeemed us to God by thy blood. ~ Robert Murray McCheyne (1813-1843)

IN HUMILITY

Let this mind be in you, which was also in Christ Jesus . . . But made
himself of no reputation, and took upon him the form of a servant
and was made in the likeness of men . . . he humbled himself,
and became obedient unto death, even the death of the cross.

PHILIPPIANS 2:5, 7, 8 KJV

Although Jesus made His entry on the stage of life so humbly and silently; although the citizens of Bethlehem dreamed not what had happened in their midst; although the emperor of Rome knew not that his decree had influenced the nativity of a king who was yet to bear rule, not only over the Roman world, but over many a land where Rome's eagles never flew; although the history of mankind went thundering forward next morning in the channels of its ordinary interests, quite unconscious of the event which had happened, yet it did not altogether escape notice. As the babe leaped in the womb of the aged Elizabeth when the mother of her Lord approached her, so when He who brought the new world with Him appeared, there sprang up anticipation and forebodings of the truth in various representatives of the old world that was passing. There went through sensitive and waiting soul, here and there, a dim and half-conscious thrill, which drew them round the Infant's cradle. Look at the group which gathered to gaze on Him! It represented in miniature the whole of His future history.

~ James Stalker (1848-1927)

HE IS A GOD OF POWER

. . .far above all principality and power and might and dominion, and every name that is named, not only in this age but also in that which is to come.
———— EPHESIANS 1:21 NKJV ————

There is no want of power in God to cast wicked men into hell at any moment. Men's hands cannot be strong when God rises up. The strongest have no power to resist Him, nor can any deliver out of His hands. He is not only able to cast wicked men into hell, but He can most easily do it. Sometimes an earthly prince meets with a great deal of difficulty to subdue a rebel, who has found means to fortify himself, and has made himself strong by the numbers of his followers. But it is not so with God. . .Though hand join in hand, and vast multitudes of God's enemies combine and associate themselves, they are easily broken in pieces. They are as great heaps of light chaff before the whirlwind; or large quantities of dry stubble before devouring flames. We find it easy to tread on and crush a worm that we see crawling on the earth; so it is easy for us to cut or singe a slender thread that any thing hangs by: thus easy is it for God, when He pleases, to cast His enemies down to hell. What are we, that we should think to stand before Him, at whose rebuke the earth trembles, and before whom the rocks are thrown down? ~ Jonathan Edwards (1703-1758)

A JOYOUS HEART

. . .the joy of the LORD is your strength.
NEHEMIAH 8:10 KJV

"THE sad heart tires in a mile," is a frequent proverb. What a difference there is between the energy of the healthy, joyous heart and the forced activity of the morbid and depressed one! The one leaps to its task, the other creeps to it. The one discovers its meat and drink in self-sacrifice, the other limps, and stoops, and crawls. If you want to be strong for life's work, be sure to keep a glad heart. But, be equally sure to be glad with the joy of Lord. There is a counterfeit of it in the world, of which we must beware — an outward merry-making, jesting, and mad laughter, which hides an aching and miserable heart. . .Ours must be the joy of the Lord. It begins with the assurance of forgiveness and acceptance in the Beloved. It is nourished in trial and tribulation, which veil outward sources of consolation, and lead us to rejoice in God through our Lord Jesus. . .It lives not in the gifts of God, but in God Himself. It is the fruit of the Spirit, who begets in us love, joy, peace, long-suffering. Get the Lord Himself to fill your soul, and joy will be as natural as the murmur of a brook to its flow. ~ F. B. Meyer (1847-1929)

CHRIST, THE TEACHER

*"Rabbi, we know that You are a teacher come from God;
for no one can do these signs that You do unless God is with him."*
—— JOHN 3:2 NKJV ——

John calls Jesus "Word of God." What is a word? It is the invisible thought taking form: Wordsworth says, "Language is the incarnation of thought." Spoken words are sounds, articulate and significant: sounds in which there is soul. Written words are visible signs of intelligence and intellect; thought has determined their exact form, order, relation. God is represented as pure Spirit, and cannot be known by sense. He would communicate with man, and so puts His thought and love in a visible form in Christ, who is therefore beautifully called the living 'Word of God.' As God does everything perfectly, we are justified in looking for such an expression of His mind and heart in His incarnate Son as shall excel all other revelations of Himself. In Christ, as the Word of God, we may properly expect to find the clear and unmistakable stamp of the divine mind. In His teaching there must be a divine authority, majesty, originality, spirituality, vitality, essential worth and practical power, such as no merely human teaching could display.
~ Jonathan Edwards (1703-1758)

PSALM 8

O LORD, our Lord, how wondrous great Is thine exalted name!
The glories of thy heav'nly state Let men and babes proclaim.
When I behold thy works on high, The moon that rules the night,
And stars that well adorn the sky, Those moving worlds of light.
Lord, what is man, or all his race, Who dwells so far below,
That thou should visit him with grace, And love his nature so?
That thine eternal Son should bear To take a mortal form;
Made lower than His angels are, To save a dying worm?
Yet while He lived on earth unknown, And men would not adore,
The obedient seas and fishes own His Godhead and His power.
The waves lay spread beneath His feet; And fish, at His command,
Bring their large shoals to Peter's net, Bring tribute to His hand.
Those lesser glories of the Son Shone through the fleshly cloud;
Now, we behold Him on His throne, And men confess Him God.
Let Him be crowned with majesty, Who bowed His head to death;
And be His honors sounded high, By all things that have breath.
Jesus, our Lord, how wondrous great Is thine exalted name!
The glories of thy heavenly state Let the whole earth proclaim.
~ King David (10th Century B.C.) and Isaac Watts (1674–1748)

For this reason God gave them up to vile passions. For even their women exchanged the natural use for what is against nature. Likewise also the men, leaving the natural use of the woman, burned in their lust for one another, men with men committing what is shameful, and receiving in themselves the penalty of their error which was due. And even as they did not like to retain God in their knowledge, God gave them over to a debased mind, to do those things which are not fitting; being filled with all unrighteousness, sexual immorality, wickedness, covetousness, maliciousness; full of envy, murder, strife, deceit, evil-mindedness; they are whisperers, backbiters, haters of God, violent, proud, boasters, inventors of evil things, disobedient to parents, undiscerning, untrustworthy, unloving, unforgiving, unmerciful; who, knowing the righteous judgment of God, that those who practice such things are deserving of death, not only do the same but also approve of those who practice them.

ROMANS 1:26-32 NKJV

STANDING FIRM

GROW IN KNOWLEDGE

. . . grow in the grace and knowledge of our Lord and Savior. . .
—————— II PETER 3:18 NKJV ——————

The knowledge of a person is not the same as the knowledge of a creed or of a thought or of a book. We are to grow in the knowledge of Christ, which includes but is more than the intellectual apprehension of the truths concerning Him. He might turn the injunction into — "Increase your acquaintance with your Savior." Many Christians never get to be any more intimate with Him than they were when they were first introduced to Him. They are on a kind of bowing acquaintance with their Master, and have little more than that. We sometimes begin an acquaintance which we think promises to ripen into a friendship, but are disappointed. Circumstances or some want of congeniality which is discovered prevents its growth. So with not a few professing Christians. They have got no nearer to Jesus Christ than when they first knew Him. Their friendship has not grown. It has never reached the stage where all restraints are laid aside and there is perfect confidence. "Grow in the knowledge of your Lord and Savior Jesus Christ." Get more and more intimate with Him, nearer to Him, and franker and more cordial with Him day by day. ~ Alexander Maclaren (1826-1910)

CALVARY'S CROSS

. . .Jesus, the author and finisher of our faith. . .endured the cross. . .
HEBREWS 12:2 NKJV

We take a Red Cross, and with it symbolize the ministry of healing. Our poets and hymn-writers sing to us of "the wondrous cross," "the blessed cross." But all this ought not to hide from us the fact that originally the cross was a thing unspeakable, shameful, and degrading. "Cursed is everyone that hangeth on a tree," said Paul, quoting Deuteronomy. That was how Jewish feeling expressed it; and Roman sentiment was the same. "This cruelest, most hideous of punishments," said Cicero, using words in which you can almost hear the shudder — "crudelissimum taeterrimumque supplicium." "Never may it," he said elsewhere, "come near the bodies of Roman citizens, never near their thoughts or eyes or ears!" Devised in the first instance in semi-barbaric Oriental lands, death by crucifixion was reserved by the Romans for slaves and for criminals of the most abandoned kind. It was a fate of utter ignominy . . . That the Messiah should die such a death was utterly beyond belief. Yet so it was. Everything which Christ ever touched — the cross included — he adorned and transfigured and haloed with splendour and beauty; but let us never forget out of what appalling depths He has set the cross on high. ~ James S. Stewart (1783-1858)

PERSONAL REVELATION OF GOD

In the beginning was the Word, and the Word
was with God, and the Word was God.
—— JOHN 1:1 NKJV ——

No one can too fully understand, or too deeply feel, the necessity of taking home the Bible with all it contains, as a message sent from Heaven to him; nor can too earnestly desire or seek the promised Spirit to teach him the true spiritual import of all its contents. He must have the Bible made a personal revelation of God to his own soul. It must become his own book. He must know Christ for himself. He must know him in his different relations. He must know him in his blessed and infinite fullness, or he cannot abide in him, and unless he abide in Christ, he can bring forth none of the fruits of holiness. 'Except a man abide in me, he is cast forth as a branch, and is withered.' [John 15:6].
~ Charles G. Finney (1792-1875)

THE DWELLING PLACE OF GOD

In my Father's house are many mansions. . .
I go to prepare a place for you.

JOHN 14:2 KJV

There are some people who depend so much upon their reason that they reason away God. They say God is not a person we can ever see. They say God is a Spirit. So He is, but He is a person too; and became a man and walked the earth once. Scripture tells us very plainly that God has a dwelling-place. There is no doubt whatsoever about that. A place indicates personality. God's dwelling-place is in heaven. He has a dwelling-place, and we are going to be inmates of it. Therefore we shall see Him. . .We believe this is just as much a place and just as much a city as is New York, London or Paris. We believe in it a good deal more, because earthly cities will pass away, but this city will remain forever. It has foundations whose builder and maker is God. Some of the grandest cities the world has ever known have not had foundations strong enough to last. ~ Dwight L. Moody (1837-1899)

STANDING FIRM

I WANT TO BE LIKE YOU, LORD!

And walk in love, as Christ also hath loved us, and given himself for us an offering and a sacrifice to God for a sweetsmelling savour.
———— EPHESIANS 5:2 KJV ————

O Thou who hast redeemed me to be a Son of God, and called me from vanity to inherit all things, I praise Thee, that having loved me and given Thyself for me, Thou commandest us saying, As I have loved you, so do ye also love one another. Wherein Thou hast commanded all men, so to love me, as to lay down their lives for my peace and welfare. Since Love is the end for which heaven and earth was made, enable me to see and discern the sweetness of so great a treasure. And since Thou hast advanced me into the Throne of God, in the bosom of all Angels and men; commanding them by this precept, to give me an union and communion with Thee in their dearest affection; in their highest esteem; and in the most near and inward room and seat in their hearts; give me the grace which Saint Paul prayed for, that I may be acceptable to the Saints, fill me with Thy Holy Spirit, and make my soul and life beautiful, make me all wisdom, goodness and love, that I may be worthy to be esteemed and accepted of them. That being delighted also with their felicity, I may be crowned with Thine, and with their glory.
~ Thomas Traherne (1636-1674)

STANDING FIRM

CHRIST CALLS HIS DISCIPLES

Then said Jesus unto his disciples, If any man will come after me,
let him deny himself, and take up his cross, and follow me.

MATTHEW 16:24 KJV

Overturning the overweening opinion we form of our own virtue, and detecting the hypocrisy in which we delight, it removes our pernicious carnal confidence, teaching us, when thus humbled, to recline on God alone, so that we neither are oppressed nor despond. Then victory is followed by hope, inasmuch as the Lord, by performing what he has promised, establishes his truth in regard to the future. Were these the only reasons, it is surely plain how necessary it is for us to bear the cross. It is of no little importance to be rid of your self-love, and made fully conscious of your weakness; so impressed with a sense of your weakness as to learn to distrust yourself—to distrust yourself so as to transfer your confidence to God, reclining on him with such heartfelt confidence as to trust in his aid, and continue invincible to the end, standing by his grace so as to perceive that he is true to his promises, and so assured of the certainty of his promises as to be strong in hope. ~ John Calvin (1509-1564)

Therefore you are inexcusable, O man, whoever you are who judge, for in whatever you judge another you condemn yourself; for you who judge practice the same things. But we know that the judgment of God is according to truth against those who practice such things. And do you think this, O man, you who judge those practicing such things, and doing the same, that you will escape the judgment of God? Or do you despise the riches of His goodness, forbearance, and longsuffering, not knowing that the goodness of God leads you to repentance? But in accordance with your hardness and your impenitent heart you are treasuring up for yourself wrath in the day of wrath and revelation of the righteous judgment of God, who "will render to each one according to his deeds": eternal life to those who by patient continuance in doing good seek for glory, honor, and immortality; but to those who are self-seeking and do not obey the truth, but obey unrighteousness—indignation and wrath, tribulation and anguish, on every soul of man who does evil, of the Jew first and also of the Greek; but glory, honor, and peace to everyone who works what is good, to the Jew first and also to the Greek. For there is no partiality with God.

—— Romans 2:1-11 NKJV ——

STANDING FIRM

JESUS' SURRENDER OF HIMSELF

...Christ also loved the Church, and gave Himself for it; that He might
sanctify and cleanse it. . . that He might present it to himself a glorious
Church, not having spot, or wrinkle, or any such thing; but that it
should be holy and without blemish.

EPHESIANS 5:25-27 KJV

Hear still a word of God: 'Who gave Himself for us, that He might redeem us from all iniquity, and purify unto Himself a people for His own possession, zealous of good works.' Yes: it is to prepare for Himself a pure people, a people of His own, a zealous people, that Jesus gives Himself. When I receive Him, when I believe that He gave Himself to do this for me, I shall certainly experience it. I shall be purified through Him, shall be held fast as His possession, and be filled with zeal and joy to work for Him. And mark, further, how the operation of this surrender of Himself will especially be that He shall then have us entirely for Himself: 'that He might present us to Himself.' 'that He might purify us to Himself, a people of His own' . . . The surrender is a mutual one: the love comes from both sides. His giving of Himself makes such an impression on my heart, that my heart with the self-same love and joy becomes entirely His. Through giving Himself to me, He of Himself takes possession of me; He becomes mine and I His. I know that I have Jesus wholly for me, and that He has me wholly for Him. ~ Andrew Murray (1827-1917)

WALKING WITH GOD (Part 1)

. . . Enoch walked with God: and he was not; for God took him.
——— GENESIS 5:24 KJV ———

Various are the pleas and arguments which men of corrupt minds frequently urge against yielding obedience to the just and holy commands of God. But, perhaps, one of the most common objections that they make is this, that our Lord's commands are not practicable, because contrary to flesh and blood; and consequently, that he is 'an hard master, reaping where he has not sown, and gathering where he has not strewed'. These we find were the sentiments entertained by that wicked and slothful servant mentioned in the 25th of St. Matthew; and are undoubtedly the same with many which are maintained in the present wicked and adulterous generation. The Holy Ghost foreseeing this, hath taken care to inspire holy men of old, to record the examples of many holy men and women; who, even under the Old Testament dispensation, were enabled cheerfully to take Christ's yoke upon them, and counted his service perfect freedom. The large catalogue of saints, confessors, and martyrs, drawn up in the 11th chapter to the Hebrews, abundantly evidences the truth of this observation. What a great cloud of witnesses have we there presented to our view? All eminent for their faith, but some shining with a greater degree of luster than do others.
~ George Whitefield (1714-1777)

WALKING WITH GOD (Part 2)

. . . Enoch walked with God: and he was not; for God took him.
———— GENESIS 5:24 KJV ————

The proto-martyr Abel leads the van. And next to him we find Enoch mentioned, not only because he was next in order of time, but also on account of his exalted piety . . . have here a short but very full and glorious account, both of his behavior in this world, and the triumphant manner of his entry into the next. The former is contained in these words, 'And Enoch walked with God'. The latter in these, 'and he was not: for God took him'. He was not; that is, he was not found, he was not taken away in the common manner, he did not see death; for God had translated him. Who this Enoch was, does not appear so plainly . . . he seems to have been a person of public character . . . like Noah, a preacher of righteousness. And, if we may credit the apostle Jude, he was a flaming preacher. For he quotes one of his prophecies, wherein he saith, 'Behold, the Lord cometh with ten thousands of his saints, to execute judgment upon all, and to convince all that are ungodly among them, of all their ungodly deeds which they have ungodly committed, and of all their hard speeches, which ungodly sinners have spoken against him'. But whether a public or private person, he has a noble testimony given him in the lively oracles.
~ George Whitefield (1714-1777)

WALKING WITH GOD (Part 3)

. . . Enoch walked with God: and he was not; for God took him.
———— GENESIS 5:24 KJV ————

The author of the epistle to the Hebrews saith, that before his translation he had this testimony, 'that he pleased God'; and his being translated, was a proof of it beyond all doubt. And I would observe, that it was wonderful wisdom in God to translate Enoch and Elijah under the Old Testament dispensation, that hereafter, when it should be asserted that the Lord Jesus was carried into heaven, it might not seem a thing altogether incredible to the Jews; since they themselves confessed that two of their own prophets had been translated several hundred hears before. But it is not my design to detain you any longer, by enlarging, or making observations, on Enoch's short but comprehensive character: the thing I have in view being to give a discourse, as the Lord shall enable, upon a weighty and a very important subject; I mean, walking with God. 'And Enoch walked with God.' If so much as this can be truly said of you and me after our decease, we shall not have any reason to complain that we have lived in vain. ~ George Whitefield (1714-1777)

LET GOD LEAD

"But why do you call me 'Lord, Lord,'
and do not the things which I say?"
—————— L U K E 6 : 4 6 N K J V ——————

Struggle not to over do, for when it is time convenient, and thou canst be any way useful to thy Neighbour; God will call thee forth, and put thee in the employment that will best suit with thee: That thought belongs only to him, and to thee, to continue in thy rest, disengaged, and wholly resigned up to the Divine will and pleasure. Don't think that in that condition thou art idle: He is busied enough, who is always ready waiting to perform the Will of God. Who takes heed to himself for God's sake, does every thing; because, one pure Act of internal Resignation, is worth more than a hundred thousand Exercises for ones own Will. Though the Cistern be capable to contain much Water, yet it must still be without it, till Heaven favour it with Rain. Be at rest . . . humble and resigned, to every thing that God shall be pleased to do with thee, leave the care to God, for he as a Loving Father, knows best . . . conform thy self totally to his Will, perfection being founded in that, inasmuch as he who doeth the will of the Lord. . .Think not that God esteemeth him most, that doeth most. He is most beloved who is most humble. . .and most correspondent to his own Internal Inspiration, and to the Divine will and pleasure. ~ Miguel de Molinos (1628-1696)

THE CHRISTIAN LIFE

". . .what will a man give in exchange for his soul?"
—— MATTHEW 16:26 NKJV ——

There is not one command in all the Gospel for public worship. . . religion or devotion which is to govern the ordinary actions of our life is to be found in almost every verse of Scripture. Our blessed Saviour and His Apostles are wholly taken up in doctrines that relate to common life. They call us to renounce the world. . .to renounce all its goods, to fear none of its evils, to reject its joys, and have no value for its happiness: to be as new-born babes, that are born into a new state of things: to live as pilgrims in spiritual watching, in holy fear, and heavenly aspiring after another life: to take up our daily cross, to deny ourselves, to profess the blessedness of mourning, to seek the blessedness of poverty of spirit: to forsake the pride and vanity of riches, to take no thought for the morrow, to live in the profoundest state of humility, to rejoice in worldly sufferings: to reject the lust of the flesh, the lust of the eyes, and the pride of life: to bear injuries, to forgive and bless our enemies, and to love mankind as God loveth them: to give up our whole hearts and affections to God, and strive to enter through the strait gate into a life of eternal glory.

~ William Law (1686-1761)

For as many as have sinned without law will also perish without law, and as many as have sinned in the law will be judged by the law (for not the hearers of the law are just in the sight of God, but the doers of the law will be justified; for when Gentiles, who do not have the law, by nature do the things in the law, these, although not having the law, are a law to themselves, who show the work of the law written in their hearts, their conscience also bearing witness, and between themselves their thoughts accusing or else excusing them) in the day when God will judge the secrets of men by Jesus Christ, according to my gospel.

ROMANS 2:12-16 NKJV

STANDING FIRM

COURAGE

*For I am persuaded that neither death, nor life, nor angels, nor
principalities, nor powers, nor things present, nor things to come.
Nor height, nor depth, nor any other creature, shall be able to
separate us from the love of God, which is in Christ Jesus our Lord.*
———— ROMANS 8:38, 39 KJV ————

I will go anywhere, as long as it be forward. If you have men who
will only come if they know there is a good road, I don't want them. I
want men who will come if there is no road at all. I will place no value
on anything I have or may possess except in relation to the kingdom of
Christ. I determined never to stop until I had come to the end and
achieved my purpose. Fear God and work hard.
~ David Livingstone (1813–1873)

INTIMACY OF GOD

I am the good shepherd. . .and am known of mine.
—— JOHN 10:14 KJV ——

Intimacy with God is the very essence of religion, and the foundation of discipleship. It is in intercourse with Father, Son, and Spirit that the most real parts of our lives are lived; and all parts that are not lived in fellowship with Him, 'in whom we live, and move, and have our being,' are unreal, untrue, unsuccessful, and unsatisfying. The understanding of doctrine is one thing, and intimacy with God is another. They ought always to go together; but they are often seen asunder; and, when there is the former without the latter, there is a hard, proud, hollow religion. Get your teaching from God (Job 36:22; Jer. 23:30); take your doctrine from His lips; learn truth upon your knees. Beware of opinions and speculations: they become idols, and nourish pride of intellect; they furnish no food to the soul; they make you sapless and heartless; they are like winter frost-work on your windowpane, shutting out the warm sun. Let God be your companion, your bosom-friend, your instructor, your counselor.

~ F. Horatius Bonar (1808-1889)

LOVE ONE ANOTHER

This is My commandment, that you love one another
as I have loved you.

JOHN 15:12 NKJV

The disciples loved one another. This was the blessed fruit of Christ's dying precept to His disciples, and His dying prayer for them . . . They were dead to this world . . . evidence of the grace of God in them. They did not take away others' property, but they were indifferent to it . . . they had, in affection, forsaken all for Christ . . . they were of one heart and soul, when they sat so loose to the wealth of this world. In effect, they had all things common; for there was not any among them who lacked, care was taken for their supply. The money was laid at the apostles' feet. Great care ought to be taken in the distribution of public charity, that it be given to such as have need . . . those who are reduced to want for well-doing, and for the testimony of a good conscience, ought to be provided for. Here is one in particular mentioned, remarkable for this generous charity; it was Barnabas. As one designed to be a preacher of the gospel, he disentangled himself from the affairs of this life. When such dispositions prevail, and are exercised according to the circumstances of the times, the testimony will have very great power upon others. ~ Matthew Henry (1662-1714)

DEVOTED TO GOD

"He who has ears to hear, let him hear!"

LUKE 8:8 NKJV

That same state and temper of mind which makes our alms and devotions acceptable, must also make our labour, or employment, a proper offering unto God. If a man labours to be rich, and pursues his business, that he may raise himself to a state of figure and glory in the world, he is no longer serving God in his employment; he is acting under other masters, and has no more title to a reward from God, than he that gives alms, that he may be seen, or prays, that he may be heard of men. For vain and earthly desires are no more allowable in our employments, than in our alms and devotions. For these tempers of worldly pride, and vain-glory, are not only evil, when they mix with our good works, but they have the same evil nature, and make us odious to God, when they enter into the common business of our employment . . . But as our alms and devotions are not an acceptable service, but when they proceed from a heart truly devoted to God, so our common employment cannot be reckoned a service to Him, but when it is performed with the same temper and piety of heart.

~ William Law (1686-1761)

A FAITH PINNACLE

Thou wilt keep him in perfect peace, whose mind is stayed on thee:
because he trusteth in thee.
————— ISAIAH 26:3 KJV —————

The belief of the resurrection of our Lord from the dead, and of His ascension into heaven, has strengthened our faith by adding a great buttress of hope . . . shows how freely He laid down His life for us when He had it in His power thus to take it up again. With what assurance, then, is the hope of believers animated, when they reflect how great He was who suffered so great things for them while they were still in unbelief! And when men look for Him to come from heaven as the judge of quick and dead, it strikes great terror into the careless, so that they retake themselves to diligent preparation, and learn by holy living to long for His approach, instead of quaking at it on account of their evil deeds. . .what imagination can conceive, the reward He will bestow at the last, when we consider that for our comfort in this earthly journey He has given us so freely of His Spirit, that in the adversities of this life we may retain our confidence in, and love for, Him whom as yet we see not; and that He has also given to each gifts suitable for the building up of His Church, that we may do what He points out as right to be done, not only without a murmur, but even with delight?
~ St. Augustine (354-430)

DIVINE INSPIRATION

You shall therefore consecrate yourselves, and you shall be holy;
for I am holy.

LEVITICUS 11:44 NKJV

The Spirit of the triune God, breathed into . . . was that alone which made him a holy creature in the image and likeness of God. Had he not been . . . God in him and he in God . . . brought into the world as a true offspring and real birth of the Holy Spirit, no dispensation of God to fallen man would have directed him to the Holy Spirit, or ever have made mention of his inspiration in man . . . And had not the Holy Spirit been his first life, in and by which he lived, no inspired prophets among the sons of fallen Adam had ever been heard of, or any holy men speaking as they were moved by the Holy Ghost. For the thing would have been impossible, no fallen man could have been inspired by the Holy Spirit, but because the first life of man was a true and real birth of it; and also because every fallen man had, by the mercy and free grace of God, a secret remains of his first life preserved in him, though hidden, or rather swallowed up by flesh and blood; which secret remains, signified and assured to Adam by the name of a "bruiser of the serpent," or "seed of the woman," was his only capacity to be called and quickened again into his first life, by new breathings of the Holy Spirit in him. ~ William Law (1686-1761)

Indeed you are called a Jew, and rest on the law, and make your boast in God, and know His will, and approve the things that are excellent, being instructed out of the law, and are confident that you yourself are a guide to the blind, a light to those who are in darkness, an instructor of the foolish, a teacher of babes, having the form of knowledge and truth in the law. You, therefore, who teach another, do you not teach yourself? You who preach that a man should not steal, do you steal? You who say, "Do not commit adultery," do you commit adultery? You who abhor idols, do you rob temples? You who make your boast in the law, do you dishonor God through breaking the law? For "the name of God is blasphemed among the Gentiles because of you," as it is written. For circumcision is indeed profitable if you keep the law; but if you are a breaker of the law, your circumcision has become uncircumcision. Therefore, if an uncircumcised man keeps the righteous requirements of the law, will not his uncircumcision be counted as circumcision? And will not the physically uncircumcised, if he fulfills the law, judge you who, even with your written code and circumcision, are a transgressor of the law? For he is not a Jew who is one outwardly, nor is circumcision that which is outward in the flesh; but he is a Jew who is one inwardly; and circumcision is that of the heart, in the Spirit, not in the letter; whose praise is not from men but from God.

ROMANS 2:17-29 NKJV

STANDING FIRM

A CHRISTIAN MUST

So then faith comes by hearing, and hearing by the word of God.
—————— ROMANS 10:17 NKJV ——————

. . .The soul can do without everything except the word of God . . . it is rich and wants for nothing, since that is the word of life, of truth, of light, of peace, of justification, of salvation, of joy, of liberty, of wisdom, of virtue, of grace, of glory, and of every good thing. It is on this account that the prophet in a whole Psalm 119 . . . sighs for and calls upon the word of God with so many groanings and words . . . there is no more cruel stroke of the wrath of God than when He sends a famine of hearing His words just as there is no greater favour from Him than the sending forth of His word . . . Christ was sent for no other office than that of the word . . . The Apostle Paul explains what it is, namely the Gospel of God, concerning His Son, incarnate, suffering, risen, and glorified, through the Spirit, the Sanctifier. For the word of God cannot be received and honoured by any works, but by faith alone . . . the soul needs the word alone for life and justification, so it is justified by faith alone, and not by any works. For if it could be justified by any other means, it would have no need of the word, nor consequently of faith.
~ Martin Luther (1483-1546)

THY KINGDOM COME

. . .a man is justified by faith apart from the deeds of the law.

ROMANS 3:28 NKJV

Works . . . cannot glorify God, although they may be done to the glory of God, if faith be present. But at present we are inquiring, not into the quality of the works done, but into him who does them, who glorifies God, and brings forth good works. This is faith of heart, the head and the substance of all our righteousness. Hence that is a blind and perilous doctrine which teaches that the commandments are fulfilled by works. The commandments must have been fulfilled previous to any good works, and good works follow their fulfillment, as we shall see . . . we must know that in the Old Testament God sanctified to Himself every first-born male. The birthright was of great value, giving a superiority over the rest by the double honour of priesthood and kingship. For the first-born brother was priest and lord of all the rest. Under this figure was foreshown Christ, the true and only First-born of God the Father and of the Virgin Mary, and a true King and Priest, not in a fleshly and earthly sense. For His kingdom is not of this world; it is in heavenly and spiritual things that He reigns and acts as Priest; and these are righteousness, truth, wisdom, peace, salvation, etc.
~ Martin Luther (1483-1546)

THE PURPOSE OF GOD

And we know that all things work together for good to them that
love God, to them who are the called according to His purpose.
—— ROMANS 8:28 KJV ——

The purpose of God is one, and only one. It is always referred to in the singular; "Called according to His purpose." "According to the purpose...." (Eph. 1:11). "According to the eternal purpose" (Eph. 3:11). "According to His purpose and grace" (II Tim. 1:9). It is not a variety or number of things; it is just one. And what is the one, single, comprehensive purpose? The answer is Christ! "His Son, Jesus Christ." And when we ask further, What about His Son? The answer is, to have Him fill all things and to have all things in Him. That this is so is made clear in the definite statements of Scripture; "In Him were all things created, in the heavens and upon the earth, things visible and things invisible... all things have been created through Him, and unto Him." "For it was the good pleasure of the Father that in Him should all the fullness dwell" (Colossians 1:16, 19). "Whom He appointed heir of all things, through Whom also He made the worlds (ages)" (Heb. 1:2) . . . So, then, in the counsels of God, all things must head up in Christ. God's occupation is with bringing Christ in, and bringing into Christ. If we would be "God's fellow-workers", this must be our single-eyed aim and business. This defines precisely the purpose of the Church.
~ Austin T. Sparks (1888-1971)

THE GRAMMAR OF GOD

'Not by might nor by power, but by My Spirit,' says the Lord of hosts.
——— ZECHARIAH 4:6 NKJV ———

The Holy Spirit has his own grammar. Grammar is useful everywhere, but when the subject is greater than can be comprehended by the rules of grammar and philosophy, it must be left behind. In grammar, analogy works very well: Christ is created. Therefore Christ is a creature. But in theology, nothing is more useless. Wherefore our eloquence must be restrained, and we must remain content with the patterns prescribed by the Holy Spirit. We do not depart [from grammar] without necessity, for the subject is ineffable and incomprehensible. A creature, in the old use of language, is that which the creator has created and distinguished from himself, but this meaning has no place in Christ the creature. There the creator and the creature are one and the same . . . as once Augustine spoke, moved by the greatest joy: "Is this not a marvelous mystery? He who is the Creator, wished to be a creature." This is to be forgiven the holy Father, who was moved by surpassing joy to speak thus . . . And the Fathers are to be forgiven, because they spoke thus because of surpassing joy, wondering that the Creator was a creature . . .it does not matter how you speak, and I am not harmed if you say: Christ is thirst, humanity, captivity, creature. ~ Martin Luther (1483-1546)

GRACE AND PEACE

Grace to you and peace. . .
I THESSALONIANS 1:1 NKJV

Grace to you and peace, etc. Nothing is more desirable than to have God propitious to us, and this is signified by grace; and then to have prosperity and success in all things flowing from him, and this is intimated by peace; for however things may seem to smile on us, if God be angry, even blessing itself is turned to a curse. The very foundation then of our felicity is the favor of God, by which we enjoy true and solid prosperity, and by which also our salvation is promoted even when we are in adversities. And then as he prays to God for peace, we must understand, that whatever good comes to us, it is the fruit of divine benevolence. Nor must we omit to notice, that he prays at the same time to the Lord Jesus Christ for these blessings. Worthily indeed is this honor rendered to him, who is not only the administrator and dispenser of his Father's bounty to us, but also works all things in connection with him. It was, however, the special object of the Apostle to show, that through him all God's blessings come to us.
~ John Calvin (1509-1564)

JUSTIFICATION

It is God who justifies.

Romans 8:33 NKJV

Justification may fitly be extended to the unremitted continuance of God's favor, from the time of our calling to the hour of death; but as Paul uses this word throughout the Epistle, for gratuitous imputation of righteousness . . . What Paul indeed had in view was to show that a more precious compensation is offered to us, than what ought to allow us to shun afflictions; for what is more desirable than to be reconciled to God, so that our miseries may no longer be tokens of a curse, nor lead us to ruin? . . . Those who are now pressed down by the cross shall be glorified; so that their sorrows and reproaches shall bring them no loss. Though glorification is not yet exhibited except in our Head, yet as we in a manner behold in him our inheritance of eternal life, his glory brings to us such assurance respecting our own glory, that our hope may be justly compared to a present possession. . . . "Those whom God now, consistently with his purpose, exercises under the cross, are called and justified, that they may have a hope of salvation, so that nothing of their glory decays during their humiliation; for though their present miseries deform it before the world, yet before God and angels it always shines forth as perfect." ~ John Calvin (1509-1564)

What advantage then has the Jew, or what is the profit of circumcision? Much in every way! Chiefly because to them were committed the oracles of God. For what if some did not believe? Will their unbelief make the faithfulness of God without effect? Certainly not! Indeed, let God be true but every man a liar. As it is written: "That You may be justified in Your words, And may overcome when You are judged." But if our unrighteousness demonstrates the righteousness of God, what shall we say? Is God unjust who inflicts wrath? (I speak as a man.) Certainly not! For then how will God judge the world? For if the truth of God has increased through my lie to His glory, why am I also still judged as a sinner? And why not say, "Let us do evil that good may come"?—as we are slanderously reported and as some affirm that we say. Their condemnation is just. What then? Are we better than they? Not at all. For we have previously charged both Jews and Greeks that they are all under sin.

—— ROMANS 3:1-9 NKJV ——

THE GREAT PHYSICIAN

. . .pray for one another, that you may be healed. The effective,
fervent prayer of a righteous man avails much.

———— JAMES 5:16 NKJV ————

If we were well accustomed to the exercise of the presence of GOD, all bodily diseases would be much alleviated thereby. GOD often permits that we should suffer a little, to purify our souls, and oblige us to continue with Him. Take courage, offer Him your pains incessantly, pray to Him for strength to endure them. Above all, get a habit of entertaining yourself often with GOD, and forget Him the least you can. Adore Him in your infirmities, offer yourself to Him from time to time; and, in the height of your sufferings, beseech Him humbly and affectionately (as a child to his father) to make you conformable to His holy will . . . GOD has many ways of drawing us to Himself. He sometimes hides Himself from us: but faith alone, which will not fail us in time of need, ought to be our support, and the foundation of our confidence, which must be all in GOD. I know not how GOD will dispose of me: I am always happy: all the world suffer; and I, who deserve the severest discipline, feel joys so continual, and so great, that I can scarce contain them . . . Let us be always with Him. Let us live and die in His presence. ~ Brother Lawrence (1749-1832)

HIS DELIGHT

Blessed is the man Who walks not in the counsel of the ungodly,
Nor stands in the path of sinners, Nor sits in the seat of the scornful;
But his delight is in the law of the Lord, And in His law
he meditates day and night.

—— PSALM 1:1, 2 NKJV ——

Proverb saith, "He that has begun well, has half done": so he that has begun to live by rule, has gone a great way towards the perfection of his life. By rule, must here be constantly understood, a religious rule observed upon a principle of duty to God. For if a man should oblige himself to be moderate in his meals, only in regard to his stomach; or abstain from drinking, only to avoid the headache; or be moderate in his sleep, through fear of a lethargy; he might be exact in these rules, without being at all the better man for them. But when he is moderate and regular in any of these things, out of a sense of Christian sobriety and self-denial, that he may offer unto God a more reasonable and holy life, then it is, that the smallest rule of this kind is naturally the beginning of great piety. For the smallest rule in these matters is of great benefit, as it teaches us some part of the government of ourselves, as it keeps up a tenderness of mind, as it presents God often to our thoughts, and brings a sense of religion into the ordinary actions of our common life. ~ William Law (1686-1771)

WORK OF AN EVANGELIST

You are My friends if you do whatever I command you.
——— JOHN 15:14 NKJV ———

The people of God need to rise up and see themselves as not only sons and daughters in God's family, but as soldiers in His army. As such, we have been commanded to fight for the souls of men and the nations of the world. We have no option to accept Christ without accepting His demands. A disciple of Jesus is by definition someone who has given Jesus authority over his life. Jesus is the King of kings. He is the Lord of lords. He is the Captain of our Salvation. And He has given us a job to do, a task to perform. If we are truly obedient disciples of Jesus Christ, we will do it. As the late evangelist Leonard Ravenhill said, we should "pray as if it all depended on God and work as if it all depended on us" until that glorious day when we have reached every creature with the Gospel, or until Jesus Christ comes back, whichever comes first. ~ Danny Lehmann (1954-)

A MERCIFUL GOD

Precious in the sight of the Lord Is the death of His saints.
———— PSALM 116:15 NKJV ————

Almighty and most merciful Father, who lovest those whom thou Punishest, and turnest away thine anger from the penitent, look down with pity upon my sorrows, and grant that the affliction which it has pleased thee to bring upon me, may awaken my conscience, enforce my resolutions of a better life, and impress upon me such conviction of thy power and goodness, that I may place in thee my only felicity, and endeavor to please thee in all my thoughts, words, and actions. Grant, O Lord, that I may not languish in fruitless and unavailing sorrow, but that I may consider from whose hand all good and evil is received, and may remember that I am punished for my sins, and hope for comfort only by repentance. Grant, O merciful God, that by the assistance of thy Holy Spirit I may repent, and be comforted, obtain that peace which the world cannot give, pass the residue of my life in humble resignation and cheerful obedience; and when it shall please thee to call me from this mortal state, resign myself into thy hands with faith and confidence, and finally obtain mercy and everlasting happiness, for the sake of Jesus Christ our Lord. Amen. ~ Samuel Johnson (1709-1784)

GODLY WISDOM

"For whoever has, to him more will be given; and whoever does not have, even what he seems to have will be taken from him."

———— LUKE 8:18 NKJV ————

If we had a religion that consisted in absurd superstitions . . . people might well be glad to have some part of their life excused from it. But as the religion of the Gospel is only the refinement and exaltation of our best faculties, as it only requires a life of the highest reason . . . to live in such tempers as are the glory of intelligent beings, to walk in such wisdom as exalts our nature, and to practise such piety as will raise us to God; who can think it grievous to live always in the spirit of such a religion, to have every part of his life full of it, but he that would think it much more grievous to be as the Angels of God in Heaven? . . . Our Saviour has assured us, it be more blessed to give than to receive, we ought to look upon those that ask our alms, as so many friends and benefactors, that come to do us a greater good than they can receive, that come to exalt our virtue, to be witnesses of our charity, to be monuments of our love, to be our advocates with God, to be to us in Christ's stead, to appear for us in the day of judgment, and to help us to a blessedness greater than our alms can bestow on them.

~ William Law (1686-1761)

THE PRESENCE OF CHRIST

But straightway Jesus spake unto them saying,
Be of good cheer; it is I; be not afraid.
———— MATTHEW 14:27 KJV ————

Think, first, of the presence of Christ lost. You know the disciples loved Christ, clung to Him, and with all their failings, they delighted in Him. But what happened? The Master went up into the mountain to pray, and sent them across the sea all alone without Him; there came a storm, and they toiled, rowed, and laboured, but the wind was against them, they made no progress, they were in danger of perishing, and how their hearts said, "Oh, if the Master only were here!" But His presence was gone. They missed Him. Once before, they had been in a storm, and Christ had said, "Peace, be still," and all was well; but here they are in darkness, danger, and terrible trouble, and no Christ to help them. Ah, isn't that the life of many a believer at times? I get into darkness, I have committed sin, the cloud is on me, I miss the face of Jesus; and for days and days I work, worry, and labour; but it is all in vain, for I miss the presence of Christ. Oh, beloved, let us write that down, — the presence of Jesus lost is the cause of all our wretchedness and failure. ~ Andrew Murray (1828-1917)

As it is written: "There is none righteous, no, not one; There is none who understands; There is none who seeks after God. They have all turned aside; They have together become unprofitable; There is none who does good, no, not one." "Their throat is an open tomb; With their tongues they have practiced deceit"; "The poison of asps is under their lips"; "Whose mouth is full of cursing and bitterness." "Their feet are swift to shed blood; Destruction and misery are in their ways; And the way of peace they have not known." "There is no fear of God before their eyes."

ROMANS 3:10-18 NKJV

STANDING FIRM

BIBLICAL WORSHIP

"God is spirit, and those who worship
Him must worship in spirit and truth."
—— JOHN 4:24 NKJV ——

I believe that the greatest challenge facing the Christian community today is to correct our misunderstanding and misrepresentation of Biblical worship. We have made people believe that worship consists only of what we do for an hour or so on Sunday mornings at the place we call the church. We have made it something we "go to" and "leave from" at the appropriate times. In doing so, we have reduced to an hour what God said must be our entire lives. "Therefore, I urge you, brothers, in view of God's mercy, to offer your bodies as living sacrifices, holy and pleasing to God—this is your spiritual act of worship." (Romans 12:1) True worship is the offering to God of one's body, one's entire life. Worship is a life given in obedience to God. When we meet together to encourage, teach, and equip for service, we are being obedient and therefore worshiping, but no more than when we obey Him anywhere else at any other time. A man may say he is going to the assembly to worship God, but he should also say he is going to the factory, the office, the school, the ball field, or the restaurant to worship God. Real worship is offering every moment and every action of every day to God. ~ Randy Cordell (1954 -)

GOD'S PROMISES

. . .David strengthened himself in the Lord his God.
——— 1 SAMUEL 30:6 NKJV ———

King David and his small army are stunned. Having returned home, they found their city in smoke and ashes. Their eyes scanned the ruins for signs of their wives and children. But they searched in vain. They were gone; taken captive by the enemy. They wept until their tear ducts were dry. Then grief turned to anger. "Stone David!" became the bitter cry from the lips of David's band of men. David was greatly distressed. Did he panic? No. For the Scripture says, "David strengthened himself in the Lord his God." He was not a helpless victim of other people's sins. From a youth he had learned that God is greater than the opposition. Remember the lion, the bear and Goliath? When faced with other people's sins, David was keeping his eye on the promises of God: "You shall overtake them" (the enemy) "You shall recover all" (family and possessions). From this we learn important lessons. To strengthen yourself in the Lord means to rely on the promises of God. That's what David did. Go and do likewise.
~ Kenneth M. Mick (1938 -)

CONSISTENT CHRISTIAN LIVING

But I discipline my body and bring it into subjection, lest, when I have preached to others, I myself should become disqualified.
————— I CORINTHIANS 9:27 NKJV —————

It's fairly easy to stand up in front of a crowd and preach or teach. The crowds may applaud and congratulate us on a job well done and people may gather to talk to us or ask questions. If we are foolish, we can walk away from those moments thinking we have lived the Christian life well and taught "sinners" how to be converted. We may even feel we have "glorified the Lord" with our effective words or singing. But, it's not in those confines that we live the Christian life. No, it's in the moments with our families when we are tired or discouraged. It's when someone in the office has misplaced the stapler or calculator. It's when things didn't work out as planned. It's when someone failed to do their job and left us with our hands full of their responsibilities. It's then that our Christianity rings true or hollow. We must live what we preach and teach. If not, we have not glorified the Lord regardless of our words and songs. He wants to be glorified in how we live our lives — down in the "nitty-gritty." That's when our words are the clearest and our songs the most beautiful. Consistent Christian living is just that — living Christian consistently. ~ Jacquelyn Sheppard (1943 –)

GOD'S DIVINE IMAGE

"Who is like You, O Lord, among the gods? Who is like You,
glorious in holiness, Fearful in praises, doing wonders?"

——— EXODUS 15:11 NKJV ———

We must never confine our idea of the image of God in man merely to man's original righteousness and holiness. People have often done that, and it has landed them in grievous trouble with regard to other doctrines. They say, you see, that the divine image in man simply meant his original righteousness and holiness; when he fell, therefore, he lost it all. But that is not so. The natural element in the divine image must be emphasized, because, as Scripture has taught us, it persists after the fall. It was there in Genesis 5; it is there in Genesis 9, and it is there in the third chapter of James. Man, even in sin, retains those elements and aspects of the divine image; they are an essential part of human nature. If he lost those he would no longer be human.

~ Martyn Lloyd-Jones (1899-1981)

THE LIFE ON WINGS

". . .they shall mount up with wings as eagles. . ."
—————— ISAIAH 40:31 KJV ——————

. . .Things look differently to us according to our "point of view." Trials assume a very different aspect when looked down upon from above, than when viewed from their own level. What seems like an impassable wall on its own level becomes an insignificant line to the eyes that see it from the top of a mountain. The snares and sorrows that assume such immense proportion while we look at them on the earthly plane, become insignificant when the soul has mounted on wings to the heavenly places above them. A friend once illustrated the difference in her friends in the following way. She said, if all three came to a spiritual mountain which had to be crossed, the first one would tunnel through it with hard and wearisome labor. The second would meander around it in an indefinite fashion, hardly knowing where she was going, and yet, because her aim was right, would get around it at last. But the third, she said, would just flap her wings and fly right over. All of us must know something about this. If any of us in the past have tried to tunnel our way through the mountains that have stood across our pathway, or have been meandering around them, let us now resolve to spread our wings and "mount up" into the clear atmosphere of God's presence. There it will be easy to overcome, or come over, the highest mountain of them all. ~ Hannah Whitall Smith (1832-1911)

PREPARED FOR BATTLE

For whatsoever is born of God overcometh the world: and this is the victory
that overcometh the world, even our faith. Who is he that overcometh the
world, but he that believeth that Jesus is the Son of God?
———— I JOHN 5:4, 5 KJV ————

We can be so earthly-minded, fighting our fight in the earthly realm, that we are of no value in the heavenly battle. We fire our cannons in the wrong realm. If we are not fighting in heavenly places, we will fight in earthly ones. If we are not doing battle with the powers of darkness, we will fight people instead. There is something within us that gets incensed at injustice, something that rises up in protest of wrongdoing. If we do not take that into the heavenly places, resist the enemy, and pray for a change, we will fight people. We should fight issues in society, but not people. Fighting people never advances the Kingdom of God, no matter how right the issues. God's Kingdom is advanced through God and His response to our prayer, and through our Spirit-led actions. Every adversity is a prime opportunity for Christians to have a right reaction, to give glory to God, to uphold His character, and to defeat the devil. ~ Dean Sherman (1945 -)

Now we know that whatever the law says, it says to those who are under the law, that every mouth may be stopped, and all the world may become guilty before God. Therefore by the deeds of the law no flesh will be justified in His sight, for by the law is the knowledge of sin. But now the righteousness of God apart from the law is revealed, being witnessed by the Law and the Prophets, even the righteousness of God, through faith in Jesus Christ, to all and on all who believe. For there is no difference; for all have sinned and fall short of the glory of God, being justified freely by His grace through the redemption that is in Christ Jesus, whom God set forth as a propitiation by His blood, through faith, to demonstrate His righteousness, because in His forbearance God had passed over the sins that were previously committed, to demonstrate at the present time His righteousness, that He might be just and the justifier of the one who has faith in Jesus. Where is boasting then? It is excluded. By what law? Of works? No, but by the law of faith.

ROMANS 3:19-27 NKJV

STANDING FIRM

TREASURE IN EARTHEN VESSELS

*But we have this treasure in earthen vessels, that the excellence of
the power may be of God and not of us.*
II CORINTHIANS 4:7 NKJV

The principle of the world is "self-glorification," and the principle of the world is "exalt of the Christian is "self-crucifixion." The principle of the world is "exalt yourself," and the principle of the Christian is "crucify yourself." The principle of men is greatness, bigness, pomp, and show; the principle of the cross is death. Therefore, whenever a man has seen the glory of God in the face of Jesus Christ . . . at once he comes right into a head-on collision within his own personal living, with all of his principles and motives upon which he has lived until this moment . . . . if there is to be a continual manifestation of Holy Spirit life, there must be a constant submission to the crucifixion of the flesh, not simply sometimes, but always . . . Why is it that so many Christians behave like kindergarten children? Because they have not seen His face! . . . And the cost in the Christian life . . . . Deep down in the Christian's life, always and all the time, there is to be a "no" to every demand that the flesh may make for recognition, and every demand that the flesh may make for approval, and every demand that the flesh may make for vindication. Always the Christian must bear about in his body the marks of the Lord Jesus. ~ Alan Redpath (1907 -)

THE WORD OF CHRIST

Let the word of Christ dwell in you richly in all wisdom;
teaching and admonishing one another in psalms
and hymns and spiritual songs,
singing with grace in your hearts to the Lord.

—— COLOSSIANS 3:16 KJV ——

"All the earth" was to know and own the presence of God in the midst of His people. They could know nothing of the precious relationship involved in the title "Jehovah." This latter was for the assembly of Israel alone. They were to know not only His presence in their midst, but His blessed mode of acting. To the world He was Elohim, to His beloved people He was Jehovah. Well may these exquisite touches command our heart's admiration. Oh, the living depths, the moral glories, of that peerless Revelation which our Father has graciously penned for our comfort and edification! We must confess it gives us unspeakable delight to dwell on these things and point them out to the reader, in this infidel day when the divine inspiration of Holy Scripture is boldly called in question, in parts where we should least expect it. But we have something better to do just now that replying to the contemptible assaults of infidelity. We are thoroughly persuaded that the most effective safeguard against all such assaults is to have the Word of Christ dwelling in us richly, in all its living, formative power. To the heart thus filled and fortified, the most plausible and powerful arguments of all infidel writers are but as the pattering of rain on the window. ~ C. H. Mackintosh (1820-1896)

THE WORD OF ENCOURAGEMENT TO BATTLE

Finally, my brethren, be strong in the Lord, and in the power of his might.
——— EPHESIANS 6:10 KJV ———

A soul deeply possessed with fear, and dispirited with strong apprehensions of danger, is in no posture for counsel. As we see in any army when put to flight by some sudden alarm, or apprehension of danger, it is hard rallying them into order until the fright occasioned thereby is over; therefore the apostle first raiseth up their spirits, 'be strong in the Lord.' As if he should say, Perhaps some drooping souls find their hearts fail them, while they see their enemies so strong, and they so weak; so numerous, and they so few; so well appointed, and they so naked and unarmed; so skillful and expert at arms, but they green and raw soldiers . . . with undaunted courage march on, and be strong in the Lord, on whose performance lies the stress of battle, and not on your skill or strength. It is not the least of a minister's care and skill in dividing the word, so to press the Christian's duty, as not to oppress his spirit with the weight of it, by laying it on the creature's own shoulders, and not on the Lord's strength, as here our apostle teacheth us. In this verse . . . We have, A familiar appellation, 'my brethren,' An exhortation, 'be strong,' A cautionary direction annexed to the exhortation, 'in the Lord,' An encouraging amplification of the direction, 'and in the power of his might,' or in his mighty power.
~ William Gurnall (1617-1679)

UNION WITH CHRIST

Oh, love the Lord, all you His saints! For the Lord preserves
the faithful, And fully repays the proud person.
PSALM 31:23 NKJV

Christ wants above all else that we come into union with Himself. Since that union can come only through an act of willing surrender, Christ calls at a certain point for an act of obedience. He does not confuse us with a babel of voices. He is specific. He demands an utter abandonment of heart and will. The state of surrender both in its origin and in the continuance will be realized around some single act of obedience. At that given point the word of command is: "This do, and life is thine." In that uttered word of His—not any words of His, or His teachings in general but His uttered and particular and specific will at the moment—there is spirit and life, yea, "all the light and might of God." Whatsoever He saith unto you, do it!

~ L. E. Maxwell (1895-1984)

STAND UP! — STAND UP FOR JESUS

Stand up! — stand up for Jesus, ye soldiers of the Cross!
Lift high His royal banner, it must not suffer loss.
From vict'ry unto vict'ry His army shall He lead
Till ev'ry foe is vanquished and Christ is Lord indeed.
Stand up! — stand up for Jesus! The trumpet-call obey;
Forth to the mighty conflict in this His glorious day!
Ye that are men, now serve Him against unnumbered foes;
Let courage rise with danger and strength to strength oppose.
Stand up! — stand up for Jesus! Stand in His strength alone;
The arm of flesh will fail you, ye dare not trust your own.
Put on the Gospel armor, each piece put on with prayer;
Where duty calls or danger, be never wanting there.
Stand up! — stand up for Jesus! The strife will not be long;
This day the noise of battle, the next, the victor's song.
To him that overcometh a crown of life shall be;
He with the King of Glory shall reign eternally.
~ George Duffield (1818-1888)

GOOD FROM BAD

Happy are the people who are in such a state; Happy are the people whose God is the Lord!

PSALM 144:15 NKJV

God's Presence can be the catalyst to turn evil events and situations into good ones. We could compare it to the process that a photographer goes through to develop a negative into a beautiful print. (The word "negative" is intriguing here.) When we hold a photo negative up to a light, all objects are reversed: black is white, white is black. Further, the character lineaments of any face in the picture are not clear. Once plunged into the developing solution, what photographers call "the latent image" is revealed in the print — darkness turns to light and lo, we have a beautiful picture . . . When we praise God by an act of the will . . . first we accept present circumstances, then we take up a positive position. By beginning to praise Him for the evil, we take our less-than-good situation and plunge in into the photographer's fluid — the presence of God.

~ Catherine Marshall (1899-1987)

Therefore we conclude that a man is justified by faith apart from the deeds of the law. Or is He the God of the Jews only? Is He not also the God of the Gentiles? Yes, of the Gentiles also, since there is one God who will justify the circumcised by faith and the uncircumcised through faith.
Do we then make void the law through faith?
Certainly not! On the contrary, we establish the law.

ROMANS 3:28-31 NKJV

STANDING FIRM

CALL FOR CHASTITY

"Be holy, for I am holy."

I PETER 1:16 NKJV

Could I influence the thought of contemporary youth and set the intent of their hearts, minds and souls upon one subject in particular, that subject would be chastity. For I believe that of all the cardinal virtues that youth might aspire after, it is the one most under attack in our society. Chastity means sexual purity. It means abstinence from sex, except for sex in the marriage bond between male and female. Chastity has found favor with noble persons both inside and outside of Christianity. Degradation unchecked knows no shame, no limits. So it is not surprising that in recent decades, pornography and the sexual abuse of children have become major problems. Practicing homosexuals demand special treatment. Sexologists seek to have incest legitimized. Did men and women and youth desire purity and fidelity as much as they cuddle up to temptation and lust, we would be freed as individuals, and as a nation, from the sordid costs of unbridled sexual passion and perversion. Oh that our churches, our literature, our schools and our politics might resound with the call to chastity. Sex is as fire: purposeful in its proper bounds, the bounds of committed marriage, but destructive outside of those boundaries.

~ Raymond V. Banner (1937-)

THE RETURN OF THE BELOVED

Rest in the LORD, and wait patiently for him. . .
—————— PSALM 37:7 KJV ——————

THOUGH God has no other desire than to impart Himself to the loving soul that seeks Him, yet He frequently conceals Himself from it, that it may be roused from sloth, and impelled to seek Him with fidelity and love. But with what abundant goodness does He recompense the faithfulness of his beloved! And how often are these apparent withdrawings of Himself succeeded by the caresses of love! At these seasons we are apt to believe that it proves our fidelity, and evinces a greater ardor of affection to seek Him by an exertion of our own strength and activity; or that such a course will induce Him the more speedily to revisit us. No, dear souls, believe me, this is not the best way in this degree of prayer; with patient love, with self-abasement and humiliation, with the reiterated breathings of an ardent but peaceful affection, and with silence full of veneration, you must await the return of the Beloved. Thus only can you demonstrate that it is HIMSELF alone, and his good pleasure, that you seek; and not the selfish delights of your own sensations in loving Him.

~ Jeanne Marie Vouvier de la Mothe Guyon (1647–1711)

THE KINGDOM OF GOD

"Now I know that the Lord is greater than all the gods; for in the very thing in which they behaved proudly, He was above them."
E X O D U S 18:11 N K J V

The famous clock in Strasburg Cathedral has a mechanism so complicated, that it seems to the ignorant and superstitious almost a work of superhuman skill. The abused and offended maker, yet unpaid for his work, came one day and touched its secret springs, and it stopped. All the patience and ingenuity of a nation's mechanics and artisans failed to restore its disordered mechanism and set it in motion. Afterward, when his grievances were redressed, that maker came again, touched the inner springs and set it again in motion, and all its multiplied parts revolved again obedient to his will. When thus, by a touch, he suspended and restored those marvelous movements, he gave to any doubting mind proof that he was the maker — certainly the master, of that clock. And when Jesus of Nazareth brings to a stop the mechanism of nature, makes its mighty wheels turn back or in any way arrests its grand movement — more than all, when He cannot only stop, but start again, the mysterious clock of human life, He gives to an honest mind overwhelming proof that God is with him. For a malignant power might arrest or destroy, but only He could reconstruct and restore! ~ Arthur T. Pierson (1867-1911)

LANGUAGE OF LOVE

Your kingdom come. Your will be done On earth as it is in heaven.
———— MATTHEW 6:10 NKJV ————

When we come to inquire what the matter of Jesus' preaching consisted of, we perhaps naturally expect to find Him expounding the system of doctrine which we are ourselves acquainted with, in the forms, say, of the Catechism or the Confession of Faith. But what we find is very different. He did not make use of any system of doctrine. We can scarcely doubt, indeed, that all the numerous and varied ideas of His preaching, as well as those which He never expressed, co-existed in His mind as one world of rounded truth. But they did not so co-exist in His teaching. He did not use theological phraseology, speaking of the Trinity, of predestination, of effectual calling, although the ideas which these terms cover underlay His words, and is it the undoubted task of science to bring them forth. But He spoke in the language of life, and concentrated His preaching on a few burning points, that touched the heart, the conscience, and the time. The central idea and the commonest phrase of His preaching was "the kingdom of God." — Jesus announced that it had come, and that He had brought it. The time of waiting was fulfilled. ~ James Stalker (1848-1927)

WHAT WE HAVE AND DON'T HAVE

But as it is written: "Eye has not seen, nor ear heard,
Nor have entered into the heart of man The things which God
has prepared for those who love Him."
———— I CORINTHIANS 2:9 NKJV ————

Often, when we think we have something, we don't, or when we think we don't have something, we do. This concept was vividly dramatized in the fall of a powerful high-tech company. For years, employees had given their lives to build this company and were rewarded richly in company stock. Some, near retirement, had a million dollars or more in company stock, more than enough to give them a comfortable, even delightful, retirement. Then the company fell overnight from an accounting scandal. What these trusting people thought they had, a comfortable retirement income, they didn't have. Their stock was almost worthless. What they thought they didn't have, worry about insufficient money for older years, they did have. These were real live people living out a real live drama before our eyes. As we remember their story, we are reminded that they, and we, are tempted to think we have self-sufficiency in circumstances such as this. But what we thought we had, self-sufficiency, we didn't have. What we thought we didn't have, insufficiency, we had. From a human viewpoint, we could despair. Then we realize that God's all-sufficiency can transcend both our self-sufficiency and our insufficiency.

~V. Gilbert Beers (1928-)

SHELTER OF THE MOST HIGH

Hear my cry, O God; Attend to my prayer. From the end of the earth
I will cry to You, When my heart is overwhelmed; Lead me to the rock
that is higher than I. For You have been a shelter for me,
A strong tower from the enemy. I will abide in Your tabernacle forever;
I will trust in the shelter of Your wings.

PSALM 61:1-4 NKJV

During the time when Indonesia was almost taken over by the Communists our Baptist Hospital was to be demonstrated against with the ultimate goal of destroying it and the missionaries who worked there. We were given three days to prepare. Needless to say, prayer was THE preparation. The day of the demonstration came. Thousands had gathered at the soccer field with their knives and kerosene cans ready to march to the excitement. My husband, Jim, had already gone over to the hospital and was seeing the few patients who dared to venture out. My Christian helpers and I gathered around the dining table. As a child of missionaries growing up in China, I was quite used to trusting God during dangerous times. Reading Psalm 91 we all were encouraged and reminded that we serve a Faithful, All Powerful God who would protect us, our three little girls, other missionaries and our Christian Indonesians. God did answer all of our prayers in Kediri because when the word came from the Communist leaders, "Destroy" there was only silence and one by one the three thousand people dropped their rocks, turned around and went home. God proved once again, we "live in the shelter of the Most High." ~ Joyce S. Carpenter (1931-)

What then shall we say that Abraham our father has found according to the flesh? For if Abraham was justified by works, he has something to boast about, but not before God. For what does the Scripture say? "Abraham believed God, and it was accounted to him for righteousness." Now to him who works, the wages are not counted as grace but as debt. But to him who does not work but believes on Him who justifies the ungodly, his faith is accounted for righteousness, just as David also describes the blessedness of the man to whom God imputes righteousness apart from works: "Blessed are those whose lawless deeds are forgiven, And whose sins are covered; Blessed is the man to whom the Lord shall not impute sin."

—— ROMANS 4:1-8 NKJV ——

STANDING FIRM

BEWARE OF BACKSLIDING

Behold what manner of love the Father has bestowed on us,
that we should be called children of God!
———— I JOHN 3:1 NKJV ————

'There is no condemnation to them that are in Christ Jesus;' but if you cannot fall finally, you may fall foully, and may go with broken bones all your days. Take care of backslidings; for Jesus Christ's sake, do not grieve the Holy Ghost. You may never recover your comfort while you live. I have paid dear for backsliding. Our hearts are so cursedly wicked, that if you take not care, if you do not keep up a constant watch, your wicked hearts will deceive you, and draw you aside. It will be sad to be under the scourge of a correcting Father . . . Let me, therefore, exhort you that have got peace to keep a close walk with Christ. I am grieved with the loose walk of those that are Christians, that have had discoveries of Jesus Christ; there is so little difference betwixt them and other people, that I scarce know which is the true Christian. Christians are afraid to speak of God, they run down with the stream; if they come into worldly company, they will talk of the world as if they were in their element; this you would not do when you had the first discoveries of Christ's love; you could talk then of Christ's love for ever, when the candle of the Lord shined upon your soul.

~ George Whitefield (1714-1770)

STAND FOR THE TRUTH

Great peace have those who love Your law,
And nothing causes them to stumble.
—— P SALM 119:165 NKJV ——

As God can send a nation of people no greater blessing than to give them faithful, sincere, and upright ministers, so the greatest curse that God can possibly send upon a people in this world, is to give them over to blind, unregenerate, carnal, lukewarm, and unskilled guides. And yet, in all ages, we find that there have been many wolves in sheep's clothing, many that daubed with untempered mortar, that prophesied smoother things than God did allow. As it was formerly, so it is now; there are many that corrupt the Word of God and deal deceitfully with it. It was so in a special manner in the prophet Jeremiah's time; and he, faithful to his Lord, faithful to that God who employed him, did not fail from time to time to open his mouth against them, and to bear a noble testimony to the honor of that God in whose name he from time to time spake. . . . This is what I design at present, that I may deliver my soul, that I may be free from the blood of those to whom I preach — that I may not fail to declare the whole counsel of God. I shall, from the words of the text, endeavor to show you what you must undergo, and what must be wrought in you before you can speak peace to your hearts.
~ George Whitefield (1714-1770)

FULLNESS OF JOY

...the joy of the LORD is your strength...
——— NEHEMIAH 8:10 KJV ———

O! What heart can conceive, what tongue can express, with what unspeakable joy and consolation shall we then look back on our past sincere and hearty services. Think you then, my dear hearers, we shall repent we had done too much; or rather think you not, we shall be ashamed that we did no more; and blush we were so backward to give up all to God; when he intended hereafter to give us himself? Let me...exhort you, my brethren, to have always before you the unspeakable happiness of enjoying God. And think withal, that every degree of holiness you neglect, every act of piety you omit, is a jewel taken out of your crown, a degree of blessedness lost in the vision of God. O! Do but always think and act thus, and you will no longer be laboring to compound matters between God and the world; but, on the contrary, be daily endeavoring to give up yourselves more and more unto him; you will be always watching, always praying, always aspiring after farther degrees of purity and love, and consequently always preparing yourselves for a fuller sight and enjoyment of that God, in whose presence there is fullness of joy, and at whose right-hand there are pleasures for ever more. Amen! Amen!

~ George Whitefield (1714-1770)

GOD REMAINS UNCHANGED AND UNCHANGEABLE

And their sins and iniquities will I remember no more.
HEBREWS 10:17 KJV

Our faith becomes a fixed attitude, once it begins to rest in this wonderful fact. Then it can be, if necessary, "rejected indeed of men, but chosen of God, and precious" (1 Peter 2:4 ASV). This is the steadying influence most believers are in need of today. A century ago, J.B. Stoney wrote: "The blessed God never alters nor diverges from the acceptance in which He has received us because of the death and resurrection of Jesus Christ. Alas! we diverge from the state in which God can ever be toward us as recorded in Romans 5:1-11. Many suppose that because they are conscious of sins, that hence they must renew their acceptance with God." The truth is that God has not altered. His eye rests on the work accomplished by Christ for the believer. When you are not walking in the Spirit you are in the flesh: you have turned to the old man which was crucified on the cross (Romans 6:6). You have to be restored to fellowship, and when you are, you find your acceptance with God unchanged and unchangeable . . . He certainly will judge the flesh if we do not, but He never departs from the love which He has expressed to the prodigal, and we find . . . His love, blessed be His Name, had never changed."

~ Miles Stanford (1914 -1999)

A SABBATH REST

Come to Me, all you who labor and are heavy laden,
and I will give you rest.
—— MATTHEW 11:28 NKJV ——

There is a famous story about a time when Martin Luther was facing a very busy day. The work he needed to do required more time than he had at his disposal. He is recorded as remarking to one of his friends, "I have so much to do that I shall spend the first three hours in prayer!" The spiritual truth of this is hard for our natural minds to grasp. If we give God His due — first place in our lives — we will accomplish more, even though the time we actually have to work with is less. Living in Sabbath rest, whether it be one day in seven, or simply abiding in the Sabbath rest promised by Jesus, is a statement of faith that we are ceasing from our work, just as God ceased from His (Hebrews 4:10). We are declaring by our actions that our work will be even more productive when it is done God's way, which includes Sabbath rest. This acknowledgement of our weakness enables God to work on our behalf. ~ Danny Lehmann (1954 -)

HEIRS OF GOD

And said, Verily I say unto you, Except ye be converted, and become as little children, ye shall not enter into the kingdom of heaven.

———— MATTHEW 18:3 KJV ————

Christ says that except we "become like children, you shall not enter into the Kingdom of heaven." But it is impossible to get the child-spirit until the servant-spirit has disappeared. Notice, I do not say the spirit of service, but the servant-spirit. Every good child is filled with the spirit of service, but shouldn't have the servant-spirit. The child serves from love. The servant works for wages. If a child of loving parents would get the idea that its parents would not give him food and clothing unless he earned them in some way, all the sweetness of the relationship between parent and child would be destroyed. I knew a little girl who did get this idea, and who went around the neighborhood asking at the doors for work so that she might earn a little money to buy herself some clothes. It nearly broke the hearts of her parents when they discovered it. Legal Christians grieve the heart of their Heavenly Father, far more than they know, by letting the servant-spirit creep into their relationship with Him. As soon as we begin to "work for our living" in spiritual things, we have stepped out of the son's place into the servant's, and have fallen from grace.

~ Hannah Whitall Smith (1832-1911)

*Does this blessedness then come upon the circumcised only, or
upon the uncircumcised also? For we say that faith was
accounted to Abraham for righteousness. How then was it
accounted? While he was circumcised, or uncircumcised? Not
while circumcised, but while uncircumcised. And he received the
sign of circumcision, a seal of the righteousness of the faith which
he had while still uncircumcised, that he might be the father of
all those who believe, though they are uncircumcised, that
righteousness might be imputed to them also, and the father of
circumcision to those who not only are of the circumcision, but
who also walk in the steps of the faith which our father Abraham
had while still uncircumcised. For the promise that he would be
the heir of the world was not to Abraham or to his seed through
the law, but through the righteousness of faith. For if those who
are of the law are heirs, faith is made void and the promise made
of no effect, because the law brings about wrath; for where there
is no law there is no transgression.*

——— ROMANS 4:9-15 NKJV ———

JESUS CALLS US FRIENDS

And when he is come, he will reprove the world of sin,
and of righteousness, and of judgment.
JOHN 16:8 KJV

These words contain part of a gracious promise, which the blessed Jesus was pleased to make to his weeping and sorrowful disciples. The time was now drawing near, in which the Son of man was first to be lifted up on the cross, and afterwards to heaven. Kind, wondrous kind! had this merciful High-priest been to His disciples, during the time of His tabernacling amongst them. He had compassion on their infirmities, answered for them when assaulted by their enemies, and set them right when out of the way, either in principle or practice. He neither called nor used them as servants, but as friends; and He revealed his secrets to them from time to time. He opened their understandings, that they might understand the scriptures; explained to them the hidden mysteries of the kingdom of God, when He spoke to others in parables: nay, He became the servant of them all, and even condescended to wash their feet. The thoughts of parting with so dear and loving a Master as this, especially for a long season, must needs affect them much. ~ George Whitfield (1714-1770)

A FOREVER COMMITMENT!

. . . walk worthy of the Lord unto all pleasing, being fruitful in
every good work, and increasing in the knowledge of God;
Strengthened with all might, according to his glorious power,
unto all patience and longsuffering with joyfulness . . .

—————— COLOSSIANS 1:10, 11 KJV ——————

We can never take a vacation from Christianity. We cannot put God or Satan on hold. We can never say, "God understands if I just coast for a while. He knows my tragedy, my circumstances, my hurt. He will give me a little time to lick my wounds." God does indeed understand our struggle, pain and grief, but He intends for us to live in victory, not in defeat. He offers us grace to be more than conquerors. And though He understands, there is one who will never make allowances for us—Satan. When a root of bitterness surfaces, we must deal with it immediately. It is relatively easy to uproot a tree when it is a small shoot. But when the tree is full-grown, uprooting it becomes a monumental task. The roots have spread so far and are so large that it can take tractors, dynamite, and a lot of digging and chopping. This is exactly what it is like when we allow bitterness and other bad attitudes to linger. It pays to respond quickly. When we notice that we are bitter toward someone, we must not let the sun go down before we have dealt with our bitterness. We must pull it out of our lives before it begins to spread and go deeper. If we tolerate bitterness, rebellion, independence, pride, or unbelief, we cannot live in victory.

~ Dean Sherman (1945-)

THE NEW COVENANT

"This cup is the new covenant. . ."
I CORINTHIANS 11:25 NKJV

The Lord's Supper is a covenant meal . . . It is of great importance to understand the New Covenant thoroughly. It is something quite different from the Old Covenant — infinitely better and more glorious. The Old Covenant which God made with Israel was indeed glorious, but yet not adapted for sinful man, because he could not fulfill it. God gave to His people His perfect law, with the glorious promises of His help, His guidance, His blessing, if they should continue in the observance of it. But man in his inner life was still under the power of sin: he was lacking in the strength requisite for abiding in the covenant of His God. God promised to make a New Covenant. . . . God promised to bestow the most complete forgiveness of sins and to take man altogether into His favor . . . to communicate to him His law, not externally as written on tables, but inwardly and in his heart, so that he should have strength to fulfill its precepts. He was to give him a new heart and a new spirit — in truth, His own Holy Spirit. Man was not called on in the first instance to promise that he would walk in God's law. God rather took the initiative in promising that He would enable him to do so.
~ Andrew Murray (1828-1917)

SELF-EXAMINATION

I will instruct thee and teach thee in the way which
thou shalt go: I will guide thee with mine eye.

——— PSALM 32:8 KJV ———

True proving of ourselves consists of three parts: 1) In the first place, let everyone in his own heart reflect on his sin and condemnation, in order that he may loathe himself and humble himself before God: seeing that the wrath of God against sin is so great that, rather than suffer it to remain unpunished, He punished it in His dear Son Jesus Christ, in the bitter and ignominious death of the Cross. 2) In the second place, let everyone examine his heart as to whether he also believes this sure promise of God, that only on the ground of the suffering and death of Jesus Christ all his sins are forgiven him, and the perfect righteousness of Christ is bestowed upon him and imputed to him as his own: yea, as completely as if he himself in his own person had atoned for all his sins and performed all righteousness. 3) In the third place, let everyone examine his conscience as to whether he is prepared, henceforth and with his whole life, to manifest true thankfulness toward God the Lord, and to walk uprightly in God's sight. All who are so disposed, God will assuredly receive into His favor, and regard as worthy communicants at the table of His Son Jesus Christ. On the other hand, those that have no such testimony in their hearts, eat and drink judgment to themselves.

~ Andrew Murray (1828-1917)

PRAYER AND FAITH

And all things, whatever ye shall ask in prayer, believing, ye shall receive.
———— MATTHEW 21:22 KJV ————

Faith does the impossible because it brings God to undertake for us, and nothing is impossible with God. How great—without qualification or limitation is the power of faith! If doubt be banished from the heart, and unbelief made stranger there, what we ask of God shall surely come to pass, and a believer hath vouchsafed to him "whatsoever he saith." Prayer projects faith on God, and God on the world. Only God can move mountains, but faith and prayer move God. In His cursing of the fig-tree our Lord demonstrated His power. Following that, He proceeded to declare, that large powers were committed to faith and prayer, not in order to kill but to make alive, not to blast but to bless. ~ E. M. Bounds (1835-1913)

GOD'S PEACEMAKERS

Blessed are the Peacemakers: for they shall be called the children of God.
—— MATTHEW 5:9 KJV ——

If a man go and carry to men the great message of a reconciled and a reconciling God manifest in Jesus Christ, and bringing Peace between men and God, he will have done more to sweeten society and put an end to hostility than I think he will be likely to do by any other method. Christian men and women, whatever else you and I are here for, we are here mainly that we may preach, by lip and life, the great message that in Christ is our Peace, and. . .there is no nobler office for Christians than to seek to damp down all these devil's flames of envy and jealousy and mutual animosity. We have to do it, first, by making very sure that we do not answer scorn with scorn, gibes with gibes, hate with hate, but "seek to overcome evil with good." It takes two to make a quarrel, and your most hostile antagonist cannot break the Peace unless you help him. If you are resolved to keep it, kept it will be.

~ Alexander Maclaren (1826-1910)

Therefore it is of faith that it might be according to grace, so that the promise might be sure to all the seed, not only to those who are of the law, but also to those who are of the faith of Abraham, who is the father of us all (as it is written, "I have made you a father of many nations") in the presence of Him whom he believed—God, who gives life to the dead and calls those things which do not exist as though they did; who, contrary to hope, in hope believed, so that he became the father of many nations, according to what was spoken, "So shall your descendants be." And not being weak in faith, he did not consider his own body, already dead (since he was about a hundred years old), and the deadness of Sarah's womb. He did not waver at the promise of God through unbelief, but was strengthened in faith, giving glory to God, and being fully convinced that what He had promised He was also able to perform. And therefore "it was accounted to him for righteousness." Now it was not written for his sake alone that it was imputed to him, but also for us. It shall be imputed to us who believe in Him who raised up Jesus our Lord from the dead, who was delivered up because of our offenses, and was raised because of our justification.

ROMANS 4:16-25 NKJV

A NEW AND LIVING WAY

"Ponder the path of thy feet, and let all thy ways be established."
——— E X O D U S 2 0 : 1 2 K J V ———

Take heed thou dost not turn into those lanes which lead out of the way. There are crooked paths, paths in which men go astray, paths that lead to death and damnation, but take heed of all those. Some of them are dangerous because of practice, some because of opinion, but mind them not; mind the path before thee, look right before thee, turn neither to the right hand nor to the left, but let thine eyes look right on, even right before thee; Turn not to the right hand nor to the left. "Remove thy foot far from evil." This counsel being not so seriously taken as given, is the reason of that starting from opinion to opinion, reeling this way and that way, out of this lane into that lane, and so missing the way to the kingdom. Tho the way to heaven be but one, yet there are many crooked lanes and by-paths that shoot down upon it, as I may say. And again, notwithstanding the kingdom of heaven be the biggest city, yet usually those by-paths are most beaten, most travelers go those ways; and therefore the way to heaven is hard to be found, and as hard to be kept in, by reason of these. . .the scarlet streams of Christ's blood run throughout the way to the kingdom of heaven; therefore mind that, see if thou do not find the besprinkling of the blood of Christ in the way, and if thou do, be of good cheer, thou art in the right way. . . ~ John Bunyan (1628-1688)

HONORING YOUR FAMILY

Honour thy father and thy mother: that thy days may be long
upon the land which the LORD thy God giveth thee.

EXODUS 20:12 KJV

"Honor thy father and thy mother" is one of the Ten Commandments. While Christ hung upon the cross he remembered his own mother Mary and charged the beloved Apostle John to care for her. Caring for and serving the weak and needy and old and sick has been a mark of Christianity from its inception and this application is most pertinent to the members of one's own family. The church father Gregory of Nazianzus was raised in a devout Christian family. In his example of deeds and funeral orations of words Gregory exemplified this tender aspect of Christianity when he returned to his hometown of Nazianzus to take charge of the affairs of his dead brother and then served as in succession his beloved sister, father and mother died. Sometimes the child must give many years of physical assistance and bear the emotional burdens and restrictions of such care. Some times there have been ruptures in family relations where forgiveness, humility and submissive self sacrifice are necessary for the sanctified carrying out of such service. Such service and ministering is often tedious and burdensome, seldom glamorous. But it can be made sweet and rewarding by the grace of God and the spirit of Him who "came, not to be ministered unto but to minister. . ." ~ Raymond V. Banner (1937-)

GRACE, MERCY, AND PEACE

Grace be with you, mercy, and peace, from God the Father,
and from the Lord Jesus Christ, the Son of the Father, in truth and love.
———— II John 1:3 KJV ————

"Grace, Mercy, and Peace," stand related to each other in a very interesting manner as it were, from the fountain head, and slowly trace the course of the blessing down to its lodgment in the heart of man. There is the fountain, and the stream, and, if I may so say, the great still lake in the soul, into which its waters flow, and which the flowing waters make. There is the sun, and the beam, and the brightness grows deep in the heart of man. Grace, referring solely to the Divine attitude and thought: Mercy, the manifestation of grace in act, referring to the workings of that great Godhead in its relation to humanity: and Peace, which is the issue in the soul of the fluttering down upon it of the Mercy which is the activity of the Grace. So these three come down . . . a great, solemn, marble staircase from the heights of the Divine Mind . . . down to the level of earth; and the blessings which are shed along the earth . . . All begins with Grace; and the end and purpose of Grace, when it flashes into deed, and becomes Mercy, is to fill my soul with quiet repose, and shed across all the turbulent sea of human love a great calm, a beam of sunshine that gilds, and miraculously stills while it gilds, the waves. ~ Alexander Maclaren (1826 –1910)

A CALL TO BE HOLY

. . .be holy and without blame before Him. . .
——— EPHESIANS 1:4 NKJV ———

We must come out from the world and be separate, and must not be conformed to it in our characters . . . no longer share in its spirit or its ways. Our conversation must be in Heaven, and we must seek those things that are above . . . We must walk through the world as Christ walked . . . have the mind that was in Him. As pilgrims and strangers we must abstain from fleshly lusts that war against the soul. As good soldiers of Jesus Christ, we must disentangle ourselves from the affairs of this life as far as possible . . . We must abstain from all appearance of evil. We must be kind one to another, tenderhearted, forgiving one another, even as God, for Christ's sake, hath forgiven us. We must not resent injuries or unkindness, but must return good for evil, and turn the other cheek to the hand that smites us. We must take always the lowest place among our fellowmen; and seek not our own honor, but the honor of others. We must be gentle, and meek, and yielding; not standing up for our own rights, but for the rights of others. All that we do must be done for the glory of God. And, to sum it all up, since He which hath called us is holy, so we must be holy. . .
~ Hannah Whitall Smith (1832-1911)

GROWTH

But grow in grace, and in the knowledge
of our Lord and Saviour Jesus Christ.
———— II PETER 3:18 KJV ————

These are the last words of an old man, written down as his legacy to us. He was himself a striking example of his own precept. It would be interesting study to examine these two letters of the Apostle Peter in order to construct from them a picture of what he became, and to contrast it with his own earlier self when full of self confidence, rashness, and instability. It took a lifetime for Simon, the son of Jonas, to grow into Peter; but it was done. And the very faults of the character became strength. What he had proved possible in his own case he commands and commends to us, and from the height to which he has reached, he looks upwards to the infinite ascent which he knows he will attain when he puts off this tabernacle; and then downwards to his brethren, bidding them, too, climb and aspire. His last word is like that of the great Roman Catholic Apostle to the East Indies: "Forward!" He is like some trumpeter on the battlefield who spends his last breath in sounding an advance. Immortal hope animates his dying injunction: "Grow! Grow in Grace, and in the knowledge of our Lord and Savior."
~ Alexander Maclaren (1826-1910)

SEEING THE CREATOR
IN HIS CREATION

But as God has distributed to each one,
as the Lord has called each one, so let him walk.

———— I CORINTHIANS 7:17 NKJV ————

How far you go in life depends on your being tender with the young, compassionate with the aged, sympathetic with the striving and tolerant of the weak and strong. Because someday in your life you will have been all of these. I love to think of nature as an unlimited broadcasting station, through which God speaks to us every hour, if we will only tune in. Ninety-nine percent of the failures come from people who have the habit of making excuses.

Our creator is the same and never changes despite the names given Him by people here and in all parts of the world. Even if we gave Him no name at all, He would still be there, within us, waiting to give us good on this earth.

When I was young, I said to God, "God, tell me the mystery of the universe." But God answered, that knowledge is for me alone. So I said, "God, tell me the mystery of the peanut." Then God said, "Well, George, that's more nearly your size." Reading about nature is fine, but if a person walks in the woods and listens carefully, he can learn more than what is in books, for they speak with the voice of God. Where there is no vision, there is no hope.

~ George Washington Carver (1860-1943)

Therefore, having been justified by faith, we have peace with God through our Lord Jesus Christ, through whom also we have access by faith into this grace in which we stand, and rejoice in hope of the glory of God. And not only that, but we also glory in tribulations, knowing that tribulation produces perseverance; and perseverance, character; and character, hope. Now hope does not disappoint, because the love of God has been poured out in our hearts by the Holy Spirit who was given to us.

—— ROMANS 5:1-5 NKJV ——

STANDING FIRM

FOLLOWING AFTER GOD

But they that wait upon the LORD shall renew their strength;
they shall mount up with wings as eagles; they shall run,
and not be weary; and they shall walk, and not faint.

———— ISAIAH 40:31 KJV ————

To those who set their gaze on Christ, no present from which He wishes them to remove can be so good for them as the new conditions into which He would have them pass. It is hard to leave the spot, though it be in the desert, where we have so long encamped that it has come to look like home. We may look with regret on the circle of black ashes on the sand where our little fire glinted cheerily, and our feet may ache and our hearts ache more as we begin our tramp once again, but we must set ourselves to meet the God appointed change cheerfully, in the confidence that nothing will be left behind which it is not good to lose, nor anything met, which does not bring a blessing, however its first aspect may be harsh or sad . . . A heart that waits and watches for God's direction, that uses common sense as well as faith to unravel small and great perplexities, and is willing to sit loose to the present, however pleasant, in order that it may not miss the indications which say "Arise! this is not your rest" — fulfills the conditions on which, if we keep them, we may be sure that He will guide us by the right way, and bring us at last to the city of habitation. ~ Alexander Maclaren (1826-1910)

HE WILL DO

He that believeth on me, the works that I do shall he do also; and greater
works than these shall he do; because I go unto my Father. And whatsoever
ye shall ask in my name, that will I do, that the Father may be glorified
in the Son. If ye shall ask anything in my name, I will do it.
—— JOHN 14:12-14 KJV ——

How wonderful are these statements of what God will do in answer to prayer! Of how great importance these ringing words, prefaced, as they are, with the most solemn verity! Faith in Christ is the basis of all working, and of all praying. All wonderful works depend on wonderful praying, and all praying is done in the Name of Jesus Christ. Amazing lesson, of wondrous simplicity, is this praying in the name of the Lord Jesus! All other conditions are depreciated, everything else is renounced, save Jesus only. The name of Christ — the Person of our Lord and Savior Jesus Christ — must be supremely sovereign, in the hour and article of prayer. If Jesus dwell at the fountain of my life; if the currents of His life have displaced and superseded all self-currents; if implicit obedience to Him be the inspiration and force of every movement of my life, then He can safely commit the praying to my will, and pledge Himself, by an obligation as profound as His own nature, that whatsoever is asked shall be granted. Nothing can be clearer, more distinct, more unlimited both in application and extent, than the exhortation and urgency of Christ, "Have faith in God."

~ E. M. Bounds (1835-1913)

ZION'S JOY

*Sing, O Daughter of Zion; shout, O Israel; be glad and rejoice with
all the heart, O daughter of Jerusalem. . . . he will rejoice over thee with joy;
he will rest in his love, he will joy over thee with singing.*

ZEPHANIAH 3:14, 17 KJV

WHAT A WONDERFUL RUSH of exuberant gladness there is in
these words! The swift, short clauses, the triple invocation in the former
verse, the triple promise in the latter, the heaped together synonyms all
help the impression. The very words seem to dance with joy. But more
remarkable than this is the parallelism between the two verses. Zion is
called to rejoice in God because God rejoices in her. She is to shout for
joy and sing because God's joy too has a voice, and breaks out into
singing. For every throb of joy in man's heart, there is a wave of
gladness in God's. The notes of our praise are at once the echoes and
the occasions of His. We are to be glad because He is glad: He is glad
because we are so. We sing for joy, and He joys over us with singing
because we do. We are solemnly warned by "profound thinkers" of
letting the shadow of our emotions fall upon God. No doubt there is a
real danger there; but there is a worse danger, that of conceiving of a
God who has no life and heart; and it is better to hold fast by this —
that in Him is that which corresponds to what in us is gladness.

~ Alexander Maclaren (1826-1919)

IN THE BODY

. . .glorify God in your body, and in your spirit, which are God's.
I CORINTHIANS 6:20 KJV

God having made the heavens and the earth, which do not feel the happiness of their being, He has willed to make beings who should know it, and who should compose a body of thinking members. For our members do not feel the happiness of their union, of their wonderful intelligence, of the care which has been taken to infuse into them minds, and to make them grow and endure. How happy they would be if they saw and felt it! But for this they would need to have intelligence to know it, and good-will to consent to that of the universal soul. But if, having received intelligence, they employed it to retain nourishment for themselves without allowing it to pass to the other members, they would be not only unjust, but also miserable, and would hate rather than love themselves; their blessedness, as well as their duty, consisting in their consent to the guidance of the whole soul to which they belong, which loves them better than they love themselves. To be a member is to have neither life, being, nor movement, except through the spirit of the body, and for the body. ~ Blaise Pascal (1623-1662)

PRAYER FOR REVIVAL

*For I will pour water upon him that is thirsty, and floods upon
the dry ground: I will pour my Spirit upon thy seed, and my
blessing upon thine offspring: And they shall spring up as among
the grass, as willows by the water courses.*

———— Isaiah 44:3, 4 KJV ————

God has given much honor to His ministers, but not the privilege
of pouring out the Spirit. He keeps that in His own hand: "I will pour."
"It is not by might, nor by power, but by My Spirit, saith the Lord of
hosts." Alas! we would have little hope, if it depended upon ministers,
for where are our men of might now? God is as able to do it today as He
was at the day of Pentecost; but men are taken up with ministers, and
not with God. As long as you look to a minister, God cannot pour, for
you would say it came from man. Prayer is more powerful than
preaching. It is prayer that gives preaching all its power. I observe that
some Christians are very ready to censure ministers and to complain of
their preaching, of their coldness, their unfaithfulness. God forbid that
I should ever defend unfaithful preaching, or coldness, or deadness, in
the ambassador of Christ! May my right hand sooner forget its
cunning! But I do say, where lies the blame of unfaithfulness? Where,
but in the lack of faithful praying? Why, the very hands of Moses would
have fallen down, had they not been held up by his faithful people.
~ Robert Murray McCheyne (1813-1843)

THE INNER LIFE

*I counsel thee to buy of me gold tried in the fire, that thou
mayest be rich; and white raiment that thou mayest be clothed,
and that the shame of thy nakedness do not appear; and anoint
thine eyes with eyesalve, that thou mayest see.*

REVELATION 3:18 KJV

What men stand most in need of, is the knowledge of God. They know, to be sure, by dint of reading, that history gives an account of a certain series of miracles and marked providences; they have reflected seriously on the corruption and instability of worldly things; they are even, perhaps, convinced that the reformation of their lives on certain principles of morality is desirable in order to their salvation; but the whole of the edifice is destitute of foundation; this pious and Christian exterior possesses no soul. The living principle which animates every true believer, God, the all and in all, the author and the sovereign of all, is wanting. He is, in all things, infinite — in wisdom power and love, — and what wonder, if everything that comes from his hand should partake of the same infinite character and set at nought the efforts of human reason. ~ Jeanne Marie Vouvier de la Mothe Guyon (1647–1711)

For when we were still without strength, in due time Christ died for the ungodly. For scarcely for a righteous man will one die; yet perhaps for a good man someone would even dare to die. But God demonstrates His own love toward us, in that while we were still sinners, Christ died for us. Much more then, having now been justified by His blood, we shall be saved from wrath through Him. For if when we were enemies we were reconciled to God through the death of His Son, much more, having been reconciled, we shall be saved by His life. And not only that, but we also rejoice in God through our Lord Jesus Christ, through whom we have now received the reconciliation.

—— ROMANS 5:6-11 NKJV ——

STANDING FIRM

THE ADVENT OF OUR KING

The advent of our King Our prayers must now employ,
And we must hymns of welcome sing In strains of holy joy.
The everlasting Son Incarnate deigns to be;
Himself a servant's form puts on To set His servants free.
O Zion's Daughter, rise To meet thy lowly King,
Nor let thy faithless heart despise The peace He comes to bring.
As Judge, on clouds of light, He soon will come again
And His true members all unite With Him in heaven to reign.
Before the dawning day Let sin's dark deeds be gone,
The old man all be put away, The new man all put on.
All glory to the Son, Who comes to set us free,
With Father, Spirit, ever One, Through all eternity.
~ Charles Coffin (1676-1749)

THE FATHER'S LOVE

Behold what manner of love the Father has bestowed on us. . .
—— I JOHN 3:1 NKJV ——

Learn this solemn truth that the Father loves you, the Father wants you to be saved, the Father wants you to believe on the Son; the very Father who commanded Christ to lay down his life for sinners. You will notice from this that the Father is clear from the blood of all men. He does not want you to perish. "Turn ye, turn ye. why will ye die?" He is not willing that any should perish. "He willeth all men to be saved, and to come to the knowledge of the truth." He does not want you to perish. He commands Christ to go into the world, and lay down his life for sinners. Oh! it is true: the Father does not want you to perish. "God so loved the world, that he gave his only begotten Son." "God sent not his Son into the world to condemn the world; but that the world through him might be saved." God the Father is as earnest in your salvation as Christ is. It was God's part to send the Son, and the Son's part to come and die. And as God the Son has done his part, so God the Father has done his. So that, sinners, if you perish, it is because you will not come to him, that you may have life. ~ Robert Murray McCheyne (1813-1843)

THE GREAT APOSTASY AND THE GREAT TRIBULATION

"But of that day and hour no one knows. . .but My Father only."
—————— MATTHEW 24:36 NKJV ——————

The Bible teaches repeatedly that toward the end of time there will be a great falling away. Iniquity will increase, and the love of many will wax cold. Wickedness crying to high heaven will result in a terrible tribulation "such as hath not been from the beginning of the world until now, no, nor ever shall be" Matthew 24:21 ASV. If those days were not shortened no flesh would be saved; but they will be shortened for the sake of the elect. The Bible also refers to striking signs as marking the beginning of the end. There will be wars, famines, and earthquakes in diverse places, which are called the beginning of travail, to be followed by the rebirth of the universe; and also fearful portents in heaven, when the powers of the heavens will be shaken. After these signs the Son of Man will be seen coming on the clouds of heaven. Some believe that the coming of Christ is imminent, that is, may now occur at any time. But the Bible teaches us that the events and signs mentioned in the foregoing must precede the return. From God's point of view the coming is always near; but no one can determine the exact time, not even the angels nor the Son of Man.

~ Louis Berkoff (1809-1833)

AFFLICTION

Surely it is meet to be said unto God, I have born chastisement.
I will not offend any more: That which I see not teach thou me:
if I have done iniquity, I will do no more.

———— JOB 34:31, 32 KJV ————

This world is a world of trouble: "Man that is born of woman, is of few days, and full of trouble." "We dwell in cottages of clay, our foundation is in the dust, we are crushed before the moth," Job 4:19. This world has sometimes been called "a vale of tears." Trials come into all your dwellings; the children of God are not excepted; there is a need be that you be in many temptations. "Count it not strange when you fall into diverse temptations, as though some strange thing happened unto you." If this be so, of how great importance is it, that you and I be prepared to meet it. The darkest thunder cloud only covers the heavens for a time . . . Remember, it is right to learn contentment. What right have you to complain? What right have you to challenge God's dealings with you? If little children were to take upon them to decide upon the proceedings of both houses of Parliament, what would you think of it? And what right have you to challenge God's government? We should say, with Job, "The Lord gave, and the Lord hath taken away; blessed be the name of the Lord." ~ Robert Murray McCheyne (1813-1843)

RIGHT MOTIVES

For the love of Christ compels us, because we judge thus:
that if One died for all, then all died. . .
—— II CORINTHIANS 5:14 NKJV ——

One of our greatest privileges as human beings is that we bear the imprint of our Maker. We are created in the image of God, and a key aspect of this image is volition of free choice. This is what separates us from the rest of creation. God could have created us to simply follow animal instincts. He also could have created us as robotic automations to fulfill His will. Instead, He "took a chance" and gave us this aspect of His own nature. He chose to do so because He knew that the deepest relationships form only when free choice is involved. One of the reasons we study God's character is that we see how aspects of His character (love, kindness, goodness, faithfulness, etc.) motivate Him to take certain actions. For example, ". . . God so loved the world that He *gave* . . ." (John 3:16, emphasis mine). This great verse shows that He gave His Son as an atoning sacrifice for our sins out of a motive of love for us. Having strong motives also drives the work of evangelism.
~ Danny Lehmann (1954-)

SURRENDER

. . .yield yourselves unto God.

ROMANS 6:13 KJV

Have you confessed, renounced and surrendered? If you have, then all you have to do is to believe. God will then give you a supernatural faith and you will be able to trust Him for the fullness of the Holy Spirit. Remember, the Holy Spirit is more anxious to fill you than you are to be filled. Nature abhors a vacuum. So it is with the Holy Ghost. As soon as your heart is ready He will come in and then He will complete the transformation until you are finally changed into Christlikeness. There may not be any great emotional experience. God never promises it. No two are filled the same. When there is a lot of sin there may be a tremendous experience. When there is a big dam and it is suddenly taken away, there will be a mighty rush and roar as the water pours over. If there is no great dam, then, as you quietly yield, He will flow in in His fullness and fill you without any tremendous upheaval, but it will be real nevertheless. The result will be seen in your ministry. You will be used by God. Conviction will grip the hearts of those to whom you preach, or witness. God will work in you and through you for His glory. ~ Oswald J. Smith (1889–1986)

Therefore, just as through one man sin entered the world, and death through sin, and thus death spread to all men, because all sinned—(For until the law sin was in the world, but sin is not imputed when there is no law. Nevertheless death reigned from Adam to Moses, even over those who had not sinned according to the likeness of the transgression of Adam, who is a type of Him who was to come. But the free gift is not like the offense. For if by the one man's offense many died, much more the grace of God and the gift by the grace of the one Man, Jesus Christ, abounded to many. And the gift is not like that which came through the one who sinned. For the judgment which came from one offense resulted in condemnation, but the free gift which came from many offenses resulted in justification. For if by the one man's offense death reigned through the one, much more those who receive abundance of grace and of the gift of righteousness will reign in life through the One, Jesus Christ.)

Romans 5:12-17 NKJV

AN EXHORTATION TO HUMILITY

The fear of the Lord is the instruction of wisdom,
And before honor is humility.

—————— PROVERBS 15:33 NKJV ——————

Let us therefore, brethren, be of humble mind, laying aside all haughtiness, and pride, and foolishness, and angry feelings; and let us act according to that which is written (for the Holy Spirit saith, "Let not the wise man glory in his wisdom, neither let the mighty man glory in his might, neither let the rich man glory in his riches; but let him that glorieth glory in the Lord, in diligently seeking Him, and doing judgment and righteousness"), being especially mindful of the words of the Lord Jesus which He spake, teaching us meekness and long-suffering. For thus He spoke: "Be ye merciful, that ye may obtain mercy; forgive, that it may be forgiven to you; as ye do, so shall it be done unto you; as ye judge, so shall ye be judged; as ye are kind, so shall kindness be shown to you; with what measure ye mete, with the same it shall be measured to you." By this precept and by these rules let us establish ourselves, that we walk with all humility in obedience to His holy words. For the holy word saith, "On whom shall I look, but on him that is meek and peaceable, and that trembleth at My words?"
~ Philip Schaff (1819-1893)

FROM GROANS TO PRAISE

Let the saints be joyful in glory . . .
———— PSALM 149:5 KJV ————

Truly we are more than conquerors through Him that loved us; for we can give thanks before the fight is done. Yes, even in the thickest of the battle we can look up to Jesus, and cry, Thanks to God. The moment a soul groaning under corruption rests the eye on Jesus, that moment his groans are changed into songs of praise. In Jesus you discover a fountain to wash away the guilt of all your sin. In Jesus you discover grace sufficient for you, — grace to hold you up to the end — and a sure promise that sin shall soon be rooted out all together. "Fear not, I have redeemed thee. I have called thee by My name; thou art Mine." Ah, this turns our groans into songs of praise! How often a psalm begins with groans and ends with praises! This is the daily experience of all the Lord's people. Is it yours? Try yourselves by this. Oh, if you know not the believer's song of praise, you will never cast your crowns with them at the feet of Jesus! Dear believers, be content to glory in your infirmities, that the power of Christ may rest upon you. Glory, glory, glory to the Lamb! ~ Robert Murray McCheyne (1813-1843)

CONSECRATED WHOLLY TO GOD

My soul melteth for heaviness:
strengthen thou me according unto thy word.
—— PSALM 119:28 KJV ——

But who am I, and what is my people, that we should be able to offer so willingly after this sort? For all things come of Thee, and of Thine own have we given Thee. To be and abide in continual dependence upon God. Become nothing, begin to understand that you are nothing but an earthen vessel into which God will shine down the treasure of His love. Blessed is the man who knows what it is to be nothing, to be just an empty vessel meet for God's use. Work, the Apostle says, for it is God who worketh in you to will and to do. Brethren, come and take tonight the place of deep, deep dependence on God. And then take the place of child-like trust and expectancy. Count upon your God to do for you everything that you can desire of Him. Honour God as a God who gives liberally. Honour God and believe that He asks nothing from you but what He is going first to give. And then come praise and surrender and consecration. Praise Him for it! Let every sacrifice to Him be a thank-offering. What are we going to consecrate? First of all our lives. ~ Andrew Murray (1828-1917)

THE DOOR

Then said Jesus unto them again, Verily, verily, I say unto you, I am the door
of the sheep. All that ever came before me are thieves and robbers: but the
sheep did not hear them. I am the door: by me if any man enter in, he shall
be saved, and shall go in and out, and find pasture. The thief cometh not,
but for to steal, and to kill, and to destroy: I am come that they might have
life, and that they might have it more abundantly.

JOHN 10:7–10 KJV

Christ is the kindest of all teachers. He was speaking to a crowd of ignorant and prejudiced Jews, and yet how kindly he deals with them. He told them one parable, but they understood not. "This parable spake Jesus unto them; but they understood not what things they were he spake unto them." And yet, we are told, Christ spake unto them again. He hath given them a description of the true and false shepherd, and of the door into the sheepfold; but they seem to have been at a loss to know what the door meant; therefore he says, "Verily, verily, I say unto you, I am the door of the sheep." You see how kindly he tries to instruct them. My brethren, Christ is the same kind teacher still. Are there not many stupid and prejudiced persons here? And yet has he not given you "precept upon precept, precept upon precept; line upon line, line upon line; here a little, and there a little," Isaiah 13:28.

~ Robert Murray McCheyne (1813-1843)

MAKING HIM KING!

Because the LORD hath loved his people,
he hath made thee king over them.

II CHRONICLES 2:11 KJV

God's loving appointment in making Jesus King will be apparent when we remember how beautiful He is in his personal character; how closely He is identified with our nature; the might of his arm with which He shields, the patience wherewith He bears, the redemption which He has wrought out and brought in for all who believe. What could God's love have done better to approve itself? Is He your King? Never till He is so, will you know the fulness of God's love. Those who question or refuse his authority are always in doubt about the love of God to themselves and to the world. Those, on the other hand, who acknowledge his claims, and crown Him as King, suddenly find themselves admitted to a standpoint of vision in which doubts and disputations vanish, and the secret love of God is unfolded. Then they experience the wise and gentle tendance of the Divine love in its most entrancing characteristics. All is love where Jesus reigns. Nothing is more indicative of God's benevolence than his incessant appeal to men to make Jesus King. "Go, spread your trophies at his feet, And crown Him Lord of all!" ~ F.B. Meyer (1847-1929)

RUNNING THE RACE

Know ye not that they which run in a race run all,
but one receiveth the prize? So run, that ye may obtain.
—————— I CORINTHIANS 9:24 KJV ——————

It's not the beginning of the race that's difficult. The hardest part of the race is just before we cross the finish line. We start out, fresh and lively, confident as we set our pace. But, somewhere along the way, we begin to grow tired and weary. Our feet and legs seem like wood and we stumble along, grasping with our hands to keep from falling. Sometimes we are blessed with a "second wind" and we pick up the pace and run faster, gaining strides and making up for lost time. At other times, just before we hit the ground, we feel a Strong Arm or someone's prayers that lifts us up until we are back in the race. Sometimes we look around to see those who took themselves out of the race and it causes us to doubt our own strength. "If they fell, how can I succeed?" we ask. Yet, it's not how another runs the race that determines our success. No, it's whether or not we keep our eyes on Jesus and run towards the finish line — even we can't see it. It's His face that we must keep before us regardless of what the world says or does and regardless of how badly our feet are hurting. We run on — because of the cross and for the crown. ~ Jacquelyn Sheppard (1943-)

Therefore, as through one man's offense judgment came to all men, resulting in condemnation, even so through one Man's righteous act the free gift came to all men, resulting in justification of life. For as by one man's disobedience many were made sinners, so also by one Man's obedience many will be made righteous. Moreover the law entered that the offense might abound. But where sin abounded, grace abounded much more, so that as sin reigned in death, even so grace might reign through righteousness to eternal life through Jesus Christ our Lord.

ROMANS 5:18-21 NKJV

WALK WITH CHRIST

We took sweet counsel together,
and walked unto the house of God in company.
———— PSALM 55:14 KJV ————

"There is a path which no fool knoweth, and which the vulture's eye hath not seen: the lion's whelps have not trodden it, nor the fierce lion passed by it." What an unspeakable mercy for one who really desires to walk with God, to know that there is a way for him to walk in! God has prepared a pathway for His redeemed in which they may walk with all possible certainty, calmness and fixedness. It is the privilege of every child of God, and every servant of Christ, to be as sure that he is in God's way as that his soul should be saved. This may seem a strong statement; but the question is, Is it true? If it be true, it cannot be too strong. No doubt it may, in the judgment of some, savor a little of self confidence and dogmatism to assert, in such a day as that in which we live, and in the midst of such a scene as that through which we're passing, that we are sure of being in God's path. . . . the selfsame voice that tells us of God's salvation for our souls, tells us also of God's pathway for our feet. ~ C.H. Mackintosh (1820-1896)

WALK OF FAITH

So Jesus answered and said to them, "Have faith in God."
MARK 11:22 NKJV

The blessed apostle declares himself not ashamed of The gospel; "for it is The power of God unto salvation to everyone that believeth; to The Jew first, and also to The Greek. For therein is The righteousness of God revealed, on The principle of faith, to faith: as it is written, The just shall live by faith . . . but that no man is justified by The law in The sight of God, it is evident: For, The just shall live by faith." Finally, in The tenth of Hebrews, where The object is to exhort believers to hold fast their confidence, we read, "Cast not away therefore your confidence, which hath great recompense of reward. For ye have need of patience, that, after ye have done The will of God, ye might receive The promise. For yet a little while, He that shall come will come, and will not tarry. Now The just shall live by faith." Here we have faith presented not only as The ground of righteousness, but as The vital principle by which we are to live, day by day, from The starting-post to The goal of The Christian course. There is no other way of righteousness, no other way of living, but by faith. It is by faith we are justified, and by faith we live. By faith we stand, and By faith we walk. ~ C.H. Mackintosh (1820-1896)

SAVIOR OF THE NATIONS, COME

Savior of the nations, come, Virgin's Son, make here Thy home!
Marvel now, O heaven and earth, That the Lord chose such a birth.
Not by human flesh and blood, By the Spirit of our God,
Was the Word of God made flesh — Woman's Offspring, pure and fresh.
Wondrous birth! O wondrous Child Of the Virgin undefiled!
Though by all the world disowned, Still to be in heaven enthroned.
From the Father forth He came And returneth to the same,
Captive leading death and hell — High the song of triumph swell!
Thou, the Father's only Son, Hast o'er sin the victory won.
Boundless shall Thy kingdom be When shall we its glories see?
Brightly doth Thy manger shine, Glorious is its light divine
Let not sin o'ercloud this light; Ever be our faith thus bright.
Praise to God the Father sing, Praise to God the Son, our King,
Praise to God the Spirit be Ever and eternally.
~ Martin Luther (1483-1546)

TRAIN UP A CHILD

Train up a child in the way he should go:
and when he is old, he will not depart from it.
———— PROVERBS 22:6 KJV ————

The world is old, and we have the experience of nearly six thousand years to help us. We live in days when there is a mighty zeal for education in every quarter. We hear of new schools rising on all sides. We are told of new systems, and new books for the young, of every sort and description. And still for all this, the vast majority of children are manifestly not trained in the way they should go, for when they grow up to man's estate, they do not walk with God. The plain truth is, the Lord's commandment in our text is not regarded; and therefore the Lord's promise in our text is not fulfilled. I know that you cannot convert your child. I know well that they who are born again are born, not of the will of man, but of God. But I know also that God says expressly, "Train up a child in the way he should go," and that He never laid a command on man which He would not give man Grace to perform . . . It is just in the going forward that God will meet us. The path of obedience is the way in which He gives the blessing. We have only to do as the servants were commanded at the marriage feast in Cana, to fill the water pots with water, and we may safely leave it to the Lord to turn that water into wine. ~ J.C. Ryle (1816-1900)

HE SEEKS US

For the Son of man is come to seek and to save that which was lost.
—— LUKE 19:10 KJV ——

It is simply and only a question of becoming acquainted with God, and getting to know what He is, and what He does, and what He feels. Comfort and peace never come from anything we know about ourselves, but only and always from what we know about Him. We may spend our days in what we call our religious duties, and we may fill our devotions with fervor, and still may be miserable. Nothing can set our hearts at rest but a real acquaintance with God; for, after all, everything in our salvation must depend upon Him in the last instance; and, according as He is worthy or not of our confidence, so must necessarily be our comfort. If we were planning to take a dangerous voyage, our first question would be as to the sort of captain we were to have. Our common sense would tell us that if the captain were untrustworthy, no amount of trustworthiness on our part would make the voyage safe; and it would be his character and not our own that would be the thing of paramount importance to us. ~ Hannah Whitall Smith (1832-1911)

PERSONAL OIL

'Give us some of your oil. . .'
MATTHEW 25:8 NKJV

No one can give of his oil to another . . . A man can give light, but he cannot give oil. The latter is the gift of God alone. "The wise answered, saying, Not so; lest there be not enough for us and you, but go ye rather to them that sell and buy for yourselves. And while they went to buy, the Bridegroom came, and they that were ready went in with him to the marriage; and the door was shut." It is of no use looking to Christian friends to help us or prop us up. No use in flying hither and thither for some one to lean upon. . .our creed, or our sacraments. We want oil. Not from man, not from the church, not from the saints, not from the fathers. We must get it from God; and He, blessed be His name, gives freely. "The Gift of God is eternal life, through Jesus Christ our Lord." No man can believe, or get life for another. Each must have to do with God for himself. The link which connects the soul with Christ is intensely individual. There is no such thing as second-hand faith. A man may teach us religion, or theology, or the letter of Scripture; but he cannot give us oil; he cannot give us faith; he cannot give us life. "It is the gift of God." ~ C.H. Mackintosh (1820-1896)

What shall we say then? Shall we continue in sin that grace may abound? Certainly not! How shall we who died to sin live any longer in it? Or do you not know that as many of us as were baptized into Christ Jesus were baptized into His death? Therefore we were buried with Him through baptism into death, that just as Christ was raised from the dead by the glory of the Father, even so we also should walk in newness of life. For if we have been united together in the likeness of His death, certainly we also shall be in the likeness of His resurrection, knowing this, that our old man was crucified with Him, that the body of sin might be done away with, that we should no longer be slaves of sin. For he who has died has been freed from sin.

ROMANS 6:1-7 NKJV

STANDING FIRM

PRECIOUS CHRIST

Unto you therefore which believe he is precious. . .

——— 1 PETER 2:7 KJV ———

UNTO BELIEVERS JESUS CHRIST IS PRECIOUS. In Himself He is of inestimable preciousness, for He is the very God of very God. He is moreover, perfect man without sin. The precious gopher wood of his humanity is overlaid with the pure gold of his divinity. He is a mine of jewels, and a mountain of gems. He is altogether lovely, but, alas! this blind world seeth not his beauty. The painted harlotries of that which, Madam Bubble, the world can see, and all men wonder after her. This life, its joy, its lust, its gains, its honours, — these have beauty in the eye of the unregenerate man, but in Christ he sees nothing which he can admire. He hears his name as a common word, and looks upon his cross as a thing in which he has no interest, neglects his gospel, despises his Word, and, perhaps, vents fierce spite upon his people. But not so the believer. The man who has been brought to know that Christ is the only foundation upon which the soul can build its eternal home, he who has been taught that Jesus Christ is the first and the last, the Alpha and the Omega, the author and the finisher of faith, thinks not lightly of Christ. He calls him all his salvation and all his desire; the only glorious and lovely one. ~ Charles H. Spurgeon (1834-1892)

TO CHRIST WE OWE OUR RIGHTEOUSNESS

. . .by the obedience of one shall many be made righteous.

—— ROMANS 5:19 KJV ——

'Through the obedience of the One shall the many be made righteous.' These words tell us what we owe to Christ. As in Adam we were made sinners, in Christ we are made righteous. The words tell us, too, to what in Christ it is we owe our righteousness. As Adam's disobedience made us sinners, the obedience of Christ makes us righteous. To the obedience of Christ we owe everything. Among the treasures of our inheritance in Christ this is one of the richest . . . You are familiar with the blessed truth of justification by faith . . . The object of Christ's life of obedience was threefold: (1) As an Example, to show us what true obedience was. (2) As our Surety, by His obedience to fulfill all righteousness for us. (3) As our Head, to prepare a new and obedient nature to impart to us. So He died, too, to show us that His obedience means a readiness to obey to the uttermost, to die for God; that it means the vicarious endurance and atonement of the guilt of our disobedience; that it means a death to sin as an entrance to the life of God for Him and for us. ~ Andrew Murray (1828-1917)

EFFECTIVE PRAYER

Oh that I knew where I might find him! that I might come even to his seat!
I would order my cause before him, and fill my mouth with arguments.

————— JOB 23:3, 4 KJV —————

Put these three things together, the deep spirituality which recognizes prayer as being real conversation with the invisible God — much distinctness which is the reality of prayer, asking for what we know we want — and much fervency, believing the thing to be necessary, and therefore resolving to obtain it if it can be had by prayer, and above all these, complete submission, leaving it still with the Master's will; —commingle all these, and you have a clear idea of what it is to order your cause before the Lord. Still prayer itself is an art which only the Holy Ghost can teach us. He is the giver of all prayer. Pray for prayer — pray till you can pray; pray to be helped to pray, and give not up praying because you cannot pray, for it is when you think you cannot pray that you are most praying. Sometimes when you have no sort of comfort in your supplications, it is then that your heart all broken and cast down is really wrestling and truly prevailing with the Most High.
~ Charles H. Spurgeon (1843-1892)

SERMON ON THE MOUNT

And seeing the multitudes, He went up on a mountain. . . .Then He opened
His mouth and taught them. . .
———— MATTHEW 5:1, 2 NKJV ————

Consider the sermon which our Lord Jesus Christ spoke on the mount, as we read it in the Gospel according to Matthew . . . so far as regards the highest morals, a perfect standard of the Christian life: and this we do not rashly venture to promise, but gather it from the very words of the Lord Himself. For the sermon itself is brought to a close in such a way, that it is clear there are in it all the precepts which go to mould the life. For thus He speaks: "Therefore, whosoever heareth these words of mine, and doeth them, I will liken him unto a wise man, which built his house upon a rock: and the rain descended, and the floods came, and the winds blew, and beat upon that house; and it fell not: for it was founded upon a rock. And every one that heareth these words of mine, and doeth them not, I will liken unto a foolish man, which built his house upon the sand: and the rain descended, and the floods came, and the winds blew, and beat upon that house; and it fell: and great was the fall of it." Since, therefore, He has not simply said, "Whosoever heareth my words," but has made an addition, saying, "Whosoever heareth these words of mine," He has sufficiently indicated . . . that these sayings which He uttered on the mount so perfectly guide the life of those who may be willing to live according to them, that they may justly be compared to one building upon a rock.

~ St. Augustine (345-430)

JOY

These things I have spoken to you, that My joy may remain in you,
and that your joy may be full.

JOHN 15:11 NKJV

Joy, which was the small publicity of the pagan, is the gigantic secret of the Christian. . . . I open again the strange small book from which all Christianity came; and I am again haunted by a kind of confirmation. The tremendous figure which fills the Gospels towers in this respect, as in every other, above all the thinkers who ever thought themselves tall. His pathos was natural, almost casual. The Stoics, ancient and modern, were proud of concealing their tears. He never concealed His tears; He showed them plainly on His open face at any daily sight, such as the far sight of His native city. Yet He concealed something. Solemn supermen and imperial diplomatists are proud of restraining their anger. He never restrained His anger. He flung furniture down the front steps of the Temple, and asked men how they expected to escape the damnation of Hell. Yet He restrained something. I say it with reverence; there was in that shattering personality a thread that must be called shyness. There was something that He hid from all men when He went up a mountain to pray. There was something that He covered constantly by abrupt silence or impetuous isolation. There was some one thing that was too great for God to show us when He walked upon our earth; and I have sometimes fancied that it was His mirth. ~ Gilbert K. Chesterton (1874-1936)

REPENTANCE

Repent therefore and be converted, that your sins may be blotted out, so that times of refreshing may come from the presence of the Lord. . .
——— A C T S 3 : 1 9 N K J V ———

Our Lord denounced dreadful woes against the self-righteous Pharisees; so ministers must cut and hack them, and not spare; but say wo, wo, wo to all those that will not submit to the righteousness of Jesus Christ! I could almost say this is the last stroke the Lord Jesus gave Paul. I mean in turning him to real Christianity; for having given him a blow as a persecutor and injurious, He then brought him out of himself by revealing His person and office as a Saviour. "I am Jesus." Hence says the apostle, "I count all things but loss — that I may win Christ, and be found in Him; not having my own righteousness, which is of the law, but that which is through the faith of Christ; the righteousness which is of God by faith.". . . To be washed in His blood; to be clothed in His glorious imputed righteousness: the consequence of this imputation, or application of a Mediator's righteousness to the soul, will be a conversion from sin to holiness. They that are truly converted to Jesus, and are justified by faith in the Son of God, will take care to evidence their conversion, not only by the having grace implanted in their hearts, but by that grace diffusing itself through every faculty of the soul, and making an universal change in the whole man.
~ George Whitefield (1714-1770)

Now if we died with Christ, we believe that we shall also live with Him, knowing that Christ, having been raised from the dead, dies no more. Death no longer has dominion over Him. For the death that He died, He died to sin once for all; but the life that He lives, He lives to God. Likewise you also, reckon yourselves to be dead indeed to sin, but alive to God in Christ Jesus our Lord. Therefore do not let sin reign in your mortal body, that you should obey it in its lusts. And do not present your members as instruments of unrighteousness to sin, but present yourselves to God as being alive from the dead, and your members as instruments of righteousness to God. For sin shall not have dominion over you, for you are not under law but under grace.

ROMANS 6:8-14 NKJV

STANDING FIRM

CHRIST'S HOME IN OUR HEARTS

My kingdom is not of this world.
—— JOHN 18:36 NKJV ——

"THE kingdom of God is within you," says the Lord. Turn, then, to God with all your heart. Forsake this wretched world and your soul shall find rest. Learn to despise external things, to devote yourself to those that are within, and you will see the kingdom of God come unto you, that kingdom which is peace and joy in the Holy Spirit, gifts not given to the impious. Christ will come to you offering His consolation, if you prepare a fit dwelling for Him in your heart, whose beauty and glory, wherein He takes delight, are all from within. His visits with the inward man are frequent, His communion sweet and full of consolation, His peace great, and His intimacy wonderful indeed. Therefore, faithful soul, prepare your heart for this Bridegroom that He may come and dwell within you; He Himself says: "If any one love Me, he will keep My word, and My Father will love him, and We will come to him, and will make Our abode with him." Give place, then, to Christ, but deny entrance to all others, for when you have Christ you are rich and He is sufficient for you. He will provide for you. He will supply your every want, so that you need not trust in frail, changeable men. Christ remains forever, standing firmly with us to the end.

~ Thomas à Kempis (1380-1471)

COMMUNION WITH GOD

But if we walk in the light as He is in the light,
we have fellowship with one another...
I JOHN 1:7 NKJV

The communion of saints is twofold: 'tis their communion with God and communion with one another, (I John 1:3) That ye also may have fellowship with us, and truly our fellowship is with the Father and with His Son, Jesus Christ. Communion is a common partaking of good, either of excellency or happiness, so that when it is said the saints have communion or fellowship with the Father and with the Son, the meaning of it is that they partake with the Father and the Son of their good, which is either their excellency and glory (II Peter 1:4), Ye are made partakers of the Divine nature; Heb. 12:10, That we might be partakers of His holiness; John 17:22, 23, And the glory which Thou hast given Me I have given them, that they may be one, even as we are one, I in them and Thou in Me; or of their joy and happiness: (John 17:13) That they might have My joy fulfilled in themselves. But the Holy Ghost being the love and joy of God is His beauty and happiness, and it is in our partaking of the same Holy Spirit that our communion with God consists: (II Cor. 13:14) They are not different benefits but the same . . . for the Holy Ghost is that love and grace. . .
~ Jonathan Edwards (1703-1758)

REJOICE THE LORD IS KING!

Rejoice the Lord is King! Your Lord and King adore!
Mortals give thanks and sing, and triumph evermore.
Lift up your heart! Lift up your voice!
Rejoice! Again I say, rejoice!
Jesus, the Savior reigns, the God of truth and love:
When He had purged our stains, He took His seat above.
His kingdom cannot fail; He rules o'er earth and heaven;
The keys of death and hell are to our Jesus given.
He sits at God's right hand till all His foes submit,
And bow to His command, and fall beneath His feet:
Rejoice in glorious hope! Jesus the Judge shall come and take
His servants up to their eternal home:
We soon shall hear the archangel's voice,
the trump of God shall sound: rejoice!
~ Charles Wesley (1707-1788)

CONFLICT AND CONQUEST

"If the righteous one is scarcely saved,
Where will the ungodly and the sinner appear?"
I PETER 4:18 NKJV

Must a regenerate Christian daily pour out to God so many ardent prayers and utter so many agonizing supplications, shed so many bitter tears, be so distressed and concerned respecting his sins, find it necessary to strive so manfully against them, and in addition be compelled to endure so many temptations and afflictions; and can you, by one heartless sigh to God and a little superficial service, become an heir of salvation? Oh, no! But, do you ask, are there none then saved who do not experience such a conflict? No, none! . . . Let it not be supposed, however, that this conflict is the meritorious cause of the salvation of the righteous. Oh, no! That is to be attributed to pure sovereign grace, but it is the way to salvation, for God leads His children through conflict and conquest. You will possibly say, "If this be so narrow a way, I should dread to enter upon it; for who could always live thus?" But know, O man, that it is but for a time, and that the sufferings of this present time are not to be compared with the glory which shall hereafter be revealed to the children of God (Romans 8:18). Is the labor great? The reward is still greater. Is the contest severe? The victory is glorious. Though the battle endure for awhile, the glorious issue is certain. ~ Theodorus J. Frelinghuysen (1691-1748)

CONFORMED TO HIS IMAGE

*For our light affliction, which is but for a moment, worketh
for us a far more exceeding and eternal weight of glory. . .*
—————— II CORINTHIANS 4:17 KJV ——————

. . .in choosing us in Christ before the foundation of the world, our Heavenly Father also had in His eternal plan the sphere of service with which He intended to entrust us. In doing so, surely He had in mind that through our reaction in all the testing of Christian work and through our faithfulness or lack of it in the opportunities that He is pleased to give us, we are fashioned into the likeness of His dear Son. . . What a day it will be when the Lord welcomes us home! Indeed, it will be worth it all when we see Jesus. We will understand then, as we can never understand now, that the very wounds which so often have been inflicted upon us have been the means of conforming us to the image of the Lord Jesus Christ, and of making Him all the more precious to us. Circumstances which we have resented, situations which we have found desperately difficult, have all been the means in the hands of God of driving the nails into the self-life which so easily complains. His dealing causes us to rejoice in the midst of affliction, "For our light affliction, which is but for a moment, worketh for us a far more exceeding and eternal weight of glory." ~ Alan Redpath (1907-)

PRAYER

I desire therefore that the men pray everywhere. . .
————— I TIMOTHY 2:8 NKJV —————

God's command to "pray without ceasing" is founded on the necessity we have of his grace to preserve the life of God in the soul, which can no more subsist one moment without it, than the body can without air. Whether we think of; or speak to God, whether we act or suffer for him, all is prayer, when we have no other object than his love, and the desire of pleasing him. All that a Christian does, even in eating and sleeping, is prayer, when it is done in simplicity, according to the order of God, without either adding to or diminishing from it by his own choice. Prayer continues in the desire of the heart, though the understanding be employed on outward things. In souls filled with love, the desire to please God is a continual prayer. As the furious hate which the devil bears us is termed the roaring of a lion, so our vehement love may be termed crying after God. God only requires of his adult children, that their hearts be truly purified, and that they offer him continually the wishes and vows that naturally spring from perfect love. For these desires, being the genuine fruits of love, are the most perfect prayers that can spring from it. ~ John Wesley (1703-1788)

What then? Shall we sin because we are not under law but under grace? Certainly not! Do you not know that to whom you present yourselves slaves to obey, you are that one's slaves whom you obey, whether of sin leading to death, or of obedience leading to righteousness? But God be thanked that though you were slaves of sin, yet you obeyed from the heart that form of doctrine to which you were delivered. And having been set free from sin, you became slaves of righteousness. I speak in human terms because of the weakness of your flesh. For just as you presented your members as slaves of uncleanness, and of lawlessness leading to more lawlessness, so now present your members as slaves of righteousness for holiness. For when you were slaves of sin, you were free in regard to righteousness. What fruit did you have then in the things of which you are now ashamed? For the end of those things is death. But now having been set free from sin, and having become slaves of God, you have your fruit to holiness, and the end, everlasting life. For the wages of sin is death, but the gift of God is eternal life in Christ Jesus our Lord.

ROMANS 6:15-23 NKJV

SPIRITUAL WARFARE

Let us hold fast the profession of our faith without
wavering; (for he is faithful that promised;). . .
———— HEBREWS 10:23 KJV ————

We are called to spiritual warfare, not a sheltered life of comfort without pain. Our comfort comes from knowing who God is. We are called to be overcomers, not avoiders. We are called to establish the Kingdom of God and resist the powers of darkness. God could remove us from the planet as soon as we're saved, but He chooses to leave us here to become spiritual warriors. We must live through suffering with right reactions. We must grit our teeth and endure adversity righteously to defeat the enemy's attacks. We are the primary combatants upon whom rests the future. This is not to exclude God. He is our Creator, our Lord, and our victorious Savior. He is our strength and our hope. He has ensured the conquest of the powers of darkness. Nevertheless, He has chosen not to leave us out. He has delegated responsibility to us. He has chosen us as co-workers in the establishment of His Kingdom of darkness. God is waiting for His people to rise up and take hold of the victory He purchased on the Cross. He desires that we reach back to the Cross by praying in Jesus' name and bringing that total victory into every space and time. . .
~ Dean Sherman (1945 -)

OUT OF AND INTO

And he brought us out from thence, that he might bring us in,
to give us the land which he sware unto our fathers.

———— DEUTERONOMY 6:23 KJV ————

After Israel had crossed the river, the Captain of the Lord's host had to come and encourage Joshua, promising to take charge of the army and remain with them. You need the power of God's Spirit to enable you to overcome sin and temptation. You need to live in His fellowship — in His unbroken fellowship, without which you cannot stand or conquer. If you are to venture today, say by faith "My God, I know that Jesus Christ is willing to be the Captain of my salvation, and to conquer every enemy for me, He will keep me by faith and by His Holy Spirit; and though it be dark to me, and as if the waters would pass over my soul, and though my condition seem hopeless, I will walk forward, for God is going to bring me in to-day, and I am going to follow Him. My God, I follow Thee now into the promised land." Perhaps some have already entered in, and the angels have seen them, while they have been reading these solemn words. Is there anyone still hesitating because the waters of Jordan look threatening and impassable? Oh! Come, beloved soul; come at once, and doubt not.

~ Andrew Murray (1828-1917)

THE RISEN CHRIST

Jesus said to her, "I am the resurrection and the life.
He who believes in Me, though he may die, he shall live."
———— JOHN 11:25 NKJV ————

The risen Christ lingered on earth long enough fully to satisfy His adherents of the truth of His resurrection. They were not easily convinced. The apostles treated the reports of the holy women with scornful incredulity; Thomas doubted the testimony of the other apostles; and some of the five hundred to whom He appeared on a Galilean mountain doubted their own eyesight, and only believed when they heard His voice. The loving patience with which He treated these doubters showed that, though His bodily appearance was somewhat changed, He was still the same in heart as ever. This was pathetically shown too by the places which He visited in His glorified form. They were the old haunts where He has prayed and preached, labored and suffered — the Galilean mountain, the well-beloved lake, the Mount of Olives, the village of Bethany, and, above all, Jerusalem, the fatal city which had murdered her own Son, but which He could not cease to love. Yet there were obvious indications that He belonged no more to this lower world. There was a new reserve about his risen humanity. . . . His glorified humanity was received up into that world to which it rightfully belonged. ~ James Stalker (1848-1927)

GOD'S EXCELLENCE

. . .He has by inheritance obtained a more excellent name than they.
———— HEBREWS 1:4 NKJV ————

Intellectual pleasures consist in the beholding of spiritual excellencies and beauties, but the glorious excellency and beauty of God are far the greatest. God's excellence is the supreme excellence. When the understanding of the reasonable creature dwells here, it dwells at the fountain, and swims in a boundless, bottomless ocean. The love of God is also the most suitable entertainment of the soul of man, which naturally desires the happiness of society, or of union with some other being. The love of so glorious a being is infinitely valuable, and the discoveries of it are capable of ravishing the soul above all other love. It is suitable to the nature of an intelligent being also, as it is that kind of delight that reason approves of. There are many other delights in which men indulge themselves, which, although they are pleasing to the senses and inferior powers, yet are contrary to reason. Reason opposes the enjoyment of them, so that unless reason be suppressed and stifled, they cannot be enjoyed without a war in the soul. Reason, the noblest faculty, resists the inferior rebellious powers. And the more reason is in exercise, the more will it resist, and the greater will be the inward war and opposition. ~ Jonathan Edwards (1703-1758)

CARNAL CHRISTIANS

And I, brethren, could not speak to you as to spiritual people
but as to carnal, as to babes in Christ.
———— I CORINTHIANS 3:1 NKJV ————

Based upon the work of the Son of God on the Cross of Calvary, in which the sinner for whom He died was identified with the Substitute who died for him, the redeemed and regenerate believer is called to "reckon", or account himself " dead to sin ", because "our old man was crucified with Him." The Holy Spirit of God dwelling in his spirit can then carry out to its ultimate issue the Divine purpose that the "body of sin" -i.e., the whole continent of sin in the whole of fallen man may be "destroyed" or abolished, as the man on his part steadily and faithfully refuses to "let sin reign" . . . the "babe in Christ" knows this that the "flesh" ceases to dominate, and have control, and he rises in spirit into real union with the Ascended Lord — alive unto God in Christ Jesus. The "babe in Christ" . . . ceases to fulfill the desires of the flesh, and henceforth gives his spirit, indwelt by the Spirit of God, the domination of his entire being. It does not mean that he may not again lapse into the walk " after the flesh", but as long as he gives his mind to the "things of the Spirit", and reckons himself continually "dead indeed unto sin", he, "by the Spirit", steadfastly "makes to die" the "doings of the body" and walks in newness of life. ~ Jessie Penn-Lewis (1861-1927)

CHRISTIAN LIFE

Yet indeed I also count all things loss for the excellence
of the knowledge of Christ Jesus my Lord...
—————— PHILIPPIANS 3:8 NKJV ——————

I insist not that the life of the Christian shall breathe nothing but the perfect Gospel, though this is to be desired, and ought to be attempted. I insist not so strictly on evangelical perfection, as to refuse to acknowledge as a Christian any man who has not attained it. In this way all would be excluded from the Church, since there is no man who is not far removed from this perfection, while many, who have made but little progress, would be undeservedly rejected. What then? Let us set this before our eye as the end at which we ought constantly to aim. Let it be regarded as the goal towards which we are to run. For you cannot divide the matter with God, undertaking part of what His Word enjoins, and omitting part at pleasure. For, in the first place, God uniformly recommends integrity as the principal part of his worship, meaning by integrity real singleness of mind, devoid of gloss and fiction, and to this is opposed a double mind; as if it had been said, that the spiritual commencement of a good life is when the internal affections are sincerely devoted to God, in the cultivation of holiness and justice. ~ John Calvin (1509-1564)

Or do you not know, brethren (for I speak to those who know the law), that the law has dominion over a man as long as he lives? For the woman who has a husband is bound by the law to her husband as long as he lives. But if the husband dies, she is released from the law of her husband. So then if, while her husband lives, she marries another man, she will be called an adulteress; but if her husband dies, she is free from that law, so that she is no adulteress, though she has married another man. Therefore, my brethren, you also have become dead to the law through the body of Christ, that you may be married to another—to Him who was raised from the dead, that we should bear fruit to God. For when we were in the flesh, the sinful passions which were aroused by the law were at work in our members to bear fruit to death. But now we have been delivered from the law, having died to what we were held by, so that we should serve in the newness of the Spirit and not in the oldness of the letter.

ROMANS 7:1-6 NKJV

THE REASONABLENESS OF A RESURRECTION

Why should it be thought a thing incredible with you,
that God should raise the dead?

ACTS 26:8 KJV

The resurrection of the dead is one of the great articles of the Christian faith; and yet so it hath happened that this great article of our religion hath been made one of the chief objections against it. There is nothing that Christianity hath been more upbraided for withal, both by the heathens of old and by the infidels of later times, than the impossibility of this article; so that it is a matter of great consideration and consequence to vindicate our religion in this particular. But if the thing be evidently impossible, then it is highly unreasonable to propose it to the belief of mankind ... we may begin this blest state while we are upon earth, by "setting our hearts and affections upon the things that are above, and having our conversation in heaven, from whence also we look for a Savior, the Lord Jesus Christ, who shall change our vile bodies, that they may be fashioned like unto his glorious body, according to the working whereby he is able to subdue all things to himself." ~ John Tillotson (1630-1694)

GOD WITH US

Where can I go from Your Spirit?
Or where can I flee from Your presence?
———— PSALM 139:7 NKJV ————

There are times in our lives when delirium makes us utterly unaware of the presence of our most careful and tender nurses. A child in delirium will cry out in anguish for its mother, and will harrow her heart by its piteous lamentations and appeals, when all the while she is holding its fevered hand, and bathing its aching head, and caring for it with all the untold tenderness of a mother's love. The darkness of disease has hidden the mother from the child, but has not hidden the child from the mother. And just so it is with our God and us. The darkness of our doubts or our fears, of our sorrows or our despair, or even of our sins, cannot hide us from Him, although it may, and often does, hide Him from us. He has told us that the darkness and the light are both alike to Him; and if our faith will only lay hold of this as a fact, we will be enabled to pass through the darkest seasons in quiet trust, sure that all the while, though we cannot see nor feel Him, our God is caring for us, and will never leave nor forsake us.

~ Hannah Whitall Smith (1832-1911)

VENGEANCE IS MINE!

Do not be overcome by evil, but overcome evil with good.
ROMANS 12:21 NKJV

When two goats meet upon a narrow bridge over deep water, how do they behave? Neither of them can turn back again, neither can pass the other, because the bridge is too narrow; if they should thrust one another, they might both fall into the water and be drowned; nature, then, has taught them, that if the one lays himself down and permits the other to go over him, both remain without hurt. Even so people should rather endure to be trod upon, than to fall into debate and discord one with another. A Christian, for the sake of his own person, neither curses nor revenges himself; but faith curses and revenges itself . . . we must distinguish God and man, the person and cause. In what concerns God and his cause, we must have no patience, nor bless; as for example, when the ungodly persecute the Gospel, this touches God and his cause, and then we are not to bless or to wish good success, but rather to curse the persecutors and their proceedings . . . faith's cursing, which, rather than it would suffer God's Word to be suppressed and heresy maintained, would have all creatures go to wreck; for through heresy we lose God himself. But individuals personally ought not to revenge themselves, but to suffer all things, and according to Christ's doctrine and the nature of love, to do good to their enemies.

~ Martin Luther (1483-1546)

AN APOSTLE'S SUPREME AMBITION

That I may know him, and the power of his resurrection, and the fellowship
of his sufferings, being made conformable unto his death . . .
———— PHILIPPIANS 3:10 KJV ————

It is important in understanding the Apostle Paul to realise that he was not thinking of conformity to Christ's death as the end of all else. His real meaning was that he should increase in the knowledge of Christ, know the power of His resurrection and the fellowship of His sufferings by becoming conformed to His death. His death . . . was behind . . . and the spiritual history of the believer is in working back in what that death meant. It meant the end of the "old man", crucifixion to the world mind and will; the closing of the door to a whole system which was not Christ-centered and Christ-governed. All this had been stated and presented in Paul's earlier letters ... The meaning of Christ's death — Paul taught was to be the inner history of the believer, and this would work out — progressively — in the power of His resurrection and the fellowship of His sufferings. So that, by being conformed to His death, he would come to the fuller knowledge of Him and of that Divine power. It is ever so. The all-governing passion opens the way for the effectual, and effectuating power, by the essential basis, through the progressive principle of conformity to His death.

~ Austin T. Sparks (1888-1971)

THE MAN AFTER
GOD'S OWN HEART

". . . a man after mine own heart, which shall fulfill all my will."
ACTS 13:22 KJV

No man can be making much of his life who has not a very definite conception of what he is living for. And if you ask, at random, a dozen men what is the end of their life, you will be surprised to find how few have formed to themselves more than the most dim idea. The question of the summum bonum has ever been the most difficult for the human mind to grasp. What shall a man do with his life? What is life for? Why is it given? These have been the one great puzzle for human books and human brains; and ancient philosophy and medieval learning and modern culture alike have failed to tell us what these mean . . . The general truth of these words is simply this: that the end of life is to do God's will . . . It may seem too bright and beautiful, for all things fair have soon to come to an end. And if any cloud could cross the true Christian's sky it would be when he thought that this ideal life might cease. But God, in the riches of His forethought, has rounded off this corner of his life with a great far-reaching text, which looks above the circumstance of time, and projects his life into the vast eternity beyond. "He that doeth the will of God abideth for ever" (1 John 2:17).

~ Henry Drummond (1851-1897)

MY HEAVENLY FRIEND

Greater love has no one than this,
than to lay down one's life for his friends.
—— JOHN 15:13 NKJV ——

The precious Lord Jesus Christ is our friend. Oh, let us seek to realize this! It is not merely a religious phrase or statement, but truly He is our friend. He is the Brother "born for adversity," the one who "sticks closer than a brother." Who will never leave and never forsake us . . . He is willing not merely to grant this for a few months, or a year or two, but to the very end of our earthly pilgrimage. David, in Psalm 23 says: "Yea, though I walk through the valley of the shadow of death, I will fear no evil, for Thou art with me." Oh, how precious this is. For this "Lovely One" is coming again, and soon. Soon He will come again; and then He will take us home and there we shall be forever with Him. Oh, how precious is that bright and glorious prospect. Here again the practical point is to appropriate this to ourselves. "He is coming to take me — poor, guilty, worthless, hell-deserving me — He is coming to take me to Himself." And to the degree in which we enter into these glorious things, the joys of heaven have already commenced!

~ George Muller (1483-1586)

What shall we say then? Is the law sin? Certainly not! On the contrary, I would not have known sin except through the law. For I would not have known covetousness unless the law had said, "You shall not covet." But sin, taking opportunity by the commandment, produced in me all manner of evil desire. For apart from the law sin was dead. I was alive once without the law, but when the commandment came, sin revived and I died. And the commandment, which was to bring life, I found to bring death. For sin, taking occasion by the commandment, deceived me, and by it killed me. Therefore the law is holy, and the commandment holy and just and good. Has then what is good become death to me? Certainly not! But sin, that it might appear sin, was producing death in me through what is good, so that sin through the commandment might become exceedingly sinful.

ROMANS 7:7-13 NKJV

HIS CREATED BEAUTY

*Yet the LORD will command his lovingkindness in the daytime, and in the
night his song shall be with me, and my prayer unto the God of my life.*
———— Psalm 42:8 KJV ————

Had I been alive in Adam's stead, how should I have admired the
Glories of the World! What a confluence of thoughts and wonders, and
joys, and thanksgivings would have replenished me in the sight of so
magnificent a theatre, so bright a dwelling place; so great a temple, so
stately a house replenished with all kind of treasure, raised out of
nothing and created for me and for me alone. Shall I now despise them?
When I consider the heavens which Thou hast made, the moon and
stars, which are the works of Thy fingers: what is man that Thou art
mindful of him, or the son of man that Thou visiteth him! Thou hast
made him a little lower than the angels, and crowned him with glory
and honour. O what love must that needs be, that prepared such a
palace! Attended with what power! With what wisdom illuminated!
Abounding with what zeal! And how glorious must the King be, that
could out of nothing erect such a curious, so great, and so beautiful a
fabric! It was glorious while new: and is as new as it was glorious.
~ Thomas Traherne (1636-1674)

SWEET FLOW'RETS
OF THE MARTYR BAND

Sweet flow'rets of the martyr band,
Plucked by the tyrant's ruthless hand
Upon the threshold of the morn,
Like rosebuds by a tempest torn;
First victims for the incarnate Lord,
A tender flock to feel the sword;
Beside the very altar gay,
With palm and crown, ye seemed to play.
Ah, what availed King Herod's wrath?
He could not stop the Savior's path.
Alone, while others murdered lay,
In safety Christ is borne away.
O Lord, the Virgin-born,
to Thee Eternal praise and glory be,
Whom with the Father we adore
And Holy Ghost forevermore. Amen.
~ Henry W. Baker (1821-1877)

GOD IS . . .

For the Lord is the great God, And the great King above all gods.
———— PSALM 95:3 NKJV ————

Admitting that Jesus was indeed the God-man, the hope is vain of either escaping or explaining the mystery which invests Him; for He presents the phenomenon of history, original, unique, solitary; no being like Him, before or after. Here is a combination heretofore supposed to be contradictory and impossible! God is infinite; space cannot contain Him, nor time limit Him. Man is finite, fenced in by definite bounds. How can the unlimited and limited combine and unite? All our previous notions of things are contradicted in the God-man. God is omnipresent; yet here is God, submitting to the laws and limits of a human body, which can occupy but one place at any one time, and must, by the law of locomotion, take time for a transfer from one place to place. God is omniscient; yet here is a being claiming equality with Jehovah, yet affirming that there are some things which as a man, and even as the Messiah, He knows not. God is omnipresent; yet the God-man says He "can do nothing of Himself," and that it is God dwelling in Him that "doeth the works." ~ Arthur T. Pierson (1867-1911)

APART FROM HIM, WE HAVE NOTHING

But of him are ye in Christ Jesus, who of God is made unto us wisdom, and righteousness, and sanctification, and redemption. . .
———— I CORINTHIANS 1:30 KJV ————

When people are comparative strangers to one another, they cannot receive gifts from each other comfortably. But when they are united in spirit with a bond of true love between them, no matter how great the gifts, they can be accepted without embarrassment or obligation. This principle holds true in the spiritual life. When Christians are living apart from God, they cannot be brought to accept any great gifts from Him. They feel as if they are too unworthy and do not deserve such gifts. Even when He puts the blessing into their hands, their false humility prevents them from seeing it, and they go on their way without it. But when Christians get near enough to the Lord to feel the true spirit of adoption, they are ready to accept with delight all the blessings He has in store for them. They never think anything is too much to receive. For then they discover that He is only eager, as parents are, to pour out every good gift upon His children. All things are theirs because they are Christ's, and Christ is God's.

~ Hannah Whitall Smith (1832-1911)

EASTER MONDAY

*"To Him all the prophets witness that, through His name,
whoever believes in Him will receive remission of sins."*

———— ACTS 10:43 NKJV ————

Peter, by way of proving conclusively to the world that this one
Lord, as he names Him, Jesus of Nazareth, is the true Messiah promised
of old in the Scriptures, says: "To him bear all the prophets witness."
The prophets plainly speak of such a person, one to be born of David's
flesh and blood, in the city of Bethlehem, who should suffer, die and
rise again, accomplishing just what this Jesus has accomplished and
even proven by miraculous signs. Therefore, truly the Jews and the non-
Christians have no reason to doubt concerning Christ, no reason to
await the coming of another . . . Peter, citing the testimony of the
prophets, indicates the nature of Christ's kingdom as not external
power; not temporal dominion like that of earthly lords, kings, and
emperors; not dominion over countries or control of people, property
and temporal concerns; but a spiritual, eternal kingdom, a kingdom in
the hearts of men, an authority over, and power opposed to, sin,
everlasting death and hell, a power able to redeem us from those things
and bestow upon us salvation. Salvation is ours, Peter teaches, through
the preaching of the Gospel, and is received by faith. Faith is the
obedience every man must render unto the Lord. By faith he makes
himself subject to Christ and partaker of his grace and blessings.

~ Martin Luther (1483-1586)

WEEPING MARY

". . . Woman, why are you weeping?" She said to them, "Because they have taken away my Lord, and I do not know where they have laid Him."
—————— JOHN 20:13 NKJV ——————

For as yet they did not know the Scripture, that He must rise again from the dead. Then the disciples went away again to their own homes. But Mary stood outside by the tomb weeping, and as she wept she stooped down and looked into the tomb. And she saw two angels in white sitting, one at the head and the other at the feet, where the body of Jesus had lain ... Here is a woman more forward in seeking Christ nor [than] all His eleven disciples are. Because she get not her errand that she was seeking, she could not get Christ, and therefore she will not leave, nor give over, but will wait on and seek Him. A soul that is in love with Christ, they never get their errand till they get Christ Himself. Ye that are seeking Christ, never give over seeking till ye meet with Him, for they shall at last meet with Him who lie at His door, seeking, as this woman did, who say, "I shall lie still at Thy door, let me die there if Thou likest, and albeit it should come to that, I shall die, or I go away and meet not with Him." Ye may know the ardent desire of a soul after Christ can be satisfied with nothing but Himself.

~ Samuel Rutherford (1600-1661)

For we know that the law is spiritual, but I am carnal, sold under sin. For what I am doing, I do not understand. For what I will to do, that I do not practice; but what I hate, that I do. If, then, I do what I will not to do, I agree with the law that it is good. But now, it is no longer I who do it, but sin that dwells in me. For I know that in me (that is, in my flesh) nothing good dwells; for to will is present with me, but how to perform what is good I do not find. For the good that I will to do, I do not do; but the evil I will not to do, that I practice. Now if I do what I will not to do, it is no longer I who do it, but sin that dwells in me.

ROMANS 7:14-20 NKJV

STANDING FIRM

GOD, THE AUTHOR

For ever, O LORD, thy word is settled in heaven.

PSALM 119:89 KJV

There is only one covenant of grace and it all centers around the Lord Jesus Christ. The old points forward to Him; the new reveals Him and holds Him forth to us in person. He alone is the fulfillment of everything that is promised from Genesis 3:15 onwards. It is all in Him. The original covenant with regard to redemption was fully and clearly made with Him. Sometimes you hear people saying that the Bible is not a book, but a library of books. I think I know what they mean, but you know, this sort of thing is wrong, it should never be said. This is really one book. It was written by different men, at different times, and in different places, but there is only one book and one message; it is one book with one theme, about one person. Let us follow our fathers, who always talked about 'The Book'. For that is what it is, not a library of books. It is infinitely greater, that is the glory of it, and these different men were used by the Holy Spirit to write this one book, inspired by the Author. ~ Martyn Lloyd-Jones (1899-1981)

REALITY

My little children, let us not love in word or in tongue,
but in deed and in truth.

I JOHN 3:18 NKJV

God looks for reality. "He did not love us in word or in tongue, but in deed and in truth; and He looks for a response from us — a response clear, full, and distinct; a response coming out in a life of good works, a life yielding mellow clusters of the "fruits of righteousness which are by Christ Jesus, to the glory and praise of God." — Ought we not diligently to seek to promote love and good works? And how can this be most effectually accomplished? Surely by walking in love ourselves, and faithfully treading the path of good works in our own private life. For ourselves, we confess we are thoroughly sick of hollow profession. High truth on the lips and low practice in daily life, is one of the crying evils of our day. We talk of grace; but fail in common righteousness — fail in the plainest moral duties in our daily private life. We boast of our "position" and our "standing;" but we are deplorably lax as to our "condition" and "state." May the Lord, in His infinite goodness, stir up all hearts to more thorough earnestness, in the pursuit of good works, so that we may more fully adorn the doctrine of God our Savior in all things! ~ C.H. Mackintosh (1820-1896)

TRUSTING GOD

I will put My trust in Him.
HEBREWS 2:13 NKJV

I have discovered, through personal experience and from biblical example, that human effort, self-assertion, positive thinking, and will power are of little use in the quest for godliness. Throughout my years at elementary school, I was a straight "C" student. I barely squeaked through high school, and was forced to abandon any hopes I had of going to college, because of a lack of discipline. Instead of school, I told my family, "I'm going surfing," and for the next four years, lived the life of a California beach bum, regularly blowing out my brains on drugs. At age twenty-one, a longhaired, broken, burned-out freak with barely enough discipline to hold down a job, I landed at the foot of the Cross, and was gloriously saved. Since that time, God, through His mercy and grace, has helped me to discipline my life — not because I had any natural endowment of stick-toitiveness, but because His Holy Spirit came and took up residence in my life when I surrendered to Him and trusted Him. Trust, spelled with a capital "T," is the key. If we want to better our devotional life, we must trust Him. . . . All of God's dealings with man, Christian and non-Christian, are for one purpose: to bring us to a point where we can trust Him. ~ Danny Lehmann (1954 -)

CHRISTIAN CONTENTMENT DESCRIBED

'. . . I have learned, in whatsoever state I am, therewith to be content.'
PHILIPPIANS 4:11 KJV

These words are brought in by Paul as a clear argument to persuade the Philippians that he did not seek after great things in the world, and that he sought not 'theirs' but 'them'. He did not long for great wealth. His heart was taken up with better things. 'I do not speak', he says, 'in respect of want, for whether I have or have not, my heart is fully satisfied, I have enough: I have learned in whatsoever state I am, therewith to be content.' 'I have learned' — Contentment in every condition is a great art, a spiritual mystery. It is to be learned, and to be learned as a mystery. And so in verse 12 he affirms: 'I know how to be abased, and I now how to abound: everywhere and in all things I am instructed.' The word which is translated 'instructed' is derived from the word that signifies 'mystery'; it is just as if he had said, 'I have learned the mystery of this business.' Contentment is to be learned as a great mystery, and those who are thoroughly trained in this art, which is like Samson's riddle to a natural man, have learned a deep mystery. 'I have learned it' — I do not have to learn it now, nor did I have the art at first; I have attained it, though with much ado, and now, by the grace of God, I have become the master of this art.

~ Jeremiah Burroughs (1599-1646)

DAILY FOOD

*For as the rain cometh down, and the snow from heaven,
and returneth not thither, but watereth the earth, and maketh it
bring forth and bud, that it may give seed to the sower, and bread
to the eater: So shall my word be that goeth forth out of my mouth:
it shall not return unto me void, but it shall accomplish that which
I please, and it shall prosper in the thing whereto I sent it.*

———— ISAIAH 55:10, 11 KJV ————

It is most difficult to see that daily feeding on the Word should have top priority in the lives of Christ's sheep. How can sheep have an aversion to green pastures? Nevertheless, it seems, that many have time for everything but daily Bread. Time for paperback books. Time for magazines and newspapers. Time for TV. Time for shaving, and grooming the hair. Time for every room in the house. But no time for daily Bread. Are you hungry? Hungry to know God, to know Christ, to know Truth? Are you longing to survive temptations, to stand firm, to grow in righteousness? Then, keep the dust off your Bible every day of the week. There is strong evidence that a dusty Bible and spiritual malnutrition go hand in hand. ~ Kenneth M. Mick (1938 -)

GRACE COVENANT

. . .who also made us sufficient as ministers of the new covenant,
not of the letter but of the Spirit; for the letter kills, but the Spirit gives life.
II CORINTHIANS 3:6 NKJV

When one person assigns a stipulated work to another person with the promise of a reward upon the condition of the performance of that work, there is a covenant. Nothing can be plainer than that all this is true in relation to the Father and the Son. The Father gave the Son a work to do; He sent Him into the world to perform it, and promised Him a great reward when the work was accomplished. Such is the constant representation of the Scriptures. We have, therefore, the contracting parties, the promise, and the condition. These are the essential elements of a covenant. Such being the representation of Scripture, such must be the truth to which we are bound to adhere. It is not a mere figure, but a real transaction, and should be regarded and treated as such if we would understand aright the plan of salvation. In Psalm 40, expounded by the Apostle as referring to the Messiah, it is said, "Lo, I come: in the volume of the book it is written of me, I delight to do thy will," i.e., to execute thy purpose, to carry out thy plan. Christ came, therefore, in execution of a purpose of God, to fulfill a work which had been assigned Him. ~ Charles Hodge (1797-1887)

*I find then a law, that evil is present with me, the one who wills
to do good. For I delight in the law of God according to the
inward man. But I see another law in my members, warring
against the law of my mind, and bringing me into captivity to the
law of sin which is in my members. O wretched man that I am!
Who will deliver me from this body of death? I thank God—
through Jesus Christ our Lord! So then, with the mind I myself
serve the law of God, but with the flesh the law of sin.*

ROMANS 7:21-25 NKJV

STANDING FIRM

THE RELATION OF THE WILL
OF GOD TO SANCTIFICATION

"For this is the will of God, even your sanctification . . ."
I THESSALONIANS 4:3 KJV

We take our doctrines from the Bible and our assurance from Christ. But for want of the living bright reality of His presence in our hearts we search the world all round for impulses. We search religious books for impulses, and tracts and sermons, but in vain. . . . "I am Alpha and Omega, the beginning and the end." "Christ is all and in all." The beginning of all things is in the will of God. The end of all things is in sanctification through faith in Jesus Christ. Between these two poles all spiritual life and Christian experience run. And no motive outside Christ can lead a man to Christ. If your motive to holiness is not as high as Christ it cannot make you rise to Christ. For water cannot rise above its level. "Beware, therefore, lest any man spoil you through philosophy and vain deceit, after the tradition of men, after the rudiments of the world, and not after Christ. For in Him dwelleth all the fullness of the Godhead bodily. And ye are complete in Him which is the head of all principality and power" (1 Cor. i. 30). "As ye have therefore received the Lord Jesus, so walk ye in Him." ~ Henry Drummond (1818-1888)

THE PRAYER OF RELINQUISHMENT

. . . he who does the will of God abides forever.

I JOHN 2:17 NKJV

A demanding spirit, with self-will as its rudder, blocks prayer. . . . The reason for this is that God absolutely refuses to violate our free will. Therefore, unless self-will is voluntarily given up, even God cannot move to answer prayer . . . Jesus' prayer in the Garden of Gethsemane is a pattern for us. "Dear Father . . . Please let me not have to drink this cup. Yet it is not what I want, but what You want." (Luke 22:42, PHILLIPS) . . . Even at the moment when Christ was bowing to the possibility of an awful death by crucifixion, He never forgot either the presence or the power of God. The Prayer of Relinquishment must not be interpreted negatively. It does not let us lie down in the dust of a godless universe and steel ourselves just for the worst. Rather it says: "This is my situation at the moment. I'll face the reality of it. But I'll also accept willingly whatever a loving Father sends."

~ Catherine Marshall (1914-1983)

LOVEST THOU ME?

Thine eyes did see my substance, yet being unperfect;
and in thy book all my members were written. . .
———— PSALM 139:16 KJV ————

. . . God deserves to be loved very much . . . because He loved us first, He infinite and we nothing, loved us, miserable sinners, with a love so great and so free . . . the measure of our love to God is to love immeasurably. For since our love is toward God, who is infinite and immeasurable, how can we bound or limit the love we owe Him? Besides, our love is not a gift but a debt. And since it is the Godhead who loves us . . . since it is He who loves us, I say, can we think of repaying Him grudgingly? 'I will love Thee, O Lord, my strength. The Lord is my rock and my fortress and my deliverer, my God, my strength, in whom I will trust' (Psalm 18:1). He is all that I need, all that I long for. My God and my help, I will love Thee for Thy great goodness . . . I cannot love Thee as Thou deservest to be loved, for I cannot love Thee more than my own feebleness permits. I will love Thee more when Thou deemest me worthy to receive greater capacity for loving; yet never so perfectly as Thou hast deserved of me. 'Yet Thou recordest in that book all who do what they can, even though they cannot do what they ought.' ~ Bernard of Clairvaux (1090-1153)

THE WILLING LORD

"I will: be thou clean."
—— LUKE 5:13 KJV ——

This leper must have been told about Jesus. How much is missed because people are not constantly telling what Jesus will do in this our day. Probably someone had come to that leper and said, "Jesus can heal you." And so he was filled with expectation as he saw the Lord coming down the mountain side. Lepers were not allowed to come within reach of people, they were shut out as unclean. And so in the ordinary way it would have been very difficult for him to get near because of the crowd that surrounded Jesus. But as He came down from the mount He met this poor leper. Oh, this terrible disease! There was no help for him humanly speaking, but nothing is too hard for Jesus. The man cried, "Lord, if thou wilt, thou canst make me clean." Was Jesus willing? You will never find Jesus missing an opportunity of doing good . . . He has an overflowing cup for thee, a fullness of life. He will meet you in your absolute helplessness. All things are possible if you will only believe. God has a real plan. It is so simple. Just come to Jesus. You will find Him just the same as He was in days of old.

~ Smith Wigglesworth (1859-1947)

FOR THE BEAUTY OF THE EARTH

For the beauty of the earth, For the glory of the skies;
For the love which from our birth, Over and around us lies;
Lord of all, to Thee we raise This, our hymn of grateful praise.
For the wonder of each hour, Of the day and of the night;
Hill and vale and tree and flow'r, Sun and moon, and stars of light;
Lord of all, to Thee we raise This, our hymn of grateful praise.
For the joy of ear and eye, For the heart and mind's delight;
For the mystic harmony, Linking sense to sound and sight;
Lord of all, to Thee we raise This, our hymn of grateful praise.
For the joy of human love, Brother, sister, parent, child;
Friends on Earth and friends above, For all gentle thoughts and mild;
Lord of all, to Thee we raise This, our hymn of grateful praise.
For Thy church that evermore, Lifteth holy hands above;
Off'ring up on ev'ry shore, Her pure sacrifice of love;
Lord of all, to Thee we raise This, our hymn of grateful praise.
Amen.
~ Folliott S. Pierpont (1835-1917)

THE LAW OF LOVE

"Father, into thy hands I commend my spirit."
———— LUKE 23:46 KJV ————

We may commend any brother, any sister, to the common fatherhood. And there will be moments when, filled with that spirit which is the Lord, nothing will ease our hearts of their love but the commending of all men, all our brothers, all our sisters, to the one Father. Nor shall we ever know that repose in the Father's hands, that rest of the Holy Sepulchre, which the Lord knew when the agony of death was over, when the storm of the world died away behind his retiring spirit, and he entered the regions where there is only life, and therefore all that is not music is silence, (for all noise comes of the conflict of Life and Death) — we shall never be able, I say, to rest in the bosom of the Father, till the fatherhood is fully revealed to us in the love of the brothers. For he cannot be our father save as he is their father; and if we do not see him and feel him as their father, we cannot know him as ours. Never shall we know him aright until we rejoice and exult for our race that he is the Father. He that loveth not his brother whom he hath seen, how can he love God whom he hath not seen? To rest, I say, at last, even in those hands into which the Lord commended his spirit, we must have learned already to love our neighbour as ourselves.
~ George MacDonald (1824-1905)

There is therefore now no condemnation to those who are in Christ Jesus, who do not walk according to the flesh, but according to the Spirit. For the law of the Spirit of life in Christ Jesus has made me free from the law of sin and death. For what the law could not do in that it was weak through the flesh, God did by sending His own Son in the likeness of sinful flesh, on account of sin: He condemned sin in the flesh, that the righteous requirement of the law might be fulfilled in us who do not walk according to the flesh but according to the Spirit. For those who live according to the flesh set their minds on the things of the flesh, but those who live according to the Spirit, the things of the Spirit. For to be carnally minded is death, but to be spiritually minded is life and peace. Because the carnal mind is enmity against God; for it is not subject to the law of God, nor indeed can be. So then, those who are in the flesh cannot please God. But you are not in the flesh but in the Spirit, if indeed the Spirit of God dwells in you. Now if anyone does not have the Spirit of Christ, he is not His. And if Christ is in you, the body is dead because of sin, but the Spirit is life because of righteousness. But if the Spirit of Him who raised Jesus from the dead dwells in you, He who raised Christ from the dead will also give life to your mortal bodies through His Spirit who dwells in you.

ROMANS 8:1-11 NKJV

FALSE RELIGIONS

"I am the way . . . no man cometh unto the Father, but by me."
JOHN 14:6 KJV

The world today is a world of religion. Christ came to save men from sin and religion. Adam was the founder of the first religion. Upon being caught in sin in the garden, rather than cry to God for mercy, he sewed fig leaves together to cover his nakedness. He relied on his works rather than God's grace. From that day to this, man has been incurably religious. He continues to invent religions, thinking in this way to cover his spiritual nakedness. As the fig leaves of Adam's time did not cover sin, so all the religious acts of man today cannot atone for sin. Religion can only leave a sinner hoping. Salvation makes the sinner sure. Of course, many people are sincerely religious, but they are sincerely wrong. We do not condemn them, but in the Gospel we show them a better way — the only way. God's way! . . . You have a divine Saviour who has given you victory over sin and eternal life. The heathens are marching blindly on to death. ~ Dick Hillis (1913-)

BEHOLD THE SURE FOUNDATION — STONE

Behold the sure Foundation — stone
Which God in Zion lays
To build our heavenly hopes upon
And His eternal praise.
Chosen of God, to sinners dear,
Let saints adore the name;
They trust their whole salvation here,
Nor shall they suffer shame.
The foolish builders, scribe and priest,
Reject it with disdain;
Yet on this rock the Church shall rest
And envy rage in vain.
What though the gates of hell withstood
Yet must this building rise.
'Tis Thine own work, Almighty God,
And wondrous in our eyes.
~ Isaac Watts (1674-1748)

THE SPHERE OF A NEW LIFE

But of Him you are in Christ Jesus. . .
I CORINTHIANS 1:30 NKJV

Christ becomes to us the sphere of new power in becoming the sphere of new life. A sphere contains an atmosphere, and that atmosphere may be quite different from that which is outside; it may have different qualities, and be capable of supporting life in a far higher degree. So, what we could not do, outside of Christ, becomes both natural and possible in Him, because we have new appetites, desires, and affinities. The old passions, habits, bondage, are displaced by a new life, capacity, and freedom. ~ A. T. Pierson (1867-1911)

ALL THE WAY MY SAVIOUR LEADS ME

All the way my Saviour leads me; What have I to ask beside?
Can I doubt His faithful mercies, Who through life has been my guide?
Heav'nly peace, divinest comfort, Here by faith in Him do dwell;
For I know whate'er befall me, Jesus doeth all things well.
All the way my Saviour leads me, Cheers each winding path I tread;
Gives me strength for every trial, Feeds me with the living bread.
Though my weary steps may falter, And my soul athirst may be,
Gushing from the Rock before me, Lo, a spring of joy I see.
All the way my Saviour leads me, O the fullness of His love!
Perfect rest in me is promised, In my Father's house above;
When my spirit, clothed immortal, Wings its flight to realms of day,
This my song through endless ages: "Jesus led me all the way."
~ Fanny J. Crosby (1820-1915)

LOVE THY NEIGHBOUR

". . . Thou shalt love thy neighbor as thyself."
MATTHEW 22:39 KJV

It is possible to love our neighbour as ourselves. Our Lord never spoke hyperbolically, although, indeed, that is the supposition on which many unconsciously interpret his words, in order to be able to persuade themselves that they believe them. We may see that it is possible before we attain to it; for our perceptions of truth are always in advance of our condition. True, no man can see it perfectly until he is it; but we must see it, that we may be it. A man who knows that he does not yet love his neighbour as himself may believe in such a condition, may even see that there is no other goal of human perfection, nothing else to which the universe is speeding, propelled by the Father's will. Let him labour on, and not faint at the thought that God's day is a thousand years: his millennium is likewise one day — yea, this day, for we have him, The Love, in us, working even now the far end . . . A man must not choose his neighbour; he must take the neighbour that God sends him. In him, whoever he be, lies, hidden or revealed, a beautiful brother. The neighbour is just the man who is next to you at the moment, the man with whom any business has brought you in contact.

~ George MacDonald (1824-1905)

THE CHURCH OF NECESSITY

. . . That thou mayest know how thou oughtest to behave
thyself in the house of God, which is the church of
the living God, the pillar and ground of the truth.
———— I TIMOTHY 3:15 KJV ————

Many Christians stay in trouble, grow little, or even go astray and ruin their lives. This is often because they are lone "free lance" Christians and not closely connected to a real church. The church is God's means of taking care of His children in this age — the church age. A wolf will destroy a sheep that is off alone in the wilderness, so Satan has to find Christians that aren't under the care, authority, and discipline of a local church. We must get rid of the idea that the church is a building or an address to hold meetings. Nor is the church a "preaching point" or performance that an audience attends for information or worse, for entertainment. All churches claim great doctrinal truths on paper but do they make the Lord Jesus Christ the head by first upholding the truth of God's Word? Is the Word of God being taught in depth and power? Are Christians caring for one another? Is sin dealt with or just tolerated and ignored? Is there time for worship and praise to the Lord or just meaningless rounds of activity? Such a church might not be the largest, or fastest growing, or most prestigious, but it won't necessarily be small or stagnant either. It will be one where the Lord and His Word are taken seriously and His sheep are cared for and care for one another. ~ Dr. John Hey (1939-)

Therefore, brethren, we are debtors—not to the flesh, to live according to the flesh. For if you live according to the flesh you will die; but if by the Spirit you put to death the deeds of the body, you will live. For as many as are led by the Spirit of God, these are sons of God. For you did not receive the spirit of bondage again to fear, but you received the Spirit of adoption by whom we cry out, "Abba, Father." The Spirit Himself bears witness with our spirit that we are children of God, and if children, then heirs—heirs of God and joint heirs with Christ, if indeed we suffer with Him, that we may also be glorified together. For I consider that the sufferings of this present time are not worthy to be compared with the glory which shall be revealed in us. For the earnest expectation of the creation eagerly waits for the revealing of the sons of God. For the creation was subjected to futility, not willingly, but because of Him who subjected it in hope; because the creation itself also will be delivered from the bondage of corruption into the glorious liberty of the children of God. For we know that the whole creation groans and labors with birth pangs together until now. Not only that, but we also who have the firstfruits of the Spirit, even we ourselves groan within ourselves, eagerly waiting for the adoption, the redemption of our body. For we were saved in this hope, but hope that is seen is not hope; for why does one still hope for what he sees? But if we hope for what we do not see, we eagerly wait for it with perseverance.

———— ROMANS 8:12-25 NKJV ————

STANDING FIRM

THE GOLDEN MILESTONE
OF THE AGES

. . .Hear the word of the Lord!
JEREMIAH 22:29 NKJV

The Bible is the Golden Milestone of the ages. It has been for thousands of years the grand center of all the noblest thought, purest love, and holiest life of the world . . . From this great book proceeds the inspiration of the best literature, the most unselfish philanthropy, the most faultless morality, which the world has ever known. Whence came the Bible? Is this the accidental point of all this convergence; or is it the designed focus of all this light, love and life? Was this golden pillar erected by one infinitely more august than the foremost of Caesars, to be the center and source of all human progress? Did God put the Bible in the very forum of the nations, that by all paths men might, in the honest search after truth, find in this their goal; and that, from this, as a starting point, every true lover of God and man might proceed in his noble career of service? This is the decisive test. No literary excellence, no scientific accuracy, No perfection, as a book, could atone for one vital error in ethical teaching or moral percept, in a volume which claims the high dignity of being a guide to the human soul, in matters of faith and life, doctrine and duty! ~ Arthur T. Pierson (1867-1911)

THE UNERRING WORD OF GOD

Thy word is a lamp unto my feet, and a light unto my path.

PSALM 119:105 KJV

Nature is full of wants with corresponding supplies; of appetites or cravings with their gratifications and satisfactions. The wing of the bird tells of the air on which it may float; the fin of the fish, of the water through which it may glide; the ball of the joint, of the socket; the eye is a prophecy of the light, and the ear of sound. So universal is this correspondence that wherever we find a craving, and adaptation, or a lack, we look with unerring certainty for something else filling the craving, meeting the adaptation, supplying the lack. Emerson closed a protracted argument with a literary skeptic in these Forcible words: "Sir, I hold that God, who keeps His word with the birds and fishes in all their migratory instinct, will keep His word with man." And Bryant, in his "Lines to a Waterfowl," with great beauty, points out the lesson taught by this wonderful correspondence and correlation, in these lines: He who, from zone to zone, guides, through the boundless sky, thy certain flight, In the long way that I must tread along, Will lead my steps aright! The Bible declares and exhibits such an object, exactly adapted to fill and fulfill all this need. ~ Arthur T. Pierson (1867-1911)

BEFORE JEHOVAH'S AWE-FULL THRONE

FROM PSALM 100

Before Jehovah's awe-full throne,
Ye nations, bow with sacred joy.

Know that the Lord is God alone;
He can create and He destroy.

His sov'reign power, without our aid,
Made us of clay and formed us men;

And when like wandering sheep we strayed,
He brought us to His fold again.

We are His people, we His care,
Our souls and all our mortal frame.

What lasting honors shall we rear,
Almighty Maker, to Thy name?

We'll crowd Thy gates with thankful songs,
High as the heavens our voices raise;

And earth, with her ten thousand tongues,
Shall fill Thy courts with sounding praise.

Wide as the world is Thy command,
Vast as eternity Thy love;

Firm as a rock Thy truth must stand
When rolling years shall cease to move.

~ Isaac Watts (1674-1748)

HELPLESS WITHOUT GOD

Let us therefore come boldly unto the throne of grace,
that we may obtain mercy, and find grace to help in time of need.
———— HEBREWS 4:16 KJV ————

A dear friend of mine who was quite a lover of the chase, told me the following story: 'Rising early one morning,' he said, 'I heard the baying of a score of deerhounds in pursuit of their quarry. Looking away to a broad, open field in front of me, I saw a young fawn making its way across, and giving signs, moreover, that its race was well-nigh run. Reaching the rails of the enclosure, it leaped over and crouched within ten feet from where I stood. A moment later two of the hounds came over, when the fawn ran in my direction and pushed its head between my legs. I lifted the little thing to my breast, and, swinging round and round, fought off the dogs. I felt, just then, that all the dogs in the West could not, and should not capture that fawn after its weakness had appealed to my strength.' So is it, when human helplessness appeals to Almighty God. Well do I remember when the hounds of sin were after my soul, until, at last, I ran into the arms of Almighty God. ~ A. C. Dixon (1854-1925)

THE LORD, MY STRENGTH

The Lord is my strength and song. . .He is my God, and I will praise Him. . .
——— EXODUS 15:2 NKJV ———

Who am I, and what is my nature? What evil is there not in me and my deeds; or if not in my deeds, my words; or if not in my words, my will? But thou, O Lord, art good and merciful, and thy right hand didst reach into the depth of my death and didst empty out the abyss of corruption from the bottom of my heart . . . now I did not will to do what I willed, and began to will to do what thou didst will. But where was my free will during all those years and from what deep and secret retreat was it called forth in a single moment, whereby I gave my neck to thy "easy yoke" and my shoulders to thy "light burden," O Christ Jesus, "my Strength and my Redeemer"? . . .Thou didst cast them away, and in their place thou didst enter in thyself — sweeter than all pleasure, though not to flesh and blood; brighter than all light, but more veiled than all mystery; more exalted than all honor, though not to them that are exalted in their own eyes. Now was my soul free from the gnawing cares . . . scratching the itch of lust. And I prattled like a child to thee, O Lord my God—my light, my riches, and my salvation.
~ St. Augustine (345-440)

THE NECESSITY OF PRAYER

Thou shalt make thy prayer unto him, and he shall hear thee . . .
JOB 22:27 KJV

It is the initial quality in the heart of any man who essays to talk to the Unseen. He must, out of sheer helplessness, stretch forth hands of faith. He must believe, where he cannot prove. In the ultimate issue, prayer is simply faith, claiming its natural yet marvelous prerogatives — faith taking possession of its illimitable inheritance. True godliness is just as true, steady, and persevering in the realm of faith as it is in the province of prayer. Moreover: when faith ceases to pray, it ceases to live. We turn to a saying of our Lord, which there is need to emphasize, since it is the very keystone of the arch of faith and prayer. "Therefore I say unto you, What things soever ye desire when ye pray, believe that ye receive them, and ye shall have them." We should ponder well that statement — "Believe that ye receive them, and ye shall have them." Here is described a faith which realizes, which appropriates, which takes. Such faith is a consciousness of the Divine, an experienced communion, a realized certainty. ~ Edward M. Bounds (1835-1913)

Likewise the Spirit also helps in our weaknesses. For we do not know what we should pray for as we ought, but the Spirit Himself makes intercession for us with groanings which cannot be uttered. Now He who searches the hearts knows what the mind of the Spirit is, because He makes intercession for the saints according to the will of God. And we know that all things work together for good to those who love God, to those who are the called according to His purpose. For whom He foreknew, He also predestined to be conformed to the image of His Son, that He might be the firstborn among many brethren. Moreover whom He predestined, these He also called; whom He called, these He also justified; and whom He justified, these He also glorified.

ROMANS 8:26-30 NKJV

STANDING FIRM

BLESSINGS FROM THOSE WE BLESS

'It is more blessed to give than to receive.'
ACTS 20:35 NKJV

I'm a father of five wonderful grown children, one now already in heaven, and the grandfather of eleven awesome grandchildren. For more than half a century, my wife Arlie and I have made it a crusade to bless our children, their mates, and their children. It is the Christian thing to do, isn't it? We always expected the blessings to flow "downward" through the generations. But increasingly we have discovered a reverse flow of blessings. The more we try to bless the next generations, the more we discover greater blessings from them. We who thought we were the "blessers" suddenly become the blessed, and those we expected to be the blessed have become the "blessers." Those we blessed with wise counsel, love, generosity, role modeling and a hundred other gifts, now bless us with wise counsel, love, generosity, role modeling and a hundred other gifts. Perhaps we can carry this thought upward a bit. We expect that God is always the "blesser" and we are always the blessed. But is it not true that when we return our gifts to God we bless God? What an awesome thought that we, those blessed by God, can return blessing to Him? ~ V. Gilbert Beers (1928-)

WHAT A FRIEND WE HAVE IN JESUS

What a friend we have in Jesus, All our sins and griefs to bear;
What a privilege to carry Ev'rything to God in prayer!
O what peace we often forfeit, O what needless pain we bear.
Just because we do not carry Ev'rything to God in prayer.
Have we trials and temptations? Is there trouble anywhere?
We should never be discouraged; Take it to the Lord in prayer.
Can we find a friend so faithful, Who will all our sorrows share?
Jesus knows our ev'ry weakness; Take it to the Lord in prayer.
Are we weak and heavy-laden, Cumbered with a load of care?
Precious Saviour, still our refuge; Take it to the Lord in prayer.
Do thy friends despise, forsake thee? Take it to the Lord in prayer;
In His arms He'll take and shield thee, Thou wilt find a solace there.
~ Joseph Scriven (1819-1886)

HOLDING ON

*Wait on the LORD: be of good courage, and he shall
strengthen thine heart: wait, I say, on the LORD.*

PSALM 27:14 KJV

God's will is as great as God, as high as heaven, yet as easy as love.
For love knows no hardness, and feels no yoke. It desires no yielding to
its poverty in anything it loves. Let God be greater, and His will sterner,
love will be stronger and obedience but more true. Let not God come
down to me, slacken truth for me, make His will weaker for me: my
interests, as subject, are safer with my King, are greater with the
greatness of my King — only give me love, pure, burning love and
loyalty to Him, and I shall climb from law to law through grace and
glory, to the place beside the throne where the angels do His will. There
are two ways, therefore, of looking at God's will — one looking at the
love side of it, the other at the law; the one ending in triumph, the other
in despair; the one a liberty, the other a slavery.

~ Henry Drummond (1851-1897)

I KNOW IN MY HEART
THAT HE HAS RISEN

*Mary Magdalene came and told the disciples that she had seen the Lord,
and that He had spoken these things to her.*

JOHN 20:18 NKJV

Christ's appearing first to Mary Magdalene was without question his finest assurance to women throughout the ages that he values us, that he died for us, that he rose for us. He could have appeared before his beloved disciple John, he could have sent his spirited disciple Peter to proclaim his resurrection to the world, but that undeniable fact is, Jesus chose Mary Magdalene. He chose a woman. Yes, he did. How do I know that Jesus has risen? Because he has risen to the throne of my own heart. I have seen him work miracles in my life, one after another, big and small. He has changed my desires; he has remodeled my thinking; he has shown me how to love the unlovable, forgive the unforgivable (including myself), and move the unmovable barriers in my path. The undeniable gospel is this: a transformed life. ~ Liz Curtis Higgs (1954-)

DESIRE FOR RIGHTEOUSNESS

Blessed are those who hunger and thirst for righteousness,
For they shall be filled.

MATTHEW 5:6 NKJV

It is written of our blessed Lord, "Thou hast loved righteousness, and hated iniquity; therefore God, even thy God, hath anointed thee with the oil of gladness above thy fellows." It is the purpose of God that we, as we are indwelt by the Spirit of His Son, should likewise love righteousness and hate iniquity. I see that there is a place for us in Christ Jesus where we are no longer under condemnation but where the heavens are always open to us. I see that God has a realm of divine life opening up to us where there are boundless possibilities, where there is limitless power, where there are untold resources, where we have victory over all the power of the devil. I believe that, as we are filled with the desire to press on into this life of true holiness, desiring only the glory of God, there is nothing that can hinder our true advancement.
~ Smith Wigglesworth (1859-1947)

FAITH

For we walk by faith, not by sight . . .
—— II CORINTHIANS 5:7 KJV ——

A work of grace in the soul discovereth itself, either to him that hath it, or to standers-by. To him that hath it, thus: It gives him conviction of sin, especially the defilement of his nature, and the sin of unbelief, for the sake of which he is sure to be damned, if he findeth not mercy at God's hand, by faith in Jesus Christ. This sight and sense of things worketh in him sorrow and shame for sin. He findeth, moreover, revealed in him the Saviour of the world, and the absolute necessity of closing with him for life; at the which he findeth hungerings and thirstings after him; to which hungerings, etc., the promise is made. Now, according to the strength or weakness of his faith in his Saviour, so is his joy and peace, so is his love to holiness, so are his desires to know him more, and also to serve him in this world. But though, I say it discovereth itself thus unto him, yet it is but seldom that he is able to conclude that this is a work of grace; because his corruptions now, and his abused reason, make his mind to misjudge in this matter: therefore in him that hath this work there is required a very sound judgment, before he can with steadiness conclude that this is a work of grace.

~ John Bunyan (1628-1688)

What then shall we say to these things? If God is for us, who can be against us? He who did not spare His own Son, but delivered Him up for us all, how shall He not with Him also freely give us all things? Who shall bring a charge against God's elect? It is God who justifies. Who is he who condemns? It is Christ who died, and furthermore is also risen, who is even at the right hand of God, who also makes intercession for us. Who shall separate us from the love of Christ? Shall tribulation, or distress, or persecution, or famine, or nakedness, or peril, or sword? As it is written: "For Your sake we are killed all day long; We are accounted as sheep for the slaughter." Yet in all these things we are more than conquerors through Him who loved us. For I am persuaded that neither death nor life, nor angels nor principalities nor powers, nor things present nor things to come, nor height nor depth, nor any other created thing, shall be able to separate us from the love of God which is in Christ Jesus our Lord.

ROMANS 8:31-39 NKJV

STANDING FIRM

HOLY SPIRIT WORK

'Not by might nor by power, but by My Spirit,' Says the Lord of hosts.
—————— ZECHARIAH 4:6 NKJV ——————

The redeemed are not sanctified without Christ, who is made to them sanctification; hence the work of the Spirit must embrace the Incarnation of the Word and the work of the Messiah. But the work of Messiah involves preparatory working in the Patriarchs and Prophets of Israel, and later activity in the Apostles . . . Likewise this revelation involves the conditions of man's nature and the historical development of the race; hence the Holy Spirit is concerned in the formation of the human mind and the unfolding of the spirit of humanity . . . man's condition depends on that of the earth . . . and no less on the actions of spirits, be they angels or demons from other spheres . . . the Spirit's work must touch the entire host of heaven and earth. To avoid a mechanical idea of His work as though it began and ended at random . . . it must not be determined nor limited till it extends to all the influences that affect the sanctification of the Church. The Holy Spirit is God, therefore sovereign; hence He cannot depend on these influences, but completely controls them. For this He must be able to operate them; so His work must be honored in all the host of heaven, in man and in his history, in the preparation of Scripture, in the Incarnation of the Word, in the salvation of the elect.

~ Abraham Kuyper (1837-1920)

O PERFECT LIFE OF LOVE

O perfect life of love! All, all, is finished now,
All that He left His throne above To do for us below.
No work is left undone Of all the Father willed;
His toil, His sorrows, one by one, The Scriptures have fulfilled.
No pain that we can share But He has felt its smart;
All forms of human grief and care Have pierced that tender heart.
And on His thorn-crowned head And on His sinless soul
Our sins in all that guilt were laid That He might make us whole.
In perfect love He dies; For me He dies, for me.
O all-atoning Sacrifice, I cling by faith to Thee.
In every time of need, Before the judgment-throne,
Thy works, O Lamb of God, I'll plead, Thy merits, not mine own.
Yet work, O Lord, in me As Thou for me hast wrought,
And let my love the answer be To grace Thy love has brought.
~ Henry W. Baker (1821-1877)

GOD'S CALL

And the LORD came, and stood, and called
as at other times, Samuel, Samuel.

I SAMUEL 3:10 KJV

We may know God's call when it grows in intensity. — If an impression comes into your soul, and you are not quite sure of its origin, pray over it; above all, act on it so far as possible, follow in the direction in which it leads — and as you lift up your soul before God, it will wax or wane. If it wanes at all, abandon it. If it waxes follow it, though all hell attempt to stay you. We may test God's call by the assistance of godly friends. — The aged Eli perceived that the Lord had called the child, and gave him good advice as to the manner in which he should respond to it. Our special gifts and the drift of our circumstances will also assuredly concur in one of God's calls. We may test God's call by its effect on us. — Does it lead to self-denial? Does it induce us to leave the comfortable bed and step into the cold? Does it drive us forth to minister to others? Does it make us more unselfish, loving, tender, modest, humble? Whatever is to the humbling of our pride, and the glory of God, may be truly deemed God's call. Be quick to respond, and fearlessly deliver the message the Lord has given you.

~ F.B. Meyer (1847-1929)

THE ART OF MANFISHING

"Follow me, and I will make you fishers of men."
———— MATTHEW 4:19 KJV ————

O power and life from God in ordinances is sweet. Seek it for thyself, and seek it for thy hearers. Acknowledge thine own weakness and uselessness without it, and so cry incessantly for it, that the Lord may drive the fish into the net, when thou art spreading it out. Have an eye to this power, when thou art preaching; and think not thou to convert men by the force of reason: if thou do, thou wilt be beguiled. What an honorable thing is it to be fishers of men! How great an honor shouldst thou esteem it, to be a catcher of souls! We are workers together with God, says the apostle. If God has ever so honored thee, O that thou knewest it that thou mightst bless his holy name, that ever made such a poor fool as thee to be a co-worker with him. God has owned thee to do good to those who were before caught. O my soul, bless thou the Lord. Lord, what am I, or what is my father's house, that thou hast brought me to this? ~ Thomas Boston (1677-1732)

ALIVE IN CHRIST

Let not sin therefore reign in your mortal body,
that ye should obey it in the lusts thereof.
Neither yield ye your members as instruments
of unrighteousness unto sin:
but yield yourselves unto God
as those that are alive from the dead,
and your members as instruments
of righteousness unto God.

—— ROMANS 6:12, 13 KJV ——

"Present yourselves unto God, as alive from the dead". This defines for us the point at which consecration begins. For what is here referred to is not the consecration of anything belonging to the old creation, but only of that which has passed through death to resurrection. The 'presenting' spoken of is the outcome of my knowing my old man to be crucified. Knowing, reckoning, presenting to God: that is the Divine order. When I really know I am crucified with Him, then spontaneously I reckon myself dead; and when I know that I am raised with Him from the dead, then likewise I reckon myself "alive unto God in Christ Jesus," for both the death and the resurrection side of the Cross are to be accepted by faith. When this point is reached, giving myself to Him follows. In resurrection He is the source of my life — indeed He is my life; so I cannot but present everything to Him, for all is His, not mine . . . Presenting myself to God means that henceforth I consider my whole life as now belonging to the Lord. ~ Watchman Nee (1903-1972)

OUR ABSURDITIES

*Whoever humbles himself as this little child
is the greatest in the kingdom of heaven.*

MATTHEW 18:4 NKJV

Once we reread the Gospels, watching for Christ's wit, we find it everywhere. "They are blind leaders of the blind. And if the blind leads the blind, both will fall into a ditch." (Matt. 15:14). Thus if we will read them carefully, the Gospels give us a picture of Christ who would not let people be unobservant about life, about the actions of others, or most of all, about themselves. He wanted them awakened at every level of their being. And so He used every weapon of language and thought and communication to achieve His goals. Most effective were banter, the humorous thrust and sardonic comments about those who put on airs and think more highly of themselves than they should. As one of sound and balanced mind, He could not observe humankind and fail to see our incongruities and absurdities. He does see, and He laughs along with us. ~ Catherine Marshall (1914-1983)

I tell the truth in Christ, I am not lying, my conscience also bearing me witness in the Holy Spirit, that I have great sorrow and continual grief in my heart. For I could wish that I myself were accursed from Christ for my brethren, my countrymen according to the flesh, who are Israelites, to whom pertain the adoption, the glory, the covenants, the giving of the law, the service of God, and the promises; of whom are the fathers and from whom, according to the flesh, Christ came, who is over all, the eternally blessed God. Amen.

—— ROMANS 9:1-5 NKJV ——

IN THE BEGINNING GOD CREATED!
(Part 1)

In the beginning God created the heaven and the earth.

GENESIS 1:1 KJV

I stop struck with admiration at this thought. What shall I first say? Where shall I begin my story? Shall I show forth the vanity of the Gentiles? Shall I exalt the truth of our faith? The philosophers of Greece have made much ado to explain nature, and not one of their systems has remained firm and unshaken, each being overturned by its successor. It is vain to refute them; they are sufficient in themselves to destroy one another. Those who were too ignorant to rise to a knowledge of a God, could not allow that an intelligent cause presided at the birth of the Universe; a primary error that involved them in sad consequences. Some had recourse to material principles and attributed the origin of the Universe to the elements of the world. Others imagined that atoms, and indivisible bodies, molecules and ducts, form, by their union, the nature of the visible world. Atoms reuniting or separating, produce births and deaths and the most durable bodies only owe their consistency to the strength of their mutual adhesion: a true spider's web woven by these writers who give to heaven, to earth, and to sea so weak an origin and so little consistency! It is because they knew not how to say "In the beginning God created the heaven and the earth." ~ Henry Wace (1836-1924)

IN THE BEGINNING GOD CREATED!
(Part 2)

In the beginning God created the heaven and the earth.
———— GENESIS 1:1 KJV ————

What a glorious order! He first establishes a beginning, so that it might not be supposed that the world never had a beginning. Then he adds "Created" to show that which was made was a very small part of the power of the Creator. In the same way that the potter, after having made with equal pains a great number of vessels, has not exhausted either his art or his talent; thus the Maker of the Universe, whose creative power, far from being bounded by one world, could extend to the infinite, needed only the impulse of His will to bring the immensities of the visible world into being. If then the world has a beginning, and if it has been created, enquire who gave it this beginning, and who was the Creator: or rather, in the fear that human reasonings may make you wander from the truth, Moses has anticipated enquiry by engraving in our hearts, as a seal and a safeguard, the awful name of God: "In the beginning God created" — It is He, beneficent Nature, Goodness without measure, a worthy object of love for all beings endowed with reason, the beauty the most to be desired, the origin of all that exists, the source of life, intellectual light, impenetrable wisdom, it is He who "in the beginning created heaven and earth." ~ Henry Wace (1836-1924)

THE REALITY OF PRAYER

Who in the days of his flesh, when he had offered up prayers and
supplications with strong crying and tears unto him that was able
to save him from death, and was heard. . .
HEBREWS 5:7 KJV

The word "Prayer" expresses the largest and most comprehensive approach unto God. It gives prominence to the element of devotion. It is communion and intercourse with God. It is enjoyment of God. It is access to God. "Supplication" is a more restricted and more intense form of prayer, accompanied by a sense of personal need, limited to the seeking in an urgent manner of a supply for pressing need. "Supplication" is the very soul of prayer in the way of pleading for some one thing, greatly needed, and the need intensely felt. "Intercession" is an enlargement in prayer, a going out in broadness and fullness from self to others. Primarily, it does not centre in praying for others, but refers to the freeness, boldness and childlike confidence of the praying. It is the fullness of confiding influence in the soul's approach to God, unlimited and unhesitating in its access and its demands. This influence and confident trust is to be used for others. Prayer always, and everywhere is an immediate and confiding approach to, and a request of, God the Father. In the prayer universal and perfect, as the pattern of all praying, it is "Our Father, Who art in Heaven."
~ Edward M. Bounds (1835-1913)

WHOLE-HEARTED MEN OF PRAYER

. . .the prayer of the upright is his delight.
PROVERBS 15:8 KJV

PRAYER has to do with the entire man. Prayer takes in man in his whole being, mind, soul and body. It takes the whole man to pray, and prayer affects the entire man in its gracious results. As the whole nature of man enters into prayer, so also all that belongs to man is the beneficiary of prayer. All of man receives benefits in prayer. The whole man must be given to God in praying. The largest results in praying come to him who gives himself, all of himself, all that belongs to himself, to God. This is the secret of full consecration, and this is a condition of successful praying, and the sort of praying which brings the largest fruits. The men of olden times who wrought well in prayer, who brought the largest things to pass, who moved God to do great things, were those who were entirely given over to God in their praying. God wants, and must have, all that there is in man in answering his prayers. He must have whole-hearted men through whom to work out His purposes and plans concerning men. God must have men in their entirety. No double-minded man need apply. No vacillating man can be used. No man with a divided allegiance to God, and the world and self, can do the praying that is needed. ~ Edward M. Bounds (1835-1913)

O GOD, BE WITH US

O God, be with us, for the night is falling;
For Thy protection we to Thee are calling;
Beneath Thy shadow to our rest we yield us;
Thou, Lord, wilt shield us.
May evil fancies flee away before us;
Till morning cometh, watch, O Father, o'er us;
In soul and body Thou from harm defend us, Thine angel send us.
While we are sleeping, keep us in Thy favor;
When we awaken, let us never waver
All day to serve Thee, Thy due praise pursuing In all our doing.
Through Thy Beloved soothe the sick and weeping
And bid the captive lose his grief in sleeping;
Widows and orphans, we to Thee commend them,
Do Thou befriend them.
We have no refuge, none on earth to aid us,
Save Thee, O Father, who Thine own hast made us.
But Thy dear presence will not leave them lonely Who seek Thee only.
Thy name be hallowed and Thy kingdom given,
Thy will among us done as 'tis in heaven;
Feed us, forgive us, from all ill deliver Now and forever.

~ Herbert Petrus (1530-1571)

TRUST, NO MATTER WHAT!

Though he slay me, yet will I trust in him . . .
——— JOB 13:15 KJV ———

This was a noble expression, which has been appropriated by thousands in every subsequent age. In every friendship there is a probation, during which we narrowly watch the actions of another, as indicating the nature of his soul; but after awhile we get to such intimate knowledge and confidence, that we read and know his inner secret. We have passed from the outer court into the Holy Place of fellowship. We seem familiar with every nook and cranny of our friend's nature. And then it is comparatively unimportant how he appears to act; we know him. So it is in respect of God. At first we know Him through the testimony of others, and on the evidence of Scripture; but as time passes, with its everdeepening experiences of what God is, with those opportunities of converse that arise during years of prayer and communion, we get to know Him as He is and to trust Him implicitly. If He seems to forget and forsake us, it is only in appearance. His heart is yearning over us more than ever. God cannot do a thing which is not perfectly loving and wise and good. Oh to know Him thus! "Leaving the final issue In His hands Whose goodness knows no change, whose love is sure, Who sees, foresees, who cannot judge amiss." ~ F.B. Meyer (1847-1929)

But it is not that the word of God has taken no effect. For they are not all Israel who are of Israel, nor are they all children because they are the seed of Abraham; but, "In Isaac your seed shall be called." That is, those who are the children of the flesh, these are not the children of God; but the children of the promise are counted as the seed. For this is the word of promise: "At this time I will come and Sarah shall have a son." And not only this, but when Rebecca also had conceived by one man, even by our father Isaac (for the children not yet being born, nor having done any good or evil, that the purpose of God according to election might stand, not of works but of Him who calls), it was said to her, "The older shall serve the younger." As it is written, "Jacob I have loved, but Esau I have hated."

ROMANS 9:6-13 NKJV

HUMILITY

Before destruction the heart of a man is haughty,
And before honor is humility.

PROVERBS 18:12 NKJV

Charity and Righteousness: these two lay the foundation of the kingdom of the soul where God would dwell. And this foundation is humility. These three virtues prop and bear the whole weight and the whole edifice of all the other virtues and of all transcendence. For charity always confronts man with the unfathomable goodness of God, from which it has flowed forth, that thereby he may live worthily and remain steadfast before God, and grow in true humility and all other virtues. And righteousness places man face to face with the eternal truth of God, that he may know truth, and become enlightened, and may fulfill all virtue without erring. But humility brings man face to face with the most high mightiness of God, that he may always remain little and lowly, and may surrender himself to God, and may not stand upon his selfhood. This is the way in which a man should hold himself before God, that thereby he may grow continually in new virtues.

~ John of Ruysbroeck (1293-1381)

ALL HAIL THE POWER
OF JESUS' NAME

All hail the power of Jesus' name! Let angels prostrate fall;
Bring forth the royal diadem And crown Him Lord of all.
Crown Him, ye martyrs of our God, Who from His altar call;
Extol the Stem of Jesse's rod And crown Him Lord of all.
Ye seed of Israel's chosen race, Ye ransomed from the Fall,
Hail Him who saves you by His grace And crown Him Lord of all.
Hail Him, ye heirs of David's line, Whom David Lord did call,
The God incarnate, Man divine, And crown Him Lord of all.
Sinners, whose love can ne'er forget The wormwood and the gall,
Go, spread your trophies at His feet And crown Him Lord of all.
Let every kindred, every tribe, On this terrestrial ball
To Him all majesty ascribe And crown Him Lord of all.
Oh, that with yonder sacred throng We at His feet may fall!
We'll join the everlasting song And crown Him Lord of all.
~ Edward Perronet (1726-1792)

PRAYERS FROM THE HEART (Part 1)

O God, you led your holy apostles to ordain ministers in every place: Grant that your Church, under the guidance of the Holy Spirit, may choose suitable persons for the ministry of Word and Sacrament, and may uphold them in their work for the extension of your kingdom; through him who is the Shepherd and Bishop of our souls, Jesus Christ our Lord, who lives and reigns with you and the Holy Spirit, one God, for ever and ever. Amen

Almighty and everlasting God, by whose Spirit the whole body of your faithful people is governed and sanctified: Receive our supplications and prayers, which we offer before you for all members of your holy Church, that in their vocation and ministry they may truly and devoutly serve you; through our Lord and Savior Jesus Christ, who lives and reigns with you, in the unity of the Holy Spirit, one God, now and for ever. Amen

Almighty God, unto whom all hearts are open, all desires known, and from whom no secrets are hid: Cleanse the thoughts of our hearts by the inspiration of thy Holy Spirit, that we may perfectly love thee, and worthily magnify thy holy Name; through Christ our Lord. Amen

~ William Wilberforce (1759-1833)

PRAYERS FROM THE HEART (Part 2)

Lord God Almighty, you have made all the peoples of the earth for your glory, to serve you in freedom and in peace: Give to the people of our country a zeal for justice and the strength of forbearance, that we may use our liberty in accordance with your gracious will; through Jesus Christ our Lord, who lives and reigns with you and the Holy Spirit, one God, for ever and ever. Amen

Almighty God, who created us in your image: Grant us grace fearlessly to contend against evil and to make no peace with oppression; and, that we may reverently use our freedom, help us to employ it in the maintenance of justice in our communities and among the nations, to the glory of your holy Name; through Jesus Christ our Lord, who lives and reigns with you and the Holy Spirit, one God, now and for ever. Amen

Almighty God, the fountain of all wisdom: Enlighten by your Holy Spirit those who teach and those who learn, that, rejoicing in the knowledge of your truth, they may worship you and serve you from generation to generation; through Jesus Christ our Lord, who lives and reigns with you and the Holy Spirit, one God, for ever and ever. Amen

~ William Wilberforce (1759-1833)

PRAYERS FROM THE HEART (Part 3)

O God of unchangeable power and eternal light: Look favorably on your whole Church, that wonderful and sacred mystery; by the effectual working of your providence, carry out in tranquility the plan of salvation; let the whole world see and know that things which were cast down are being raised up, and things which had grown old are being made new, and that all things are being brought to their perfection by him through whom all things were made, your Son Jesus Christ our Lord; who lives and reigns with you, in the unity of the Holy Spirit, one God, for ever and ever. Amen

Almighty and most merciful Father, we have erred and strayed from thy ways like lost sheep, we have followed too much the devices and desires of our own hearts, we have offended against thy holy laws, we have left undone those things which we ought to have done, and we have done those things which we ought not to have done. But thou, O Lord, have mercy upon us, spare thou those who confess their faults, restore thou those who are penitent, according to thy promises declared unto mankind in Christ Jesus our Lord; and grant, O most merciful Father, for his sake, that we may hereafter live a godly, righteous, and sober life, to the glory of thy holy Name. Amen

~ William Wilberforce (1759-1833)

RELATIONSHIP PRINCIPLES

But that it may be a witness between us, and you, and our generations after us, that we might do the service of the LORD . . .

JOSHUA 22:27 KJV

I want my five children, their mates and my 13 grandchildren to know that if they ever stray from the Lord I will always have a fatted calf in my freezer. God gave me this special message on relationships on our 25th wedding anniversary. "When you slice life you always find relationships." I believe that there are at least four essentials that will make all of our relationships work. I discovered these as I thought about Jesus Christ's relationship with me as a believer. These principles are found in our four major relationships and backed up in scripture passages. My relationship with Jesus (Romans 8), my relationship with my mate (Ephesians 5), my relationship with my children (Luke 15), and my relationship with my fellow believers (Philemon). These four essential relationships are: an uncommon commitment, an uncomplicated communication, an unchangeable forgiveness and an unconditional love. ~ Robert McFarland (1939-)

What shall we say then? Is there unrighteousness with God?
Certainly not! For He says to Moses, "I will have mercy on
whomever I will have mercy, and I will have compassion on
whomever I will have compassion." So then it is not of him who
wills, nor of him who runs, but of God who shows mercy. For the
Scripture says to Pharaoh, "For this very purpose I have raised
you up, that I may show My power in you, and that My name
may be declared in all the earth." Therefore He has mercy on
whom He wills, and whom He wills He hardens. You will say to
me then, "Why does He still find fault? For who has resisted His
will?" But indeed, O man, who are you to reply against God?
Will the thing formed say to him who formed it, "Why have you
made me like this?" Does not the potter have power over the clay,
from the same lump to make one vessel for honor and another for
dishonor? What if God, wanting to show His wrath and to make
His power known, endured with much longsuffering the vessels of
wrath prepared for destruction, and that He might make known
the riches of His glory on the vessels of mercy, which He had
prepared beforehand for glory, even us whom He called,
not of the Jews only, but also of the Gentiles?

ROMANS 9:14-24 NKJV

STANDING FIRM

THE CROOK IN THE LOT

*Consider the work of God: for who can make
that straight, which he hath made crooked?*

ECCLESIASTES 7:13 KJV

Everybody's lot in this world has some crook in it. Complainers are apt to make odious comparisons. They look about, and take a distant view of the condition of others, can discern nothing in it but what is straight, and just to one's wish; so they pronounce their neighbor's lot wholly straight. But that is a false verdict; there is no perfection here; no lot out of heaven without a crook. For, as to "all the works that are done under the sun, behold, all is vanity and vexation of spirit. That which is crooked cannot be made straight." Who would have thought but that Haman's lot was very straight, while his family was in a flourishing condition, and he prospering in riches and honor, being prime minister of state in the Persian court, and standing high in the king's favor? Yet there was, at the same time, a crook in his lot, which so galled him, that "all this availed him nothing." Every one feels for himself, when he is pinched, though others do not perceive it. Nobody's lot, in this world, is wholly crooked; there are always some straight and even parts in it. Indeed, when men's passions, having gotten up, have cast a mist over their minds, they are ready to say, all is wrong with them, nothing right. But, though in hell that tale is and ever will be true, yet it is never true in this world. For there, indeed, there is not a drop of comfort allowed; but here it always holds good, that "it is of the Lord's mercies we are not consumed." ~ Thomas Boston (1677-1732)

COME, MY SOUL,
THY SUIT PREPARED

. . .the LORD appeared to Solomon in a dream by night:
and God said, Ask what I shall give thee.

I KINGS 3:5 KJV

Come, my soul, thy suit prepared, Jesus loves to answer prayer;
He Himself has bid thee pray, Therefore will not say thee nay.
Thou art coming to a King, Large petitions with thee bring;
For His grace and pow'r are such None can ever ask too much.
With my burden I begin: Lord, remove this load of sin;
Let Thy blood, for sinners spilt, Set my conscience free from guilt.
Lord, I come to Thee for rest, Take possession of my breast;
There Thy blood-bought right maintain And without a rival reign.
As the image in the glass Answers the beholder's face,
Thus unto my heart appear; Print Thine own resemblance there.
While I am a pilgrim here, Let Thy love my spirit cheer;
As my Guide, my Guard, my Friend, Lead me to my journey's end.
Show me what I have to do; Every hour my strength renew.
Let me live a life of faith; Let me die Thy people's death.

~ John Newton (1725-1807)

OBEDIENCE

Seeing ye have purified your souls in obeying to the truth . . .
———— I PETER 1:22 KJV ————

In Paul's Epistle to the Romans . . . the opening and closing verses the expression, 'the obedience of faith among all nations' (1:5; 16:26), as that for which he was made an apostle. He speaks of what God had wrought 'to make the Gentiles obedient.' He teaches that, as the obedience of Christ makes us righteous, we become the servants of obedience unto righteousness. As disobedience in Adam and in us was the one thing that wrought death, so obedience, in Christ and in us, is the one thing that the gospel makes known as the way of restoration to God and His favor. We all know how James warns us not to be hearers of the Word only but doers, and expounds how Abraham was justified, and his faith perfected, by his works. In Peter's First Epistle we have only to look at the first chapter, to see the place obedience has in his system . . . v.2 speaks to the 'Elect, in sanctification of the Spirit, unto obedience and blood-sprinkling of Jesus Christ,' and so points us to obedience as the eternal purpose of the Father, as the great object of the work of the Spirit, and a chief part of the salvation of Christ . . . 'As children of obedience,' born of it, marked by it, subject to it, 'be ye holy in all manner of conversation.' Obedience is THE VERY STARTING POINT OF TRUE HOLINESS. ~ Andrew Murray (1828-1917)

GRACIOUS LOVE

And thou shalt love the LORD thy God with all thine heart,
and with all thy soul, and with all thy might.

DEUTERONOMY 6:5 KJV

The more a true saint loves God with a gracious love, the more he desires to love Him, and the more uneasy is he at his want of love to Him; the more he hates sin, the more he desires to hate it, and laments that he has so much remaining love to it; the more he mourns for sin, the more he longs to mourn for sin; the more his heart is broke, the more he desires it should be broke the more he thirsts and longs after God and holiness, the more he longs to long, and breathe out his very soul in longings after God: the kindling and raising of gracious affections is like kindling a flame . . . So that the spiritual appetite after holiness, and an increase of holy affections is much more lively and keen in those that are eminent in holiness, than others, and more when grace and holy affections are in their most lively exercise, than at other times . . . The most that the saints have in this world, is but a taste . . . it is only an earnest of their future inheritance in their hearts. The most eminent saints in this state are but children, compared with their future, which is their proper state of maturity and perfection. . .

~ Jonathan Edwards (1703-1758)

THE WILL TO DO GOD'S WILL

If any man will do his will, he shall know of the doctrine,
whether it be of God, or whether I speak of myself.

John 7:17 KJV

It requires a well-kept life to do the will of God, and even a better kept life to will to do His will. To be willing is a rarer grace than to be doing the will of God. For he who is willing may sometimes have nothing to do, and must only be willing to wait: and it is far easier to be doing God's will than to be willing to have nothing to do — it is easier far to be working for Christ than it is to be willing to cease. No, there is nothing rarer in the world to-day than the truly willing soul, and there is nothing more worth coveting than the will to will God's will. There is no grander possession for any Christian life than the transparently simple mechanism of a sincerely obeying heart. And if we could keep the machinery clear, there would be lives in thousands doing God's will on earth even as it is done in Heaven. There would be God in many a man's career whose soul is allowed to drift — a useless thing to God and the world — with every changing wind of life, and many a noble Christian character rescued from wasting all its virtues on itself and saved for work for Christ. ~ Henry Drummond (1851-1897)

TURNING POINT

And Peter went out, and wept bitterly.

LUKE 22:62 KJV

These words indicate the turning point in the life of Peter—a crisis. There is often a question about the life of holiness. Do you grow into it? Or do you come into it by a crisis suddenly? Peter has been growing for three years under the training of Christ, but he had grown terribly downward, for the end of his growing was, he denied Jesus. And then there came a crisis. After the crisis he was a changed man, and then he began to grow aright. We must indeed grow in grace, but before we can grow in grace we must be put right . . . Just as the Lord Jesus gave the Holy Spirit to Peter, He is willing to give the Holy Spirit to you. Are you willing to receive Him? Are you willing to give up yourself entirely as an empty, helpless vessel, to receive the power of the Holy Spirit, to live, to dwell, and to work in you every day? Dear believer, God has prepared such a beautiful and such a blessed life for every one of us, and God as a Father is waiting to see why you will not come to Him and let Him fill you with the Holy Ghost. ~ Andrew Murray (1828-1917)

As He says also in Hosea: "I will call them My people, who were not My people, And her beloved, who was not beloved." "And it shall come to pass in the place where it was said to them, 'You are not My people,' There they shall be called sons of the living God." Isaiah also cries out concerning Israel: "Though the number of the children of Israel be as the sand of the sea, The remnant will be saved. For He will finish the work and cut it short in righteousness, Because the Lord will make a short work upon the earth." And as Isaiah said before: "Unless the Lord of Sabaoth had left us a seed, We would have become like Sodom, And we would have been made like Gomorrah." What shall we say then? That Gentiles, who did not pursue righteousness, have attained to righteousness, even the righteousness of faith; but Israel, pursuing the law of righteousness, has not attained to the law of righteousness. Why? Because they did not seek it by faith, but as it were, by the works of the law. For they stumbled at that stumbling stone. As it is written: "Behold, I lay in Zion a stumbling stone and rock of offense, And whoever believes on Him will not be put to shame."

ROMANS 9:25-33 NKJV

ARE YOU WASHED?

Herein is love, not that we loved God, but that he loved us. . .
———— I JOHN 4:10 KJV ————

The apostle John writes, 'But if we walk in the light, as he is in the light, we have fellowship with one another, and the blood of Jesus Christ His Son cleanseth us from all sin' (I John 1:7); and in the book of Revelation we read, 'Unto Him that loved us, and washed us from our sins in His own blood' (Revelation 1:5). Now that is a small selection of the New Testament statements, but what a selection! They are some of the pivotal passages that at once bring before us the idea of the substitute and the penal suffering, the bearing of the guilt and the guilt being punished in the substitute. And you notice the repetition of the blood. I have known people who have called themselves Christian who have said that they dislike this thought about the blood. But apart from the blood we have no redemption! 'In whom we have redemption through the blood.' It is the precious blood of Christ, the laying down of the life, the poured out life, that our redemption is secured.
~ Martyn Lloyd-Jones (1899-1981)

HOW DO YOU LIVE?

The steps of a good man are ordered by the LORD:
and he delighteth in his way.

PSALM 37:23 KJV

If men used as much care in uprooting vices and implanting virtues as they do in discussing problems, there would not be so much evil and scandal in the world, or such laxity in religious organizations. On the day of judgment, surely, we shall not be asked what we have read but what we have done; not how well we have spoken but how well we have lived. Tell me, where now are all the masters and teachers whom you knew so well in life and who were famous for their learning? . . . During life they seemed to be something; now they are seldom remembered . . . If only their lives had kept pace with their learning, then their study and reading would have been worth while. How many there are who perish because of vain worldly knowledge and too little care for serving God. They became vain in their own conceits because they chose to be great rather than humble. He is truly great who has great charity. He is truly great who is little in his own eyes and makes nothing of the highest honor. He is truly wise who looks upon all earthly things as folly that he may gain Christ. He who does God's will and renounces his own is truly very learned. . .

~ Thomas à Kempis (1380-1471)

THE CHARIOTS OF GOD (Part 1)

O my God, I trust in thee: let me not be ashamed,
let not mine enemies triumph over me.

PSALMS 25:2 KJV

The baby carried in the chariot of its mother's arms rides triumphantly through the hardest places, and does not even know they are hard. And how much more we, who are carried in the chariot of the "arms of God"! Get into your chariot, then. Take each thing that is wrong in your lives as God's chariot for you. No matter who the builder of the wrong may be, whether men or devils, by the time it reaches your side it is God's chariot for you, and is meant to carry you to a heavenly place of triumph. Shut out all the second causes, and find the Lord in it. Say, "Lord, open my eyes that I may see, not the visible enemy, but thy unseen chariots of deliverance." Accept His will in the trial, whatever it may be, and hide yourself in His arms of love. Say, "Thy will be done; Thy will be done!" over and over. Shut out every other thought but the one thought of submission to His will and of trust in His love. Make your trial thus your chariot, and you will find your soul "riding upon the heavens" with God in a way you never dreamed could be.

~Hannah Whitall Smith (1832-1911)

THE CHARIOTS OF GOD (Part 2)

By this I know that thou favourest me,
because mine enemy doth not triumph over me.

———— PSALMS 41:11 KJV ————

I have not a shadow of doubt that if all our eyes were opened today we would see our homes, and our places of business, and the streets we traverse, filled with the "chariots of God." There is no need for any one of us to walk for lack of chariots. That cross inmate of your household, who has hitherto made life a burden to you, and who has been the Juggernaut car to crush your soul into the dust, may henceforth be a glorious chariot to carry you to the heights of heavenly patience and longsuffering. That misunderstanding, that mortification, that unkindness, that disappointment, that loss, that defeat, all these are chariots waiting to carry you to the very heights of victory you have so longed to reach. Mount into them, then, with thankful hearts, and lose sight of all second causes in the shining of His love who will "carry you in His arms" safely and triumphantly over it all.

~Hannah Whitall Smith (1832-1911)

THE POWER OF PRAYER

And when they had prayed, the place was shaken
where they were assembled together; and they were all filled
with the Holy Ghost, and they spake the word of God with boldness.

ACTS 4:31 KJV

The 20th Century brought more knowledge to our world than ever before. We learned to split the atom. We learned to use nuclear energy. We defied the laws of gravity and put a man on the moon. We created wonder drugs that conquer historically old diseases and prolong life to great expectancies. We created computers and communicate within split-seconds around the world. We are surrounded by more gadgets and technologies than any other generation. Yet, with all we have in science, technology and economics, we still have very little understanding of God's promise to bestow power on us to touch the world. The Church never stands taller than when she kneels to pray; she never moves faster than when she is on her knees. Since the beginning of the Church, God has promised His powerful presence to obedient, praying believers. In Acts 4, desperate prayers of praise and petition were offered to God and the church experienced the presence of God. When the body of Christ learns to come in prayerful agreement, in unity with the Father, Son and Holy Spirit, there will be no force in the world that can withstand such power and such love. The gates of hell cannot prevail against His Church as we proclaim the whole Gospel to the whole world. ~ Glenn Sheppard (1943 -)

GOD'S MERCY
BRINGS RIGHTEOUSNESS

So then it is not of him that willeth, nor of him
that runneth, but of God that sheweth mercy.

ROMANS 9:16 KJV

Mercy then is to be found alone in Jesus Christ. Again, the righteousness of the law is to be obtained only by faith of Jesus Christ; that is, in the Son of God is the righteousness of the law to be found; for he, by his obedience to his Father, is become the end of the law for righteousness. And for the sake of his legal righteousness (which is also called the righteousness of God, because it was God in the flesh of the Lord Jesus that did accomplish it), is mercy, and grace from God extended to whoever dependeth by faith upon God by this Jesus his righteousness for it. And hence it is, that we so often read, that this Jesus is the way to the Father; that God, for Christ's sake, forgiveth us; that by the obedience of one many are made righteous, or justified; and that through this man is preached to us the forgiveness of sins; and that by him all that believe are justified from all things from which they could not be justified by the law of Moses. ~ John Bunyan (1628-1688)

Brethren, my heart's desire and prayer to God for Israel is that they may be saved. For I bear them witness that they have a zeal for God, but not according to knowledge. For they being ignorant of God's righteousness, and seeking to establish their own righteousness, have not submitted to the righteousness of God. For Christ is the end of the law for righteousness to everyone who believes. For Moses writes about the righteousness which is of the law, "The man who does those things shall live by them." But the righteousness of faith speaks in this way, "Do not say in your heart, 'Who will ascend into heaven?' "(that is, to bring Christ down from above) or, " 'Who will descend into the abyss?' " (that is, to bring Christ up from the dead).

ROMANS 10:1-7 NKJV

STANDING FIRM

CHRISTIANITY IN THE WORLD

For whatsoever is born of God overcometh the world . . .
———— I JOHN 5:4 KJV ————

It is the Son of Man before whom the nations of the world shall be gathered. It is in the presence of Humanity that we shall be charged. And the spectacle itself, the mere sight of it, will silently judge each one. Those will be there whom we have met and helped: or there, the unpitied multitude whom we neglected or despised. No other Witness need be summoned. No other charge than lovelessness shall be preferred. Be not deceived. The words which all of us shall one Day hear, sound not of theology but of life, not of churches and saints but of the hungry and the poor, not of creeds and doctrines but of shelter and clothing, not of Bibles and prayer-books but of cups of cold water in the name of Christ. Thank God the Christianity of today is coming nearer the world's need. Live to help that on. Thank God men know better, by a hairsbreadth, what religion is, what God is, who Christ is, where Christ is. Who is Christ? He who fed the hungry, clothed the naked, visited the sick. And where is Christ? Where? — whoso shall receive a little child in My name receiveth Me. And who are Christ's? Every one that loveth is born of God. ~ Henry Drummond (1851-1897)

ALTOGETHER LOVELY

. . .yea, he is altogether lovely.

SONG OF SOLOMON 5:16 KJV

. . . Our Lord Jesus makes sinners lovely. In their natural state, men are deformed and hideous to the eye of God; and as they have no love to God, so He has no delight in them. He is weary of them, and is grieved that He made men upon the earth. The Lord is angry with the wicked every day. Yet, when our Lord Jesus comes in, and covers these sinful ones with His righteousness, and, at the same time, infuses into them His life, the Lord is well pleased with them for His Son's sake. Even in heaven, the infinite Jehovah sees nothing which pleases Him like His Son. The Father from eternity loved His Only-begotten, and again and again He hath said of Him, "This is My beloved Son, in whom I am well pleased." What higher encomium can be passed upon Him? Our Lord's loveliness appears in every condition: in the manger, or in the temple; by the well, or on the sea; in the garden, or on the cross; in the tomb, or in the resurrection; in His first, or in His second coming. He is not as the herb, which flowers only at one season; or as the tree, which loses its leaves in winter; or as the moon, which waxes and wanes; or as the sea, which ebbs and flows. In every condition, and at every time, "He is altogether lovely." ~ Charles H. Spurgeon (1834-1892)

GOD WANTS HOLY MEN

And the very God of peace sanctify you wholly; and I pray
God your whole spirit and soul and body be preserved
blameless unto the coming of our Lord Jesus Christ.

I Thessalonians 5:23 KJV

Holiness is wholeness, and so God wants holy men, men whole-hearted and true, for His service and for the work of praying. These are the sort of men God wants for leaders of the hosts of Israel, and these are the kind out of which the praying class is formed . . . Man is one in all the essentials and acts and attitudes of piety. Soul, spirit and body are to unite in all things pertaining to life and godliness. The body, first of all, engages in prayer, since it assumes the praying attitude in prayer. Prostration of the body becomes us in praying as well as prostration of the soul. The attitude of the body counts much in prayer, although it is true that the heart may be haughty and lifted up, and the mind listless and wandering, and the praying a mere form, even while the knees are bent in prayer. . .The entire man must pray. The whole man, life, heart, temper, mind, are in it. Each and all join in the prayer exercise. Doubt, double-mindedness, division of the affections, are all foreign to the closest character and conduct, undefiled, made whiter than snow, are mighty potencies, and are the most seemly beauties for the closest hour, and for the struggles of prayer. ~ Edward M. Bounds (1835-1913)

AND CAN IT BE?

And can it be that I should gain An int'rest in the Savior's blood?
Died He for me who caused His pain?
For me, who Him to death pursued?
Amazing love! How can it be That Thou, my God, shouldst die for me?
'Tis mystery all! The Immortal dies!
Who can explore His strange design?
In vain the first-born seraph tries To sound the depths of love divine!
'Tis mercy all! let earth adore, Let angel-minds inquire no more.
He left His father's throne above So free, so infinite His grace!
Emptied Himself of all but love And bled for Adam's helpless race!
'Tis mercy all, immense and free For O my God, it found out me.
Long my imprisoned spirit lay Fast bound in sin and nature's night.
Thine eye diffused a quick'ning ray:
I woke—the dungeon flamed with light!
My chains fell off, my heart was free I rose,
went forth and followed Thee.
No condemnation now I dread Jesus, and all in Him, is mine!
Alive in Him, my living Head And clothed in righteousness divine
Bold I approach the 'ternal throne
And claim the crown thru Christ my own.
~ Charles Wesley (1701-1788)

EXAMINE YOURSELVES

*Now faith is the substance of things hoped for,
the evidence of things not seen.*

HEBREWS 11:1 KJV

The Holy Spirit has Paul write to each of us, "Examine yourselves, whether ye be in the faith" (2 Corinthians 13:5a), and the recommendation is certainly not out of order at the very inception of this series of studies . . . "without faith it is impossible to please him" (Hebrews 11:6a) . . . true faith must be based solely upon scriptural FACTS, for "faith cometh by hearing, and hearing by the word of God" (Romans 10:17). Unless our faith is established upon facts, it is no more than conjecture, superstition, speculation, or presumption. Hebrews 11:1 leaves no question about this: "Faith is the substance of things hoped for, the evidence of things not seen." Faith standing on the FACTS of the Word of God substantiates and gives evidence of things not seen. And everyone knows that evidence must be founded upon facts. All of us started on this principle when we were born again — our belief stood directly upon the eternal fact of the redeeming death and resurrection of our Lord and Savior Jesus Christ (1 Corinthians 15:1-4). This is the faith by which we began, and it is the same faith by which we are to "stand" and "walk" and "live." "As ye have therefore received Christ Jesus the Lord, so walk ye in him." ~ Miles Stanford (1914 -1999)

THE IMAGE OF GOD IN MAN

So God created man in his own image, in the image of God created he him; male and female created he them.

———— GENESIS 1:27 KJV ————

How hard it is for natural reason to discover a creation before revealed, or, being revealed, to believe it, the strange opinions of the old philosophers, and the infidelity of modern atheists, is too sad a demonstration ... to view nature in its cradle, and trace the outgoings of the Ancient of Days in the first instance and specimen of His creative power, is a research too great for any mortal inquiry; and we might continue our scrutiny to the end of the world ... the excellency of Christian religion, in that it is the great and only means that God has sanctified and designed to repair the breaches of humanity, to set fallen man upon his legs again, to clarify his reason, to rectify his will, and to compose and regulate his affections. The whole business of our redemption is, in short, only to rub over the defaced copy of the creation, to reprint God's image upon the soul, and, as it were, to set forth nature in a second and fairer edition; the recovery of which lost image, as it is God's pleasure to command, and our duty to endeavor, so it is in His power only to effect; to whom be rendered and ascribed, as is most due, all praise, might, majesty, and dominion, both now and forever more! ~ Robert South (1638-1716)

But what does it say? "The word is near you, in your mouth and in your heart" (that is, the word of faith which we preach): that if you confess with your mouth the Lord Jesus and believe in your heart that God has raised Him from the dead, you will be saved. For with the heart one believes unto righteousness, and with the mouth confession is made unto salvation. For the Scripture says, "Whoever believes on Him will not be put to shame." For there is no distinction between Jew and Greek, for the same Lord over all is rich to all who call upon Him. For "whoever calls on the name of the Lord shall be saved." How then shall they call on Him in whom they have not believed? And how shall they believe in Him of whom they have not heard? And how shall they hear without a preacher? And how shall they preach unless they are sent? As it is written: "How beautiful are the feet of those who preach the gospel of peace, Who bring glad tidings of good things!"

ROMANS 10:8-15 NKJV

COME, SINNERS,
TO THE GOSPEL FEAST

(LUKE 14:16-24)

COME, sinners, to the gospel feast, Let every soul be Jesu's guest;
Ye need not one be left behind, For God hath bidden all mankind.
Sent by my Lord, on you I call, The invitation is to ALL:
Come, all the world; come, sinner, thou!
All things in Christ are ready now.
Come, all ye souls by sin opprest, Ye restless wanderers after rest,
Ye poor, and maimed, and halt, and blind,
In Christ a hearty welcome find.
Come, and partake the gospel feast; Be saved from sin; in Jesus rest;
O taste the goodness of your God, And eat his flesh,
and drink his blood!
Ye vagrant souls, on you I call; (O that my voice could reach you all!)
Ye all may now be justified, Ye all may live, for Christ hath died.
My message as from God receive, Ye all may come to Christ, and live;
O let his love your hearts constrain, Nor suffer him to die in vain!
His love is mighty to compel; His conquering love consent to feel,
Yield to his love's resistless power,
And fight against your God no more.
See him set forth before your eyes, That precious, bleeding sacrifice!
His offered benefits embrace, And freely now be saved by grace.
This is the time; no more delay! This is the acceptable day,
Come in, this moment, at his call, And live for him who died for all.

~ Charles Wesley (1701-1788)

CHRISTIAN GROWTH

But grow in grace, and in the knowledge of our Lord and Saviour Jesus Christ.

———— II PETER 3:18 KJV ————

Since the Christian life matures and becomes fruitful by the principle of growth, rather than by struggle and "experiences," much time is involved. Unless we see and acquiesce to this, there is bound to be constant frustration, to say nothing of resistance to our Father's development processes for us. . . . "A student asked the President of his school whether he could not take a shorter course than the one prescribed. 'Oh yes,' replied the President, 'but then it depends upon what you want to be. When God wants to make an oak, He takes an hundred years, but when He wants to make a squash, He takes six months.'" . . . "growth is not a uniform thing in the tree or in the Christian, In some single months there is more growth than in all the year besides. During the rest of the year, however, there is solidification, without which the green timber would be useless. The period of rapid growth, when woody fiber is actually deposited between the bark and the trunk, occupies but four to six weeks" . . . there are no shortcuts to reality! . . . Unless the time factor is acknowledged from the heart, there is always danger of turning to the false enticement of a shortcut via the means of "experiences," and "blessings," where one becomes pathetically enmeshed in the vortex of ever-changing "feelings," adrift from the moorings of scriptural facts. ~ Miles Stanford (1914-1999)

OUR DUAL PROBLEM:
SINS AND SIN (Part 1)

If we confess our sins, he is faithful and just to forgive us our sins, and to cleanse us from all unrighteousness.
———— I John 1:9 KJV ————

No matter how many sins I commit, it is always the one sin principle that leads to them. I need forgiveness for my sins, but I need also deliverance from the power of sin. The former touches my conscience, the latter my life. I may receive forgiveness for all my sins, but because of my sin I have, even then, no abiding peace of mind. When God's light first shines into my heart my one cry is for forgiveness, for I realize I have committed sins before Him; but when once I have received forgiveness of sins I make a new discovery, namely, the discovery of sin, and I realize not only that I have committed sins before God but that there is something wrong within. I discover that I have the nature of a sinner. There is an inward inclination to sin, a power within that draws to sin. When that power breaks out I commit sins. I may seek and receive forgiveness, but then I sin once more. So life goes on in a vicious circle of sinning and being forgiven and then sinning again. I appreciate the blessed fact of God's forgiveness, but I want something more than that: I want deliverance. I need forgiveness for what I have done, but I need also deliverance from what I am.
~ Watchman Nee (1903-1972)

GOD'S DUAL REMEDY:
THE BLOOD AND THE CROSS (Part 2)

Being justified freely by his grace through the redemption that is in Christ
Jesus: Whom God hath set forth to be a propitiation through faith in his
blood, to declare his righteousness...

—— ROMANS 3:24, 25 KJV ——

Thus in the first eight chapters of Romans two aspects of salvation are presented to us: firstly, the forgiveness of our sins, and secondly, our deliverance from sin. But now, in keeping with this fact, we must notice a further difference. In the first part of Romans 1 to 8, we twice have reference to the Blood of the Lord Jesus, in chapter 3:25 and in chapter 5:9. In the second, a new idea is introduced in chapter 6:6, where we are said to have been "crucified" with Christ. The argument of the first part gathers round that aspect of the work of the Lord Jesus which is represented by 'the Blood' shed for our justification through "the remission of sins". This terminology is however not carried on into the second section, where the argument centers now in the aspect of His work represented by 'the Cross', that is to say, by our union with Christ in His death, burial and resurrection. This distinction is a valuable one. We shall see that the Blood deals with what we have done, whereas the Cross deals with what we are. The Blood disposes of our sins, while the Cross strikes at the root of our capacity for sin.

~ Watchman Nee (1903-1972)

GROWING IN CHRIST

I press toward the mark for the prize of
the high calling of God in Christ Jesus.

PHILIPPIANS 3:14 KJV

Graham Scroggie affirmed: "Spiritual renewal is a gradual process. All growth is progressive, and the finer the organism, the longer the process. It is from measure to measure: thirtyfold, sixtyfold, an hundredfold. It is from stage to stage: 'first the blade, then the ear, and after that, the full corn in the ear.' And it is from day to day. How varied these are! There are great days, days of decisive battles, days of crisis in spiritual history, days of triumph in Christian service, days of the right hand of God upon us. But there are also idle days, days apparently useless, when even prayer and holy service seem a burden. Are we, in any sense, renewed in these days? Yes, for any experience which makes us more aware of our need of God must contribute to spiritual progress, unless we deny the Lord who bought us." . . . It takes time to get to know ourselves; it takes time and eternity to get to know our Infinite Lord Jesus Christ. Today is the day to put our hand to the plow, and irrevocably set our heart on His goal for us — that we "may know him, and the power of his resurrection, and the fellowship of his sufferings, being made conformable unto his death" (Philippians 3:10).
~ Miles Stanford (1914-1999)

GUARDIANS AGAINST SIN

Only take heed to thyself, and keep thy soul diligently. . .
—— DEUTERONOMY 4:9 KJV ——

Every living creature possesses within himself, by the gift of God, the Ordainer of all things, certain resources for self protection. Investigate nature with attention, and you will find that the majority of brutes have an instinctive aversion from what is injurious; while, on the other hand, by a kind of natural attraction, they are impelled to the enjoyment of what is beneficial to them. Wherefore also God our Teacher has given us this grand injunction, in order that what brutes possess by nature may accrue to us by the aid of reason, and that what is performed by brutes unwittingly may be done by us through careful attention and constant exercise of our reasoning faculty. We are to be diligent guardians of the resources given to us by God, ever shunning sin as brutes shun poisons . . . Take heed to thyself, that thou mayest be able to discern between the noxious and the wholesome . . . Look well around thee, that thou mayest be delivered 'as a gazelle from the net and a bird from the snare.' It is because of her keen sight that the gazelle cannot be caught in the net. It is her keen sight that gives her her name. And the bird, if only she take heed, mounts on her light wing far above the wiles of the hunter. ~ Henry Wace (1836-1924)

But they have not all obeyed the gospel. For Isaiah says, "Lord, who has believed our report?" So then faith comes by hearing, and hearing by the word of God. But I say, have they not heard? Yes indeed: "Their sound has gone out to all the earth, And their words to the ends of the world." But I say, did Israel not know? First Moses says: "I will provoke you to jealousy by those who are not a nation, I will move you to anger by a foolish nation." But Isaiah is very bold and says: "I was found by those who did not seek Me; I was made manifest to those who did not ask for Me." But to Israel he says: "All day long I have stretched out My hands To a disobedient and contrary people."

ROMANS 10:16-21 NKJV

UNION WITH GOD

He brought me up also out of an horrible pit, out of the miry clay,
and set my feet upon a rock, and established my goings.
—— PSALM 40:2 KJV ——

. . . We should be indeed purely, simply, and wholly at one with the one eternal Will of God, or altogether without will, so that the created will should flow out into the eternal Will and be swallowed up and lost in it, so that the eternal Will alone should do and leave undone in us. Now observe what may be of use to us in attaining this object. Religious exercises cannot do this, nor words, nor works, nor any creature or work done by a creature. We must therefore give up and renounce all things, suffering them to be what they are, and enter into union with God. Yet the outward things must be; and sleeping and waking, walking and standing still, speaking and being silent, must go on as long as we live . . . when God Himself dwells in a man; as we plainly see in the case of Christ. Moreover, where there is this union, which is the outflow of the Divine light and dwells in its beams, there is no spiritual pride nor boldness of spirit, but unbounded humility and a lowly broken heart; there is also an honest and blameless walk, justice, peace, contentment, and every virtue . . . Be well assured of this.
~ Johannes Eckhart (1260-1327)

PRAYER AS DESIRING SOMEONE'S GOOD

And it shall come to pass, that before they call,
I will answer; and while they are yet speaking, I will hear.

ISAIAH 65:24 KJV

Prayer is expressed through various modes. There are petitions and intercessions; sometimes agony, tears, and fasting. I am especially intrigued by the prayer that comes wafting into our mind, that tugs at our heart as an inward desire to pray a particular blessing upon some individual, whether a loved one or a stranger. Often we have no way to trace the efficacy of such prayers. But over the years I have occasionally discovered that such "inward desire" prayers for others have been answered in a definite way. I was reminded of one such incident when coming upon the March 8, 1988 entry in my journal. I was working at the Des Moines, Iowa post office. A number of weeks prior to the journal entry I had a quiet, easy, simple inward desire to pray for a woman that I knew only slightly upon seeing her working at a distance. My prayer desire was that she would seek and find God, supposing her to be a woman of the world and without any special interest in things spiritual. Several weeks later I happened to be working near her and heard her carrying on a conversation with a Christian man. She related that she had recently come to Christ, was attending church and attempting to read and understand the Bible.

~ Raymond V. Banner (1937-)

JESUS WILL BEAR OUR GRIEFS AND CARRY OUR SORROWS

. . . A man of sorrows and acquainted with grief. . .
───────── ISAIAH 53:3 NKJV ─────────

This earth is not a stranger to tears, neither is the present the only time when they could be found in abundance. From Adam's days to ours tears have been shed, and a wail has been going up to Heaven from the broken hearted ... it is a mystery to me how all those broken hearts can keep away from Him who has come to heal them. For six thousand years that cry of sorrow has been going up to God. We find the tears of Jacob put on record, when he was told that his own son was no more. His sons and daughters tried to give him comfort, but he refused to be comforted. We are also told of the tears of King David. I can see him, as the messenger brings the news of the death of his son ... And when Christ came into the world the first sound He heard was woe—the wail of those mothers in Bethlehem; and from the manger to the Cross, He was surrounded with sorrow. We are told that He often looked up to Heaven and sighed. I believe it was because there was so much suffering around Him. It was on His right hand and on His left—everywhere on earth; and the thought that He had come to relieve the people of the earth of their burdens, and so few would accept Him, made Him sorrowful. He came for that purpose. Let the hundreds of thousands just cast their burdens on Him. He has come to bear them, as well as our sins. ~ Dwight L. Moody (1837-1899)

OUR DAILY HOMILY

. . . I have drunk neither wine nor strong drink,
but have poured out my soul before the LORD.

I SAMUEL 1:15 KJV

Is your face darkened by the bitterness of your soul? Perhaps the enemy has been vexing you sorely; or there is an unrealized hope, an unfulfilled purpose in your life; or perchance, the Lord seems to have forgotten you. Poor sufferer, there is nothing for it but to pour out your soul before the Lord. Empty out its contents in confession and prayer. God knows it all; yet tell Him, as if He knew nothing. "Ye people, pour out your hearts before Him. God is a refuge for us." "In everything, by prayer and supplication make your requests known unto God." As we pour out our bitterness, God pours in his peace. Weeping goes out of one door whilst joy enters at another. We transmit the cup of tears to the Man of Sorrows, and He hands it back to us filled with the blessings of the new covenant. Some day you will come to the spot where you wept and prayed, bringing your offering of praise and thanksgiving.
~ F. B. Meyer (1847-1929)

WE WILL BE PERFECT!

As for God, his way is perfect: the word of the
LORD is tried: he is a buckler to all those that trust him.
———— PSALM 18:30 KJV ————

We may consider the state of our minds in glory. The faculties of our souls shall then be made perfect, Hebrews 12:23, "The spirits of just men made perfect." (1.) Freed from all the clogs of the flesh, and all its influence upon them, and restraint of their powers in their operation (2.) Perfectly purified from all principles of instability and variety,—of all inclinations unto things sensual and carnal, and all contrivances of self-preservation or advancement,—being wholly transformed into the image of God in spirituality and holiness. And to take in the state of our bodies after the resurrection; even they also, in all their powers and senses, shall be made entirely subservient unto the most spiritual actings of our minds in their highest elevation by the light of glory. Hereby shall we be enabled and fitted eternally to abide in the contemplation of the glory of Christ with joy and satisfaction. The understanding shall be always perfected with the vision of God, and the affections cleave inseparably to him;—which is blessedness . . . It is Christ alone who is the likeness and image of God. When we awake in the other world, with our minds purified and rectified, the beholding of him shall be always satisfying unto us. ~ John Owen (1616-1683)

GIVING TO GOD

The LORD is my shepherd; I shall not want.
————— PSALM 23:1 NKJV —————

Tithing was a practice God asked of the Jewish people back in Old Testament times. It means giving to God through giving to others a minimum of one-tenth of one's gross income or harvest or cattle production or whatever. "Minimum" because even as Christ upholds tithing, He also strengthens it by often asking that we give away more than the base ten percent. In teaching the practice of tithing to the Jews, God was seeing to it that they would have an unending demonstration of how sound the coin of His kingdom is. To buttress this further He gave them—and us—that magnificent promise: "Bring all the tithes into the storehouse, that there may be food in My house, and try Me now in this," says the LORD of hosts, "If I will not open for you the windows of heaven and pour out for you such blessing, that there will not be room enough to receive it" (Mal 3:10). When we put God first, we won't have to worry about our supply. ~ Catherine Marshall (1914-1983)

I say then, has God cast away His people? Certainly not! For I also am an Israelite, of the seed of Abraham, of the tribe of Benjamin. God has not cast away His people whom He foreknew. Or do you not know what the Scripture says of Elijah, how he pleads with God against Israel, saying, "Lord, they have killed Your prophets and torn down Your altars, and I alone am left, and they seek my life"? But what does the divine response say to him? "I have reserved for Myself seven thousand men who have not bowed the knee to Baal." Even so then, at this present time there is a remnant according to the election of grace. And if by grace, then it is no longer of works; otherwise grace is no longer grace. But if it is of works, it is no longer grace; otherwise work is no longer work. What then? Israel has not obtained what it seeks; but the elect have obtained it, and the rest were blinded. Just as it is written: "God has given them a spirit of stupor, Eyes that they should not see And ears that they should not hear, To this very day." And David says: "Let their table become a snare and a trap, A stumbling block and a recompense to them. Let their eyes be darkened, so that they do not see, And bow down their back always."

ROMANS 11:1-10 NKJV

STANDING FIRM

COME AND DINE

". . . Behold, I have prepared my dinner. . .and all things are ready. . . "
—— MATTHEW 22:4 KJV ——

Let the King of Heaven and Earth say this to you. In honor of His Son He has prepared a great supper. There the Son bears His human nature. There are all the children of men, dear and precious to the Father, and He has caused them to be invited to the great festival of the Divine love. He is prepared to receive and honor them there as guests and friends. He will feed them with His heavenly food. He will bestow upon them the gifts and energies of everlasting life. O my soul, thou also hast received this heavenly invitation. To be asked to eat with the King of Glory: how it behooves thee to embrace and be occupied with this honor. How desirous must you be to prepare yourself for this feast. How you must long that you should be in dress and demeanor, and language and disposition, all that may be rightly expected of one who is invited to the court of the King of kings. Glorious invitation! I think of the banquet itself and what it has cost the great God to prepare it . . . I think of the blessing of the banquet. The dying are fed with the power of a heavenly life, the lost are restored to their places in the Father's house, those that thirst after God are satisfied with God Himself and with His love. Glorious invitation! ~ Andrew Murray (1828-1917)

ACCEPTANCE

*. . . being justified by faith, we have peace with
God through our Lord Jesus Christ. . .*

ROMANS 5:1 KJV

There are two questions that every believer must settle as soon as possible. The one is, Does God fully accept me? And, If so, upon what basis does He do so? This is crucial. What devastation often permeates the life of one, young or old, rich or poor, saved or unsaved, who is not sure of being accepted, even on the human level. Yet so many believers, whether "strugglers" or "vegetators," move through life without this precious fact to rest and build upon: "Having predestinated us unto the adoption of children by Jesus Christ to himself, according to the good pleasure of his will, to the praise of the glory of his grace, wherein he hath made us accepted in the beloved" (Ephesians 1:5, 6). Every believer is accepted by the Father, in Christ. The peace is God's toward us, through His Beloved Son — upon this, our peace is to be based. God is able to be at peace with us through our Lord Jesus Christ, "having made peace by the blood of his cross" (Colossians 1:20). And we must never forget that His peace is founded solely on the work of the cross, totally apart from anything whatsoever in or from us, since "God commendeth his love toward us, in that, while we were yet sinners, Christ died for us" (Romans 5:8). ~ Miles Stanford (1914-1999)

TOWARD THE GOAL

I press toward the mark for the high calling of God in Christ Jesus.
——— PHILIPPIANS 3:14 KJV ———

. . . Seeing that, in this earthly prison of the body, no man is supplied with strength sufficient to hasten in his course with due alacrity, while the greater number are so oppressed with weakness, that hesitating, and halting, and even crawling on the ground, they make little progress, let every one of us go as far as his humble ability enables him, and prosecute the journey once begun. No one will travel so badly as not daily to make some degree of progress. This, therefore, let us never cease to do, that we may daily advance in the way of the Lord; and let us not despair because of the slender measure of success. How little soever the success may correspond with our wish, our labour is not lost when to-day is better than yesterday, provided with true singleness of mind we keep our aim, and aspire to the goal, not speaking flattering things to ourselves, nor indulging our vices, but making it our constant endeavour to become better, until we attain to goodness itself. If during the whole course of our life we seek and follow, we shall at length attain it, when relieved from the infirmity of flesh we are admitted to full fellowship with God. ~ John Calvin (1509-1564)

GOD TESTS US

". . .he goeth before them, and the sheep follow him; for they know
his voice. And a stranger will they not follow, but will flee
from him, for they know not the voice of strangers."

JOHN 10:4, 5 KJV

Most people in Christian circles claim to believe the Bible and think of themselves as "hard core" Christians! Our churches proclaim the Bible to be the inerrant Word of God however, words are cheap, and no one can really be certified as a believer until a test is given. A man can claim to be the greatest athlete until he enters the Olympics and is proven. In Daniel's day the nation of Israel all claimed to be worshipers of the true God. Not until a test was given, which required them to prove their loyalty to the Living God by refusing to bow before the king's idol, were their true beliefs exposed. Shadrach, Meshach, and Abednego were not very outstanding until everyone else bowed down! After that no one else could claim orthodoxy. Paul reminds us that false teachers are permitted by God so that it will be obvious who the real believers are. The best assurance of our salvation is not what we say we believe and stand for, but rather our perseverance in the face of a test.
~ John Hey (1939 -)

FAITH AND OBEDIENCE

. . .Jesus saith unto them, "Believe ye that I am able to do this?"
They said unto him, "Yea, Lord."
—————— MATTHEW 9:28 KJV ——————

Like the man who was born blind, it goes to wash in the pool of Siloam when told to wash. Like Peter on Gennesaret it casts the net where Jesus commands, instantly, without question or doubt. Such faith takes away the stone from the grave of Lazarus promptly. A praying faith keeps the commandments of God and does those things which are well pleasing in His sight. It asks, "Lord, what wilt Thou have me to do?" and answers quickly, "Speak, Lord, Thy servant heareth." Obedience helps faith, and faith, in turn, helps obedience. To do God's will is essential to true faith, and faith is necessary to implicit obedience. ~ Edward M. Bounds (1835-1913)

EVERY MAN'S NEED OF A REFUGE

And a man shall be as an hiding place from the wind,
and a covert from the tempest; as rivers of water in a dry place,
as the shadow of a great rock in a weary land.

ISAIAH 32:2 KJV

Christ is a hiding-place from the wrath to come. Now, of course, I cannot prove that from experience, for it lies in the future; but I can prove it by an argument that is unanswerable. That argument is this: the Christ that has power to save men from the power of sin now — certainly has power to save them from the consequences of sin hereafter. Is not that a good argument? Let me add, that any religion that is not saving you from the power of sin today will not save you from the consequences of sin in eternity. There is a lot of religion in this world that is absolutely worthless. People tell you that they are Christians and that they are religious. They are saying their prayers, and doing all sorts of things. I will ask you a question: "Have you got that kind of faith in Jesus Christ that is saving you from the power of sin today?" If you have, you have that kind of faith in Jesus Christ that will save you from the consequences of sin hereafter. But if you have that kind of faith in Jesus Christ which after all is not faith, which is not saving you now, you have that kind of faith in Jesus Christ that wont save you from the penalty of sin hereafter. Friends, Jesus Christ is a refuge, a hiding-place from experience and its accusations, from the power of sin within, from the power of Satan, from the wrath to come, from all that man needs a hiding-place from. Who will come to this hiding-place. . . ~ R.A. Torrey (1856-1928)

I say then, have they stumbled that they should fall? Certainly not! But through their fall, to provoke them to jealousy, salvation has come to the Gentiles. Now if their fall is riches for the world, and their failure riches for the Gentiles, how much more their fullness! For I speak to you Gentiles; inasmuch as I am an apostle to the Gentiles, I magnify my ministry, if by any means I may provoke to jealousy those who are my flesh and save some of them. For if their being cast away is the reconciling of the world, what will their acceptance be but life from the dead? For if the firstfruit is holy, the lump is also holy; and if the root is holy, so are the branches. And if some of the branches were broken off, and you, being a wild olive tree, were grafted in among them, and with them became a partaker of the root and fatness of the olive tree, do not boast against the branches. But if you do boast, remember that you do not support the root, but the root supports you. You will say then, "Branches were broken off that I might be grafted in." Well said. Because of unbelief they were broken off, and you stand by faith. Do not be haughty, but fear. For if God did not spare the natural branches, He may not spare you either. Therefore consider the goodness and severity of God: on those who fell, severity; but toward you, goodness, if you continue in His goodness. Otherwise you also will be cut off. And they also, if they do not continue in unbelief, will be grafted in, for God is able to graft them in again. For if you were cut out of the olive tree which is wild by nature, and were grafted contrary to nature into a cultivated olive tree, how much more will these, who are natural branches, be grafted into their own olive tree?

ROMANS 11:11-24 NKJV

THE SHADOW OF THE ROCK

Because thou hast been my help, therefore
in the shadow of thy wings will I rejoice.

PSALM 63:7 KJV

Guarded by Omnipotence, the chosen of the Lord are always safe; for as they dwell in the holy place, hard by the mercy-seat, where the blood was sprinkled of old, the pillar of fire by night, the pillar of cloud by day, which ever hangs over the sanctuary, covers them also. The shadow of a rock is remarkably cooling, and so was the Lord Jesus eminently comforting to us. The shadow of a rock is more dense, more complete, and more cool than any other shade; and so the peace which Jesus gives passeth all understanding, there is none like it. No chance beam darts through the rock-shade, nor can the heat penetrate as it will do in a measure through the foliage of a forest. Jesus is a complete shelter, and blessed are they who are "under His shadow." Let them take care that they abide there, and never venture forth to answer for themselves, or to brave the accusations of Satan. As with sin, so with sorrow of every sort: the Lord is the Rock of our refuge. No sun shall smite us, nor, any heat, because we are never out of Christ. The saints know where to fly, and they use their privilege.

~ Charles H. Spurgeon (1834-1892)

THE CHILD IN THE MIDST

And he took a child, and set him in the midst of them: and when he had taken him in his arms, he said unto them, Whosoever shall receive one of such children in my name, receiveth me; and whosoever shall receive me, receiveth not me, but him that sent me.

MARK 9:36, 37 KJV

What is the kingdom of Christ? A rule of love, of truth — a rule of service. The king is the chief servant in it. "The kings of the earth have dominion: it shall not be so among you." "The Son of Man came to minister." "My Father worketh hitherto, and I work." The great Workman is the great King, labouring for his own. So he that would be greatest among them, and come nearest to the King himself, must be the servant of all. It is like king like subject in the kingdom of heaven. No rule of force, as of one kind over another kind. It is the rule of kind, of nature, of deepest nature — of God. If, then, to enter into this kingdom, we must become children, the spirit of children must be its pervading spirit throughout, from lowly subject to lowliest king. The lesson added by St. Luke to the presentation of the child is: "For he that is least among you all, the same shall be great." And St. Matthew says: "Whosoever shall humble himself as this little child, the same is greatest in the kingdom of heaven." Hence the sign that passes between king and subject. The subject kneels in homage to the kings of the earth: the heavenly king takes his subject in his arms. This is the sign of the kingdom between them. This is the all-pervading relation of the kingdom. ~ George MacDonald (1824-1905)

OBEDIENT AS JESUS WAS

Let this mind be in you which was also in Christ Jesus,
And being found in appearance as a man,
He humbled Himself and became obedient to the point of death,
even the death of the cross.

PHILIPPIANS 2:5, 8 NKJV

"We must obey God." This is the cure for servile subjection to the commandments and the doctrines of men. There must be obedience, but obedience to what? To God's authority, and to that alone. Thus the soul is preserved from the influence of infidelity on the one hand, and superstition on the other. Infidelity says, "Do as you like." Superstition says, "Do as man tells you." Faith says, "We must obey God." Here is the holy balance of the soul in the midst of the conflicting and confounding influences around us in this our day. As a servant, I am to obey my Lord; as a child, I am to hearken to my Father's commandments. Nor am I the less to do this although my fellow-servants and my brethren may not understand me. I must remember that the immediate business of my soul is with God Himself. ~ C. H. Mackintosh (1820-1896)

HE FIRST LOVED US

Ye have not chosen me, but I have chosen you, and ordained you, that ye should go and bring forth fruit, and that your fruit should remain . . .

JOHN 15:16 KJV

This is a very humbling, and at the same time, a very blessed word to the true disciple.

It was very humbling to the disciples to be told that they had not chosen Christ. Your wants were so many, your hearts were so hard, that ye have not chosen me. And yet it was exceedingly comforting to the disciples to be told that he had chosen them: "Ye have not chosen me, but I have chosen you." This showed them that his love was first with them — that he had a love for them when they were dead. And then he showed them that it was love that would make them holy: "Ye have not chosen me, but I have chosen you, and ordained you, that ye should go and bring forth fruit, and that your fruit should remain." Christ not only chooses who are to be saved, but he chooses the way; and he not only chooses the beginning and the end, he chooses the middle also.

"God hath from the beginning chosen you to salvation, through sanctification of the Spirit and belief of the truth. According as he hath chosen us in him before the foundation of the world, that we should be holy and without blame before him in love." Ephesians 1:4.

~ Robert Murray McCheyne (1813-1843)

CROWN HIM WITH MANY CROWNS

Crown Him with many crowns The Lamb upon His throne;
Hark how the heavenly anthem drowns All music but its own.
Awake, my soul, and sing Of Him who died for thee
And hail Him as thy matchless King Through all eternity.
Crown Him the Virgin's Son, The God incarnate born,
Whose arm those crimson trophies won Which now His brow adorn;
Fruit of the mystic rose, As of that rose the stem;
The root whence mercy ever flows, The Babe of Bethlehem.
Crown Him the Lord of Love. Behold His hands and side,
Rich wounds, yet visible above, In beauty glorified.
No angel in the sky Can fully bear that sight,
But downward bends his wondering eye At mysteries so bright!
Crown Him the Lord of Life Who triumphed o'er the grave
And rose victorious in the strife For those He came to save.
His glories now we sing Who died and rose on high,
Who died eternal life to bring And lives that death may die.
Crown Him the Lord of Heaven, Enthroned in worlds above,
Crown Him the King to whom is given The wondrous name of Love.
Crown Him with many crowns As thrones before Him fall;
Crown Him, ye kings, with many crowns For He is King of all.
~ Matthew Bridges (1800-1894)

KNOWING GOD

Then shall we know, if we follow on to know the LORD:
his going forth is prepared as the morning. . .
———— HOSEA 6:3 KJV ————

The Bible assumes as a self-evident fact that men can know God with at least the same degree of immediacy as they know any other person or thing that comes within the field of their experience. The same terms are used to express the knowledge of God as are used to express knowledge of physical things. "O taste and see that the Lord is good." "All thy garments smell Of myrrh, and aloes, and cassia, out of the ivory palaces." "My sheep hear my voice." "Blessed are the pure in heart, for they shall see God." These are but four of countless such passages from the Word of God. And more important than any proof text is the fact that the whole import of the Scripture is toward this belief. ~ A. W. Tozer (1897-1963)

*For I do not desire, brethren, that you should be ignorant of this
mystery, lest you should be wise in your own opinion, that
blindness in part has happened to Israel until the fullness of the
Gentiles has come in. And so all Israel will be saved, as it is
written: "The Deliverer will come out of Zion, And He will turn
away ungodliness from Jacob; For this is My covenant with them,
When I take away their sins." Concerning the gospel they are
enemies for your sake, but concerning the election they are beloved
for the sake of the fathers. For the gifts and the calling of God are
irrevocable. For as you were once disobedient to God, yet have
now obtained mercy through their disobedience, even so these also
have now been disobedient, that through the mercy shown you
they also may obtain mercy. For God has committed them all to
disobedience, that He might have mercy on all. Oh, the depth of
the riches both of the wisdom and knowledge of God! How
unsearchable are His judgments and His ways past finding out!
"For who has known the mind of the Lord? Or who has become
His counselor?" "Or who has first given to Him And it shall be
repaid to him?" For of Him and through Him and
to Him are all things, to whom be glory forever. Amen.*

—————— ROMANS 11:25-36 NKJV ——————

PROOF FULFILLED

I did not come to destroy but to fulfill.
———— MATTHEW 5:17 NKJV ————

Every sacrifice lit. . .pointed as with flaming fingers to Calvary's cross! Nay all the centuries moved as in solemn procession to lay their tributes upon Golgotha. But that age of grand fulfillment was also the age of grander prophecies. — But the prophecies, fulfilled and fulfilling before our eyes, become a new miracle. . .adapted to prove omniscience as unmistakably as the miracles of two thousand years ago proved omnipotence. Scripture is seen by us as a colossal wheel, compassing all history with its gigantic and awful rim, and full of the eyes that tell of one who sees all things! . . .We have before our very eyes some of the most awe-inspiring proofs of our holy religion. Disciples, who saw His miracles and had evidence of the senses, left us their witness to Christ. But, of many prophecies, they had only the record, while we have the evidence of or very senses to their fulfillment. — But he who can see prophecy fulfilled and not believe, is not to be persuaded by any other miracle. . .The Christian religion is the only religion that has ever dared to rest its claim upon either miracle or prophecy. The appeal to such supernatural signs is so bold, that its audacity is one proof of its genuineness. ~ Arthur T. Pierson (1867-1911)

MAKING GOOD TIME,
BUT GOING THE WRONG WAY

. . .whosoever will lose his life for my sake shall find it.
———— MATTHEW 16:25 KJV ————

A man who habitually slept as long as he could every morning, awoke one day even later than usual. Looking at the clock, he bolted out of bed, threw on some clothes, splashed cold water on his face, quickly combed his hair, gulped down a glass of milk, grabbed his briefcase, gave his wife a kiss as he ran out of the door, and raced to catch the bus. He barely got on it as it began to pull away. Dropping a coin in the meter, he lurched down the aisle toward a seat. Suddenly he looked around and breathlessly blurted out, "Where's this bus going anyway?" This story reminds me of many people today. Taken up with the rush of everyday activities, they neglect to make sure they're headed in the right direction. If we surrender our lives to God, and let Him take the controls (Matthew 16:24), we'll be on the road of joy in this life and will have eternal reward in the life to come (v. 28).

~ Richard W. De Haan (1923-2002)

OUR ONE ULTIMATE END

Finally, brethren, whatsoever things are true, whatsoever things are honest, whatsoever things are just, whatsoever things are pure, whatsoever things are lovely, whatsoever things are of good report; if there be any virtue, and if there be any praise, think on these things.

PHILIPPIANS 4:8 KJV

The royal law of heaven and earth is this, 'Thou shall love the Lord thy God with all thy heart, and with all thy soul, and with all thy mind, and with all thy strength.' The one perfect good shall be your one ultimate end. One thing shall ye desire for its own sake, the fruition of Him who is all in all. One happiness shall ye propose to your souls, even an union with Him that made them, the having 'fellowship with the Father and the Son,' the being 'joined to the Lord in one spirit.' One design ye are to pursue to the end of time, —the enjoyment of God in time and in eternity. ~ John Wesley (1703-1791)

THE INFINITE CHRIST

Behold, You desire truth in the inward parts,
And in the hidden part You will make me to know wisdom.
———— PSALM 51:6 NKJV ————

Why are love, knowledge, wisdom, and goodness said to be infinite and eternal in God, capable of no increase or decrease, but always in the same highest state of existence? Why is his power eternal and omnipotent, his presence not here, or there, but everywhere The same? No reason can be assigned, but because nothing that is temporary, limited, or bounded can be in God. It is his nature to be that which he is, and all that he is, in an infinite, unchangeable degree, admitting neither higher, nor lower, neither here nor there, but always and everywhere in the same unalterable state of infinity. If therefore wrath, rage, and resentment could be in the Deity itself, it must be an unbeginning, boundless, never-ceasing wrath, capable of no more, or less, no up or down, but always existing, always working, and breaking forth in the same strength, and everywhere equally burning in the height and depth of the abyssal Deity. There is no medium here; there must be either all or none, either no possibility of wrath, or no possibility of its having any bounds . . . For nothing can have any existence in God, but in the way and manner as his eternity, infinity, and omnipotence have their existence in him. Have you anything to object to this? ~ William Law (1686-1761)

HAVE WE NO TEARS FOR REVIVAL?

They that sow in tears shall reap in joy.

PSALM 126:5 KJV

This is the divine edict. This is more than preaching with zeal. This is more than scholarly exposition. This is more than delivering sermons of exegetical exactitude and homiletical perfection. Such a man, whether preacher or pew dweller, is appalled at the shrinking authority of the Church in the present drama of cruelty in the world. And he cringes with sorrow that men turn a deaf ear to the Gospel and willingly risk eternal hell in the process. Under this complex burden, his heart is crushed to tears. The true man of God is heartsick, grieved at the worldliness of the Church, grieved at the blindness of the Church, grieved at the corruption in the Church, grieved at the toleration of sin in the Church, grieved at the prayerlessness in the Church. He is disturbed that the corporate prayer of the Church no longer pulls down the strongholds of the devil. He is embarrassed that the Church folks no longer cry in their despair before a devil-ridden, sin-mad society, "Why could we not cast him out?" God help us. (Matthew 17:19).
~ Leonard Ravenhill (1925-1994)

LET US GO FASTER!

For God hath not given us the spirit of fear; but of power,
and of love, and of a sound mind.
————— II TIMOTHY 1:7 KJV —————

Does salvation travel as fast as sin? See how wickedness spreads. Talk about a prairie fire, it devours everything before it. Does Salvation keep pace with our ever-growing population? Make the calculation in your most favored Christian cities, and you will find we are terribly behind in the race. Do we keep pace with the devils in energy and untiring labor? Do we go as fast as death? Oh, say no more! We'll close our ears to this cold, unfeeling, stony-hearted utterance of unbelief. We must increase the speed if we are to keep pace with the yearnings of the Almighty Heart of Love that would have all men to be saved. We must go faster if we are to have a hand in the fulfillment of the prophecies. Read the sixtieth chapter of Isaiah, and think of the speed that must be reached before all that comes true. We must go faster if we would wipe out the reproach and taunts of the mocking infidels who are ever asking for living proof of God's existence. We must increase our pace before our own prayers are answered, our own expectations realized, our own relations converted, and our own consistency proved.

~ William Booth (1829-1912)

I beseech you therefore, brethren, by the mercies of God, that you present your bodies a living sacrifice, holy, acceptable to God, which is your reasonable service. And do not be conformed to this world, but be transformed by the renewing of your mind, that you may prove what is that good and acceptable and perfect will of God. For I say, through the grace given to me, to everyone who is among you, not to think of himself more highly than he ought to think, but to think soberly, as God has dealt to each one a measure of faith. For as we have many members in one body, but all the members do not have the same function, so we, being many, are one body in Christ, and individually members of one another. Having then gifts differing according to the grace that is given to us, let us use them: if prophecy, let us prophesy in proportion to our faith; or ministry, let us use it in our ministering; he who teaches, in teaching; he who exhorts, in exhortation; he who gives, with liberality; he who leads, with diligence; he who shows mercy, with cheerfulness.

ROMANS 12:1-8 NKJV

STANDING FIRM

OUR ALMIGHTY SHEPHERD

I taught Ephraim also to go, taking them by their arms...
———— HOSEA 11:3 KJV ————

Christ deals with us as you do with your children. They cannot go alone; you hold them: so does Christ by His Spirit. Breathe this prayer: "Lord, take me by the arms." John Newton says, "When a mother is teaching her child to walk on soft carpet, she will sometimes let it go, and it will fall, to teach it its weakness, but not so on the brink of a precipice." So the Lord will sometimes let you fall, like Peter on the waters, though not to your injury. The Shepherd layeth the sheep on His shoulder, it matters not how great the distance be; it matters not how high the mountains, how rough the path: our Savior-God is an Almighty Shepherd. Some of you have mountains in your way to Heaven; some of you have mountains of lusts in your hearts, and some of you have mountains of opposition: it matters not, only lie on the shoulder. He is able to keep you, even in the darkest valley He will not stumble. ~ Robert M. McCheyne (1813-1843)

WHO HAS SEEN HIM?

'God, be merciful to me a sinner!'
LUKE 18:13 NKJV

I have had a clear view of Jesus. I have seen Him, felt Him, and I have known Him in a far deeper way than simply by the outward physical appearance; I have felt the reality of His life begin to burn in my heart. I have seen in Christ the glory of a life that is totally submitted to the sovereignty of God. That glory has begun to take hold of me, and I have begun to see that this is the one life that God expects of any man He made in His own image. I have seen the marks of the cross upon Him, and by His grace the marks of the cross have been put upon me and I am no longer my own; I am bought with a price, redeemed by His precious blood. Yes, I have seen Him — not in the outward physical sense only, but in the inward sense of a deep spiritual reality. I have had a clear view of Jesus and my life will never the be same again. We all. . .the weakest, the poorest, the most sinful, the most defiled. The spiritual aristocracy of the church of Jesus Christ. . .the sinner saved by grace. It is the soul who has come like the publican of old and said, "God be merciful to me a sinner" and it is the soul bowed before Calvary and seeing (as Paul saw) the glory of God in the face of Jesus Christ. ~ Alan Redpath (1907-)

PRAY CONSTANTLY

Pray without ceasing.

I THESSALONIANS 5:17 KJV

Of all the duties enjoined by Christianity none is more essential, and yet more neglected, than prayer. Most people consider this exercise a wearisome ceremony, which they are justified in abridging as much as possible. Even those whose profession or fears lead them to pray, do it with such languor and wanderings of mind that their prayers, far from drawing down blessings, only increase their condemnation. . . . God alone can instruct us in our duty. The teachings of men, however wise and well disposed they may be, are still ineffectual, if God does not shed on the soul that light which opens the mind to truth. The imperfections of our fellow creatures cast a shade over the truths that we learn from them. Such is our weakness that we do not receive, with sufficient docility, the instructions of those who are as imperfect as ourselves. A thousand suspicions, jealousies, fears, and prejudices prevent us from profiting, as we might, by what we hear from men; and tho they announce the most serious truths, yet what they do weakens the effect of what they say. In a word, it is God alone who can perfectly teach us. ~ Francois Fénelons (1651-1715)

PRIVILEGE AND EXPERIENCE

And he said unto him, Son, thou art ever
with me, and all that I have is thine.
——— L U K E 15:31 K J V ———

"Thou are ever with me;" I am always near thee; thou canst dwell every hour of thy life in My presence, and all I have is for thee. I am a father, with a loving father's heart. I will withhold no good thing from thee. In these promises, we have the rich privilege of God's heritage. We have, in the first place, unbroken fellowship with Him. A father never sends his child away with the thought that he does not care about his child knowing that he loves him. The father longs to have his child believe that he has the light of his father's countenance upon him all the day — that, if he sends the child away to school, or anywhere that necessity compels, it is with a sense of sacrifice of parental feelings. If it be so with an earthly father, what think you of God? Does He not want every child of His to know that he is constantly living in the light of His countenance? This is the meaning of that word, "Son, thou art ever with me." . . . Let that thought into your hearts — that the child of God is called to this blessed privilege, to live every moment of his life in fellowship with God. He is called to enjoy the full light of His countenance. ~ Andrew Murray (1828-1917)

DAILY FELLOWSHIP WITH GOD

Draw near to God and He will draw near to you.
JAMES 4:8 NKJV

The first and chief need of our Christian life is, Fellowship with God. The Divine life within us comes from God, and is entirely dependent upon Him. As I need every moment afresh the air to breathe, as the sun every moment afresh sends down its light, so it is only in direct living communication with God that my soul can be strong. The manna of one day was corrupt when the next day came. I must every day have fresh grace from heaven, and I obtain it only in direct waiting upon God Himself. Begin each day by tarrying before God, and letting Him touch you. Take time to meet God. To this end, let your first act in your devotion be setting yourself still before God. In prayer, or worship, everything depends upon God taking the chief place. I must bow quietly before Him in humble faith and adoration, speaking thus within my heart: "God is. God is near. God is love, longing to communicate Himself to me. God the Almighty One, Who worketh all in all, is even now waiting to work in me, and make Himself known." Take time, till you know God is very near. When you have given God His place of honour, glory, and power, take your place of deepest lowliness, and seek to be filled with the Spirit of humility.

~ Andrew Murray (1828-1917)

LOVE

. . . the greatest of these is love.
I CORINTHIANS 13:13 NKJV

You can take nothing greater to the heathen world than the impress and reflection of the Love of God upon your own character. That is the universal language. It will take you years to speak in Chinese, or in the dialects of India. From the day you land, that language of Love, understood by all, will be pouring forth its unconscious eloquence. It is the man who is the missionary, it is not his words. His character is his message. In the heart of Africa, among the great Lakes, I have come across black men and women who remembered the only white man they ever saw before — David Livingstone; and as you cross his footsteps in that dark continent, men's faces light up as they speak of the kind Doctor who passed there years ago. They could not understand him; but they felt the Love that beat in his heart. Take into your new sphere of labor, where you also mean to lay down your life, that simple charm, and your lifework must succeed. You can take nothing greater, you need take nothing less. It is not worth while going if you take anything less. You may take every accomplishment; you may be braced for every sacrifice; but if you give your body to be burned, and have not Love, it will profit you and the cause of Christ nothing.

~ Henry Drummond (1851-1897)

Let love be without hypocrisy. Abhor what is evil. Cling to what is good. Be kindly affectionate to one another with brotherly love, in honor giving preference to one another; not lagging in diligence, fervent in spirit, serving the Lord; rejoicing in hope, patient in tribulation, continuing steadfastly in prayer; distributing to the needs of the saints, given to hospitality. Bless those who persecute you; bless and do not curse. Rejoice with those who rejoice, and weep with those who weep. Be of the same mind toward one another. Do not set your mind on high things, but associate with the humble. Do not be wise in your own opinion. Repay no one evil for evil. Have regard for good things in the sight of all men. If it is possible, as much as depends on you, live peaceably with all men. Beloved, do not avenge yourselves, but rather give place to wrath; for it is written, "Vengeance is Mine, I will repay," says the Lord. Therefore "If your enemy is hungry, feed him; If he is thirsty, give him a drink; For in so doing you will heap coals of fire on his head." Do not be overcome by evil, but overcome evil with good.

————— R OMANS 12:9-21 NKJV —————

THE WAY

But of him are ye in Christ Jesus, who of God is made unto us wisdom,
and righteousness, and sanctification, and redemption. . .
———— I CORINTHIANS 1:30 KJV ————

We know God only by Jesus Christ. Without this mediator, all communion with God is taken away; through Jesus Christ we know God. . .in proof of Jesus Christ we have the prophecies, which are solid and palpable proofs. And these prophecies, being accomplished and proved true by the event, mark the certainty of these truths and, therefore, the divinity of Christ. In Him, then, and through Him, we know God. Apart from Him, and without the Scripture, without original sin, without a necessary mediator promised and come, we cannot absolutely prove God, nor teach right doctrine and right morality. But through Jesus Christ, and in Jesus Christ, we prove God, and teach morality and doctrine. Jesus Christ is, then, the true God of men. But we know at the same time our wretchedness; for this God is none other than the Saviour of our wretchedness. So we can only know God well by knowing our iniquities. Therefore those who have known God, without knowing their wretchedness, have not glorified Him, but have glorified themselves. Not only do we know God by Jesus Christ alone, but we know ourselves only by Jesus Christ. We know life and death only through Jesus Christ. Apart from Jesus Christ, we do not know what is our life, nor our death, nor God, nor ourselves.

~ Blaise Pascal (1623-1662)

TEMPTATION (Part 1)

I pray not that thou shouldest take them out of the world,
but that thou shouldest keep them from the evil.

———— JOHN 17:15 KJV ————

As we have no strength to resist a temptation when it doth come, when we are entered into it, but shall fall under it, without a supply of sufficiency of grace from God; so to reckon that we have no power or wisdom to keep ourselves from entering into temptation, but must be kept by the power and wisdom of God, is a preserving principle, 1 Peter 1:5. We are in all things "kept by the power of God." This our Saviour instructs us in, not only by directing us to pray that we be not led into temptation, but also by his own praying for us, that we may be kept from it:, "I pray not that thou shouldest take them out of the world, but that thou shouldest keep them from the evil," — that is, the temptations of the world unto evil, unto sin, — which is all this is evil in the world; or from the evil one, who in the world makes use of the world unto temptation. Christ prays his Father to keep us, and instructs us to pray that we be so kept. It is not, then, a thing in our own power. The ways of our entering into temptation are so many, various, and imperceptible, the means of it so efficacious and powerful, — our weakness our unwatchfulness, so unspeakable, — that we cannot in the least keep or preserve ourselves from it. We fail both in wisdom and power for this work. ~ John Owen (1616–1683)

TEMPTATION (Part 2)

*I pray not that thou shouldest take them out of the world,
but that thou shouldest keep them from the evil.*

JOHN 17:15 KJV

Let the heart, then commune with itself and say, "I am poor and weak; Satan is subtle, cunning, powerful, watching constantly for advantages against my soul; the world earnest, pressing, and full of specious pleas, innumerable pretences, and ways of deceit; my own corruption violent and tumultuating, enticing, entangling, conceiving sin, and warring in me, against me; occasions and advantages of temptation innumerable in all things I have done or suffer, in all businesses and persons with whom I converse; the first beginnings of temptation insensible and plausible, so that, left unto myself, I shall not know I am ensnared, until my bonds be made strong, and sin hath got ground in my heart: therefore on God alone will I rely for preservation, and continually will I look up to him on that account." This will make the soul be always committing itself to the care of God, resting itself on him, and to do nothing, undertake nothing, etc, without asking counsel of him. ~ John Owen (1616-1683)

MARVELOUS GRACE

And of His fullness we have all received, and grace for grace.

JOHN 1:16 NKJV

I wish all professors to fall in love with grace. All our songs should be of His free grace. We are but too lazy and careless in seeking of it; it is all our riches we have here, and glory in the bud. I wish that I could set out free grace. I was the law's man, and under the law, and under a curse; but grace brought me from under that hard lord, and I rejoice that I am grace's freeholder. I pay tribute to none for heaven, seeing my land and heritage holdeth of Christ, my new King. Infinite wisdom has devised this excellent way of free-holding for sinners. It is a better way to heaven than the old way that was in Adam's days. It has this fair advantage, that no man's emptiness and want layeth an inhibition upon Christ, or hindereth His salvation; and that is far best for me. But our new Landlord putteth the names of devours, and Adam's forlorn heirs, and beggars, and the crooked and blind, in the free charters. Heaven and angels may wonder that we have got such a gate of sin and hell. Such a back-entry out of hell as Christ made, and brought out the captives by, is more than my poor shallow thoughts can comprehend.
~ Samuel Rutherford (1600-1661)

FIRMLY ESTABLISHED

As ye have therefore received Christ Jesus the Lord, so walk ye in him:
Rooted and built up in him, and stablished in the faith, as ye
have been taught, abounding therein with thanksgiving.
—— COLOSSIANS 2:6, 7 KJV ——

Be not deceived with strange doctrines, "nor give heed to fables and endless genealogies," and things in which the Jews make their boast. "Old things are passed away: behold, all things have become new." For if we still live according to the Jewish law, and the circumcision of the flesh, we deny that we have received grace. For the divinest prophets lived according to Jesus Christ. On this account also they were persecuted, being inspired by grace to fully convince the unbelieving that there is one God, the Almighty, who has manifested Himself by Jesus Christ His Son, who is His Word, not spoken, but essential. For He is not the voice of an articulate utterance, but a substance begotten by divine power, who has in all things pleased Him that sent Him. ~ Philip Schaff (1819-1893)

BROTHERLY LOVE

But above all these things put on love,
which is the bond of perfection.
————— COLOSSIANS 3:14 NKJV —————

Let us therefore, with all haste, put an end to this [state of things]; and let us fall down before the Lord, and beseech Him with tears, that He would mercifully be reconciled to us, and restore us to our former seemly and holy practice of brotherly love. For [such conduct] is the gate of righteousness, which is set open for the attainment of life, as it is written, "Open to me the gates of righteousness; I will go in by them, and will praise the Lord: this is the gate of the Lord: the righteous shall enter in by it." Although, therefore, many gates have been set open, yet this gate of righteousness is that gate in Christ by which blessed are all they that have entered in and have directed their way in holiness and righteousness, doing all things without disorder. Let a man be faithful: let him be powerful in the utterance of knowledge; let him be wise in judging of words; let him be pure in all his deeds; yet the more he seems to be superior to others [in these respects], the more humble-minded ought he to be, and to seek the common good of all, and not merely his own advantage. ~ Philip Schaff (1819-1893)

Let every soul be subject to the governing authorities. For there is no authority except from God, and the authorities that exist are appointed by God. Therefore whoever resists the authority resists the ordinance of God, and those who resist will bring judgment on themselves. For rulers are not a terror to good works, but to evil. Do you want to be unafraid of the authority? Do what is good, and you will have praise from the same. For he is God's minister to you for good. But if you do evil, be afraid; for he does not bear the sword in vain; for he is God's minister, an avenger to execute wrath on him who practices evil. Therefore you must be subject, not only because of wrath but also for conscience' sake. For because of this you also pay taxes, for they are God's ministers attending continually to this very thing. Render therefore to all their due: taxes to whom taxes are due, customs to whom customs, fear to whom fear, honor to whom honor.

Romans 13:1-7 NKJV

READY?

Prepare thy work. . .and make it fit for thyself. . .
———— PROVERBS 24:27 KJV ————

. . . We cannot shut our eyes to the fact that there is a fearful amount of laxity, unsubduedness, and self-indulgence going hand in hand with the evangelical profession of the day . . . so far as the intellect goes, into the truth of the sinner's title, who, if we are to judge from their style, deportment, and habits, are not "ready" in their moral condition — in the real state of their hearts. We are at times, we must confess, sadly cast down when we see our young friends decking their persons in the vain fashions of a vain and sinful world; feeding upon the vile literature that issues in such frightful profusion from the press; and actually singing vain songs and engaging in light and frivolous conversation. It is impossible to reconcile such with "Be ye also ready." Those who have life in Christ, who are indwelt by the Holy Ghost, will be ready. But the mere professor — the one who has the truth in the head and on the lip, but not in the heart; who has the lamp of profession, but not the Spirit of life in Christ — will be shut out into outer darkness — in the everlasting misery of gloom and hell. Let us, as we take a solemn leave of you, put this question home to your very inmost soul, "Art thou ready?" ~ C.H. Mackintosh (1820-1896)

GLORY BE TO GOD THE FATHER

And after these things I heard a great voice of much people in heaven,
saying, Alleluia; Salvation, and glory, and honour, and power,
unto the Lord our God . . .

————— REVELATION 19:1 KJV —————

Glory be to God the Father, Glory be to God the Son,
Glory be to God the Spirit: Great Jehovah, Three in One!
Glory, glory, While eternal ages run!

Glory be to Him who loved us, Washed us from each spot and stain;
Glory be to Him who bought us, Made us kings with Him to reign!
Glory, glory, To the Lamb that once was slain!

Glory to the King of angels, Glory to the Church's King,
Glory to the King of nations; Heaven and earth, your praises bring!
Glory, glory, To the King of Glory sing!

Glory, blessing, praise eternal! Thus the choir of angels sings;
Honor, riches, power, dominion! Thus its praise creation brings.
Glory, glory, Glory to the King of kings!

~ Horatius Bonar (1808-1899)

GIVE ALL UP TO CHRIST

Ye shall walk after the LORD your God, and fear him,
and keep his commandments, and obey his voice,
and ye shall serve him, and cleave unto him.
———— DEUTERONOMY 13:4 KJV ————

Deal with God, and come to Him and say, "Lord of all, I belong to Thee, I am absolutely at Thy disposal." Yield up yourselves. There may be many who cannot go as Missionaries, but oh, come, give up yourselves to God all the same to be consecrated to the work of His Kingdom. Let us bow down before Him. Let us give Him all our powers — our head to think for His Kingdom, our heart to go out in love for men, and however feeble you may be, come and say: "Lord, here I am, to live and die for Thy Kingdom. Some talk and pray about the filling of the Holy Spirit. Let them pray more and believe more. But remember the Holy Spirit came to fit men to be messengers of the Kingdom, and you cannot expect to be filled with the Spirit unless you want to live for Christ's Kingdom. You cannot expect all the love and peace and joy of heaven to come into your life and be your treasures, unless you give them up absolutely to the Kingdom of God, and possess and use them only for Him. It is the soul utterly given up to God that will receive in its emptying the fullness of the Holy Spirit. ~ Andrew Murray (1828-1917)

THE ACTIVITY OF FAITH
(OR ABRAHAM'S IMITATORS)

And the father of circumcision to them who are not of the circumcision only,
but who also walk in the steps of that faith of our father Abraham,
which he had being yet uncircumcised.

——— ROMANS 4:12 KJV ———

A faithful man is a fruitful man; faith enableth a man to be doing. Ask the question, by what power was it whereby Abraham was enabled to yield obedience to the Lord? The text answereth you, "They that walk in the footsteps" not of Abraham, but "in the footsteps of the faith of Abraham." A man would have thought the text should have run thus: They that walk in the footsteps of Abraham. That is true, too, but the apostle had another end; therefore he saith, "They that walk in the footsteps of the faith of Abraham," implying that it was the grace of faith that God bestowed on Abraham, that quickened and enabled him to perform every duty that God required of him, and called him to the performance. So that I say, the question being, whence came it that Abraham was so fruitful a Christian, what enabled him to do and to suffer what he did? Surely it was faith that was the cause that produced such effects, that helped him to perform such actions. The point then you see is evident, faith it is that causeth fruit.

~ Thomas Hooker   (1586-1647)

I AM HERE

. . .Holy. . .is the LORD of hosts: the whole earth is full of his glory.

ISAIAH 6:3 KJV

I believe that if some people had been in that very upper room itself when the Holy Ghost descended, being purblind, blinded by prejudice and passion and worldliness, they would have heard only a noise, they would have perceived no flame. If they had been with John on Patmos, they might have heard the break of the waves upon the rocks, but they never would have heard the harping of the angels. On the other hand, if Peter or John were sitting where you are now, their faces would be lighted up with supernatural light, and they would say: "Did you not see? Did you not hear? God is here. The great God has come down from the Heavens to bless these people. They have asked for it. They have claimed it. God has promised, and He has come." "Where two or three are met, I am." The Spirit of God is here and is working amongst us also, as He hath done in other times and places. He first convicts us of a cold heart, of our deep need, and of our utter undoneness, and then He comes Himself and says: "I am here."

~ F. B. Meyer (1847-1929)

> *Earth's crammed with Heaven,*
> *And every common bush aflame with God,*
> *But only he that sees takes off his shoes.*
> ELIZABETH BARRETT BROWNING

DIE, THEN!

For this reason I also suffer these things; nevertheless I am not ashamed,
for I know whom I have believed and am persuaded that
He is able to keep what I have committed to Him until that Day.

——— II TIMOTHY 1:12 NKJV ———

I call to mind a bashful young farmer in the West, who had grown up far from the atmosphere of the church and to whom the habits of religious meetings were unfamiliar, saying to me when I urged upon him to come to the prayer meeting that night in a neighbouring farmhouse, and openly confess with the mouth his need of Christ, "I never could stand up and talk in that way before people, even though I wanted to; it would kill me to do it." "Well," I replied "die then: I know how hard it is for you, but Christ commands the impossible. He told Peter to come to Him walking on the water, and as long as Peter kept his eye on the Lord, he also walked the waves. He commands you to confess Him before men and I shall expect you to do it tonight, even though you die in doing it." To the meeting this timid man came. When he rose to speak he laboured as if he were Atlas lifting the world on his shoulders. The effort crushed the cowardice out of him; for before he sat down he sang the song of the new life. By faith he attempted the impossible: he seized the ideal he knew. Christ met him in the act, and he came into a saved state. ~ L.E. Maxwell (1895-1984)

Owe no one anything except to love one another, for he who loves another has fulfilled the law. For the commandments, "You shall not commit adultery," "You shall not murder," "You shall not steal," "You shall not bear false witness," "You shall not covet," and if there is any other commandment, are all summed up in this saying, namely, "You shall love your neighbor as yourself." Love does no harm to a neighbor; therefore love is the fulfillment of the law. And do this, knowing the time, that now it is high time to awake out of sleep; for now our salvation is nearer than when we first believed. The night is far spent, the day is at hand. Therefore let us cast off the works of darkness, and let us put on the armor of light. Let us walk properly, as in the day, not in revelry and drunkenness, not in lewdness and lust, not in strife and envy. But put on the Lord Jesus Christ, and make no provision for the flesh, to fulfill its lusts.

ROMANS 13:8-14 NKJV

STANDING FIRM

GOD ORDERS BLESSINGS

But God be thanked that though you were slaves of sin, yet you obeyed from the heart that form of doctrine to which you were delivered.

ROMANS 6:17 NKJV

God does not order the wrong thing, but He uses it for our blessing; just as He used the cruelty of Joseph's wicked brethren, and the false accusations of Pharaoh's wife. In short, this way of seeing our Father in everything makes life one long thanksgiving, and gives a rest of heart, and more than that, a gayety of spirit, that is unspeakable. Someone says, "God's will on earth is always joy, always tranquillity." And since He must have His own way concerning His children, into what wonderful green pastures of inward rest, and beside what blessedly still waters of inward refreshment, is the soul led that learns this secret. If the will of God is our will, and if He always has His way, then we always have our way also, and we reign in a perpetual kingdom. He who sides with God cannot fail to win in every encounter; and whether the result shall be joy or sorrow, failure or success, death or life, we may, under all circumstances, join in the apostle's shout of victory, "Thanks be unto God, which always causeth us to triumph in Christ!"
~ Hannah Whitall Smith (1832-1911)

THE PILLAR OF CLOUD

*"Though your sins are like scarlet, They shall be as white as snow;
Though they are red like crimson, They shall be as wool."*

ISAIAH 1:18 NKJV

Lead, kindly Light, amid the encircling gloom,
Lead Thou me on!

The night is dark, and I am far from home,
Lead Thou me on!

Keep thou my feet! I do not ask to see
The distant scene—one step enough for me.

I was not ever thus, nor prayed that Thou
Shouldst lead me on; I loved to choose and see my path;
but now Lead Thou me on!

I loved the garish day, and, spite of fears,
Pride ruled my will: remember not past years!

So long thy power hath blest me, sure it still
Will lead me on,

O'er moor and fen, o'er crag and torrent,
till The night is gone,

And with the morn those angel faces smile
will lead me on.

~ John Henry Newman (1801–1890)

PRAISE HIM

And it shall come to pass in the last days, saith God,
I will pour out of my Spirit upon all flesh. . .
———— ACTS 2:17 KJV ————

The heart of the king, the heart of saint and sinner, are all in His hand. Hallelujah! for the Lord God Omnipotent reigns. Praise him for His love; for God is love. Some of you have been at sea. When far out of sight of land, you have stood high on the vessel's prow and looked round and round—one vast circle of ocean without any bound. Oh! so it is to stand in Christ justified, and to behold the love of God—a vast ocean all around you without a bottom and without a shore. Oh! praise Him for what He is. Heaven will be all praise. If you cannot praise God, you will never be there. For His mercy—for what He has done for us. The Lord has done much for me since I parted from you. We were once in the perils of waters; but the Lord saved the ship. Again and again we were in danger of plague—we nightly heard the cry of the mourner; yet no plague came near our dwelling. Again and again we were in perils of robbers—the gun of the murderous has been leveled at us; but the Lord stayed his hand. . . "Bless the Lord, O my soul!" Praise Him, O my people! for He is Good; For His mercy endures forever.
~ Robert Murray McCheyne (1813-1843)

SONG OF PRAISE TO GOD

How glorious is our heavenly King, Who reigns above the sky!
How shall a child presume to sing His dreadful majesty?
How great his power is none can tell, Nor think how large his grace;
Not men below, nor saints that dwell On high before his face.
Not angels, that stand round the Lord, Can search his secret will;
But they perform his heavenly word, And sing his praises still.
Then let me join this holy train, And my first offerings bring:
Th' eternal God will not disdain To hear an infant sing.
My heart resolves, my tongue obeys; And angels will rejoice
To hear their mighty Maker's praise Sound from a feeble voice.
~ Issac Watts (1674-1748)

EQUIPPED FOR EVERY GOOD WORK

. . . grace hath been shewed from the LORD our God . . .

EZRA 9:9 KJV

A tinkling cymbal is an instrument of music, with which a skilful player can make such melodious and heart-inflaming music. . .and yet behold the cymbal hath not life. . .but because of the art of him that plays therewith. . .such music hath been made upon it. Just thus I saw it was and will be with them who have gifts, but want saving grace, they are in the hand of Christ, as the cymbal in the hand of David. . .so Christ can use these gifted men, as with them to affect the souls of His people in His church; yet when He hath done all, hang them by as lifeless, though sounding cymbals. This consideration. . .were, for the most part, as a maul on the head of pride, and desire of vain glory; what, thought I, shall I be proud because I am a sounding brass? Is it so much to be a fiddle? Hath not the least creature that hath life, more of God in it than these?. . .a little grace, a little love, a little of the true fear of God, is better than all these gifts. . .that it is possible for a soul that can scarce give a man an answer, but with great confusion as to method, I say it is possible for them to have a thousand times more grace, and so to be more in the love and favour of the Lord than some who, by virtue of the gift of knowledge, can deliver themselves like angels.

~ John Bunyan (1628-1688)

ALL MUST MEET GOD!

The fool hath said in his heart, There is no God.

———— PSALM 14:1 KJV ————

Every one must meet God! The supreme question of life, then, is this: Are you ready to meet God? None of us can tell how soon it may be that we shall meet God. Are you ready? If not, I implore you to get ready before leaving this hall tonight. How can we meet God with joy and not with dismay? There is only one ground upon which man may meet God with joy and not with despair. That ground is the atoning blood of Jesus Christ. God is infinitely holy, and the best of us is but a sinner. The only ground upon which a sinner can meet the holy God is on the is on the ground of the shed blood, the blood of Christ. Any of us, no matter how outcast or vile, can go boldly to the Holy of Holies on the ground of the shed blood, and the best man or woman that ever walked this earth can meet God on no other ground than the shed blood. There is only one adequate preparation for the sinner to meet God, that is the acceptance of Jesus Christ as our personal Saviour, who bore all our sins on the Cross of Calvary, and as our risen Saviour who is able to set us free from the power of sin. ~ R.A. Torrey (1856-1928)

Receive one who is weak in the faith, but not to disputes over doubtful things. For one believes he may eat all things, but he who is weak eats only vegetables. Let not him who eats despise him who does not eat, and let not him who does not eat judge him who eats; for God has received him. Who are you to judge another's servant? To his own master he stands or falls. Indeed, he will be made to stand, for God is able to make him stand. One person esteems one day above another; another esteems every day alike. Let each be fully convinced in his own mind. He who observes the day, observes it to the Lord; and he who does not observe the day, to the Lord he does not observe it. He who eats, eats to the Lord, for he gives God thanks; and he who does not eat, to the Lord he does not eat, and gives God thanks. For none of us lives to himself, and no one dies to himself. For if we live, we live to the Lord; and if we die, we die to the Lord. Therefore, whether we live or die, we are the Lord's. For to this end Christ died and rose and lived again, that He might be Lord of both the dead and the living. But why do you judge your brother? Or why do you show contempt for your brother? For we shall all stand before the judgment seat of Christ. For it is written: "As I live, says the Lord, Every knee shall bow to Me, And every tongue shall confess to God."

ROMANS 14:1-11 NKJV

STANDING FIRM

TEACH THE CHILDREN

Train up a child in the way he should go,
And when he is old he will not depart from it.

———— PROVERBS 22:6 NKJV ————

"Thou shalt teach these words diligently unto thy children." And parents are commanded in the New Testament, to "bring up their children in the nurture and admonition of the Lord." The holy Psalmist acquaints us, that one great end why God did such great wonders for his people, was, "to the intent that when they grew up, they should show their children, or servants, the same." And in Deut. 6 at the 20th and following verses, God strictly commands his people to instruct their children in the true nature of the ceremonial worship, when they should inquire about it, as he supposed they would do, in time to come. And if servants and children were to be instructed in the nature of Jewish rites, much more ought they now to be initiated and grounded in the doctrines and first principles of the gospel of Christ: not only, because it is a revelation, which has brought life and immortality to a fuller and clearer light, but also, because many seducers are gone abroad into the world, who do their utmost endeavor to destroy not only the superstructure, but likewise to sap the very foundation of our most holy religion. ~ George Whitefield (1714-1770)

THE NECESSITY OF A NEW HEART

Now wouldst thou have a heart that tender is,
A heart that forward is to close with bliss;

A heart that will impressions freely take
Of the new covenant, and that will make

The best improvement of the word of grace,
And that to wickedness will not give place;

All this is in the promise, and it may
Obtained be of them that humbly pray.

Wouldst thou enjoy that spirit that is free,
And looseth those that in their spirits be

Oppressed with guilt, or filth, or unbelief;
That spirit that will, where it dwells, be chief;

Which breaketh Samson's cord as rotten thread,
And raiseth up the spirit that is dead;

That sets the will at liberty to choose
Those things that God hath promis'd to infuse

Into the humble heart? All this, I say,
The promise holdeth out to them that pray.

~John Bunyan (1628-1688)

GOD IS ALWAYS READY

And I will betroth thee unto me for ever; yea, I will betroth thee unto me in righteousness, and in judgment, and in lovingkindness, and in mercies.

——— HOSEA 2:19 KJV ———

No one ought to think that it is difficult to come to Him, though it sounds difficult and is really difficult at the beginning, and in separating oneself from and dying to all things. But when a man has once entered upon it, no life is lighter or happier or more desirable; for God is very zealous to be at all times with man, and teaches him that He will bring him to Himself if man will but follow. Man never desires anything so earnestly as God desires to bring a man to Himself, that he may know Him. God is always ready, but we are very unready; God is near to us, but we are far from Him; God is within, but we are without; God is at home, but we are strangers. The prophet saith: God guideth the redeemed through a narrow way into the broad road, so that they come into the wide and broad place; that is to say, into true freedom of the spirit, when one has become a spirit with God. May God help us to follow this course, that He may bring us to Himself.

~William Ralph Inge (1860-1954)

UNCHANGEABLE GOD

. . .Holy, holy, holy, is the LORD of hosts. . .
ISAIAH 6:3 KJV

Believers should praise God for what He is in Himself. Those that have never seen the Lord cannot praise Him. Those who have not come to Christ have never seen the King in His beauty. An unconverted man sees no loveliness in God. He sees a beauty in the blue sky—in the glorious sun—in the green earth—in the sparkling stars—in the lily of the field; but he sees no beauty in God. He has not seen Him, neither known Him; therefore there is no melody of praise in that heart. When a sinner is brought to Christ, he is brought to the Father. Jesus gave Himself for us, "that he might bring us to God." Oh! what a sight breaks in upon the soul—the infinite, eternal, unchangeable God! I know that some of you have been brought to see this sight. Oh! praise Him, then, for what He is. Praise Him for His pure, lovely holiness that cannot bear any sin in His sight. Cry, like the angels, "Holy, holy, holy, Lord God Almighty." Praise Him for His infinite wisdom that he knows the end from the beginning. In Him are hid all the treasures of wisdom and knowledge. Praise Him for His power—that all matter, all mind, is in His Hand. ~ Robert Murray McCheyne (1813-1843)

SURRENDER

For God so loved the world, that he gave his only begotten Son, that whosoever believeth in him should not perish, but have everlasting life.
───── JOHN 3:16 KJV ─────

Salvation does not mean merely deliverance from sin or the experience of personal holiness. . .If we are truly surrendered, we will never be aware of our own efforts to remain surrendered. Our entire life will be consumed with the One to whom we surrender. Beware of talking about surrender if you know nothing about it. In fact, you will never know anything about it until you understand that John 3:16 means that God completely and absolutely gave Himself to us. In our surrender, we must give ourselves to God in the same way He gave Himself for us—totally, unconditionally, and without reservation. The consequences and circumstances resulting from our surrender will never even enter our mind, because our life will be totally consumed with Him. ~ Oswald Chambers (1874-1917)

HEAVEN'S INHABITANTS

Then I saw another sign in heaven, great and marvelous. . .
———— REVELATION 15:1 NKJV ————

The society of heaven will be select. No one who studies Scripture can doubt that. There are a good many kinds of aristocracy in this world, but the aristocracy of heaven will be the aristocracy of holiness. The humblest sinner on earth will be an aristocrat there. It says in the fifty-seventh chapter of Isaiah: For thus saith the High and Lofty One that inhabiteth eternity, whose name is holy; I will dwell in the high and holy place, with him that is of a contrite and humble spirit. Now what could be plainer than that? No one that is not of a contrite and humble spirit will dwell with God in His high and holy place. If there is anything that ought to make heaven near to Christians, it is knowing that God and all their loved ones will be there. What is it that makes home so attractive? Is it because we have a beautiful home? Is it because we have beautiful lawns? Is it because we have beautiful trees around that home? Is it because we have beautiful paintings upon the walls inside? Is it because we have beautiful furniture? Is that all that makes home so attractive and so beautiful? Nay, it is the loved ones in it; it is the loved ones there. ~ Dwight L. Moody (1837-1899)

So then each of us shall give account of himself to God. Therefore let us not judge one another anymore, but rather resolve this, not to put a stumbling block or a cause to fall in our brother's way. I know and am convinced by the Lord Jesus that there is nothing unclean of itself; but to him who considers anything to be unclean, to him it is unclean. Yet if your brother is grieved because of your food, you are no longer walking in love. Do not destroy with your food the one for whom Christ died. Therefore do not let your good be spoken of as evil; for the kingdom of God is not eating and drinking, but righteousness and peace and joy in the Holy Spirit. For he who serves Christ in these things is acceptable to God and approved by men.

ROMANS 14:12-18 NKJV

HOW DO WE KNOW?

Moreover, brethren, I declare unto you the gospel . . .
By which also ye are saved. . .
———— I CORINTHIANS 15:1, 2 KJV ————

Many people think that to become a Christian means to just "believe" in believing. Many Christians have only a personal experience without objective data on which to lease their profession. This accounts for shallow living and weak testimonies of people who think they are saved, but are not. Their first trial or persecution sweeps them away. Ephesians 3 tells us this truth was verified by the Prophets who saw and recorded specific predictions hundreds of years before they occurred concerning our Lord and His Death, Burial and Resurrection; the apostles were eye-witnesses of all that happened and were willing to die for the part that Jesus Christ is alive; the Holy Spirit bears witness in our hearts with the truth. Acts records apostolic methods of preaching and in every case the objective facts were stressed and repentance and a decision were demanded. People were changed and made new creatures on the basis of truth, not feelings. There will be feelings, and experiences, but as the results of faith in the truth and not the cause. God challenges us to examine the facts — reason together with Him and believe. To not believe is to call God a liar. On what basis do you have eternal life? THE WORD OF GOD STANDS FOREVER!
~ John Hey (1939-)

THE MERCIES OF GOD

But God, who is rich in mercy, because of His great love
with which He loved us. . .made us alive together with Christ. . .
———— EPHESIANS 2:4, 5 NKJV ————

. . . For to think on the mercy of our Lord, that He hath showed to me and to thee, and to all sinful captives that sometimes were in bondage to the devil, through the greatness and multitude of our sins; how He patiently suffered us to live in our sin, and in our heinous contempts of Him, and work no revenge on us for the same, as He most justly might have done, and might most worthily have cast us down headlong into Hell, if His love had not hindered Him; but out of love He spared us, and sent His grace into our souls, taking us out of the state of heinous sins, and by His grace hath turned our will entirely unto Him, and made us thereby, for the having of Him, and for His love, to forsake all manner of sin. The remembrance of His mercy and goodness. . .may justly cause and bring into a soul a great truth and confidence in our Lord, and a full hope of salvation, and greatly inflameth the desire of love to aspire to the joys of Heaven.

~ Walter Hilton (-1396)

CHRIST'S ADVENT TO JUDGMENT

For we must all appear before the judgment seat of Christ;
that every one may receive the things done in his body,
according to that he hath done, whether it be good or bad.
II CORINTHIANS 5:10 KJV

God hath put it in our power by a timely accusation of ourselves in the tribunal of the court Christian, to prevent all the arts of aggravation which at doomsday shall load foolish and undiscerning souls. He that accuses himself of his crimes here, means to forsake them, and looks upon them on all sides, and spies out his deformity, and is taught to hate them, he is instructed and prayed for, he prevents the anger of God and defeats the devil's malice, and, by making shame the instrument of repentance, he takes away the sting, and makes that to be his medicine which otherwise would be his death: and, concerning this exercise, I shall only add what the patriarch of Alexandria told an old religious person in his hermitage. Having asked him what he found in that desert, he was answered, "Only this, to judge and condemn myself perpetually; that is the employment of my solitude." The patriarch answered, "There is no other way." By accusing ourselves we shall make the devil's malice useless, and our own consciences clear, and be reconciled to the Judge by the severities of an early repentance, and then we need to fear no accusers. ~ Jeremy Taylor (1613-1667)

THE HUMANITY OF CHRIST

Whereby are given unto us exceeding great and precious promises:
that by these ye might be partakers of the divine nature. . .
—————— II PETER 1:4 KJV ——————

. . .Think on the humanity of our Lord, as of His birth, of His Passion or of any other of His works, and feed thy thought with spiritual imagination thereof, for to move thine affection more to the love of Him. . .when it cometh freely of God's gift, with devotion and fervour of spirit, else a man will not likely find taste or devotion in it. And if he have it not with such facility and sending of God, I think it not expedient that a man should much force himself in it, as if he would get it by violence; for so doing he might hurt his head and body too, and yet be never the nearer. . .it is good for a man to have in his mind and thought sometimes our Saviour's humanity. . .and if devotion come withal, and relish or gust found in it, then to hold it and follow it for a time, but leave off soon, and hang not long thereon. And if devotion come not by thinking of the Passion, strive not, nor press too much for to have and come by such devotion or feeling in it, but take what will easily come; and if it come not easily betake thee to some other matter, wherein thou thinkest or hopest to find more devotion or gust.
~ Walter Hilton (-1396)

HIS WAYS

"For My thoughts are not your thoughts,
Nor are your ways My ways," says the Lord.
——— ISAIAH 55:8 NKJV ———

When He works, His ways and his thoughts are declared by the prophet to be as far above our ways and our thoughts as the heavens are above the earth. He makes no effort when He would execute what He has decreed; for to Him all things are equally easy; He speaks and causes the heavens and the earth to be created out of nothing, with as little difficulty as He causes water to descend or a stone to fall to the ground. His power is co-extensive with His will; when He wills, the thing is already accomplished. When the Scriptures represent Him as speaking in the creation of the world, it is not to be understood as signifying that it was necessary that the word of command should issue from Him, in order that the universe He was about to create should hear and obey His will; that word was simple and interior, neither more nor less than the thought which He conceived of what He was about to do and the will to do it. ~ Jeanne Marie Vouvier de la Mothe Guyon (1647–1711)

UNCONDITIONAL LOVE

God is love; and he that dwelleth in love dwelleth in God, and God in him.
—— I JOHN 4:16 KJV ——

It is God's love towards us that gives us everything . . .When He is able by his love to produce that love in us, He reigns within; He constitutes there our life, our peace, our happiness, and we then already begin to taste that blissful existence which He enjoys. His love towards us is stamped with his own character of infinity: it is not like ours, bounded and constrained; when He loves, all the measures of his love are infinite. He comes down from Heaven to earth to seek the creature of clay whom he loves; He becomes creature and clay with him; He gives him his flesh to eat. These are the prodigies of Divine love in which the Infinite outstrips all the affection we can manifest. He loves like a God, with a love utterly incomprehensible. It is the height of folly to seek to measure infinite love by human wisdom. Far from losing any element of its greatness in these excesses, He impresses upon his love the stamp of his own grandeur, while He manifests a delight in us bounded only by the infinite. ~ Jeanne Marie Vouvier de la Mothe Guyon (1647-1711)

Therefore let us pursue the things which make for peace and the things by which one may edify another. Do not destroy the work of God for the sake of food. All things indeed are pure, but it is evil for the man who eats with offense. It is good neither to eat meat nor drink wine nor do anything by which your brother stumbles or is offended or is made weak. Do you have faith? Have it to yourself before God. Happy is he who does not condemn himself in what he approves. But he who doubts is condemned if he eats, because he does not eat from faith; for whatever is not from faith is sin.

ROMANS 14:19-23 NKJV

STANDING FIRM

LETTER TO SUFFERING SAINTS

Let us hold fast the profession of our faith without
wavering; (for he is faithful that promised;)...

———— HEBREWS 10:23 KJV ————

"Dear, suffering lambs, for the name and command of Jesus; be valiant for His truth, and faithful, and ye will feel the presence of Christ with you. Look at Him who suffered for you, who hath bought you, and will feed you; who saith, 'Be of good comfort, I have overcome the world'; who destroys the devil and his works, and bruises the serpent's head. I say, look to Christ, your sanctuary, in whom ye have rest and peace. To you it is given not only to believe, but to suffer for His name's sake. They that will live godly in Christ Jesus, shall suffer persecution by the ungodly professors of Christ Jesus, who live out of Him. Therefore be valiant for God's truth upon the earth, and look above that spirit that makes you suffer up to Christ, who was before it was, and will be when it is gone." "Christ the Seed reigns; and His power is over all, who bruises the serpent's head, and destroys the devil and his works, and was before he was. So all of you live and walk in Christ Jesus; that nothing may be between you and God, but Christ, in whom ye have salvation, life, rest and peace with God. ~ George Fox (1624-1691)

THE WAY, THE TRUTH, AND THE LIFE

"This is My beloved Son, in whom I am well pleased. Hear Him!"
MATTHEW 17:5 NKJV

When the Lord God and His Son Jesus Christ sent me forth into the world to preach His everlasting gospel and kingdom, I was glad that I was commanded to turn people to that inward Light, Spirit, and Grace, by which all might know their salvation and their way to God; even that Divine Spirit which would lead them into all truth, and which I infallibly knew would never deceive any. But with and by this divine power and Spirit of God, and the Light of Jesus, I was to bring people off from all their own ways, to Christ, the new and living way; and from their churches, which men had made and gathered, to the Church in God, the general assembly written in heaven, of which Christ is the head. And I was to bring them off from the world's teachers, made by men, to learn of Christ, who is the Way, the Truth, and the Life, of whom the Father said, "This is my beloved Son, hear ye Him"; and off from all the world's worships, to know the Spirit of Truth in the inward parts, and to be led thereby; that in it they might worship the Father of spirits, who seeks such to worship Him. ~ George Fox (1624-1691)

TO LIVE IS CHRIST

For to me, to live is Christ, and to die is gain.
PHILIPPIANS 1:21 NKJV

The true discovery of a character is the discovery of its ideals. Paul spares us any speculation in his case. "To me to live," he says, "is Christ." This is the motto of his life, the ruling passion of it, which at once explains the nature of his success and accounts for it. He lives for Christ. "To me to live is Christ." . . . There is no fear about death being gain if we have lived for Christ. So, let it be: "To me to live is Christ." There is but one alternative — Paul's alternative, the discovery of Christ. We have all in some sense, indeed, already made that discovery. We may be as near it now as Paul when he left Jerusalem. There was no notice given that he was to change masters. The new Master simply crossed his path one day, and the great change was come. How often has He crossed our path? We know what to do the next time: we know how our life can be made worthy and great — how only; we know how death can become gain — how only. Many, indeed, tell us death must be gain. Many long for life to be done that they may rest, as they say, in the quiet grave. Let no cheap sentimentalism deceive us. Death can only be gain when to have lived was Christ. ~ Henry Drummond (1851-1897)

DO YOU LOVE ME?

. . . do you love Me? . . . Tend My sheep.

———— JOHN 21:16 NKJV ————

Jesus did not say to make converts to your way of thinking, but He said to look after His sheep, to see that they get nourished in the knowledge of Him. . .Today we have substituted doctrinal belief for personal belief, and that is why so many people are devoted to causes and so few are devoted to Jesus Christ. People do not really want to be devoted to Jesus, but only to the cause He started. Jesus Christ is deeply offensive to the educated minds of today, to those who only want Him to be their Friend, and who are unwilling to accept Him in any other way. Our Lord's primary obedience was to the will of His Father, not to the needs of people — the saving of people was the natural outcome of His obedience to the Father. If I am devoted solely to the cause of humanity, I will soon be exhausted and come to the point where my love will waver and stumble. But if I love Jesus Christ personally and passionately, I can serve humanity, even though people may treat me like a "doormat." The secret of a disciple's life is devotion to Jesus Christ. . .

~ Oswald Chambers (1874-1917)

MEN OF PRAYER

. . .rejoicing in hope, patient in tribulation,
continuing steadfastly in prayer. . .
ROMANS 12:12 NKJV

There is great need in this day for Christian business men to inform their mundane affairs with the spirit of prayer. There is a great army of successful merchants of almost every kind who are members of Christ's Church and it is high time these men attended to this matter. This is but another version of the phrase, "putting God into business," the realization and restraint of His presence and of His fear in all the secularities of life. We need the atmosphere of the prayer-closet to pervade our public sales-rooms and counting-houses. The sanctity of prayer is needed to impregnate business. We need the spirit of Sunday carried over to Monday and continued until Saturday. But this cannot be done by prayerless men, but by men of prayer. We need business men to go about their concerns with the same reverence and responsibility with which they enter the closet. Men are badly needed who are devoid of greed, but who, with all their hearts carry God with them into the secular affairs of life. . .Praying men are God's agents on earth, the representative of government of heaven, set to a specific task on the earth. ~ Edward M. Bounds (1835-1913)

GLORY AND PRAISE TO GOD

. . . unto thy name give glory. . .
—— PSALM 115:1 KJV ——

Wherefore to dignity and wisdom we must add virtue, the proper fruit of them both. Virtue seeks and finds Him who is the Author and Giver of all good, and who must be in all things glorified; otherwise, one who knows what is right yet fails to perform it, will be beaten with many stripes (Luke 12:47). Why? You may ask. Because he has failed to put his knowledge to good effect, but rather has imagined mischief upon his bed (Psalm 36:4); like a wicked servant, he has turned aside to seize the glory which, his own knowledge assured him, belonged only to his good Lord and Master. It is plain, therefore, that dignity without wisdom is useless and that wisdom without virtue is accursed. But when one possesses virtue, then wisdom and dignity are not dangerous but blessed. Such a man calls on God and lauds Him, confessing from a full heart, 'Not unto us, O Lord, not unto us, but unto Thy name give glory' (Psalm 115:1). Which is to say, 'O Lord, we claim no knowledge, no distinction for ourselves; all is Thine, since from Thee all things do come.' ~ Bernard of Clairvaux (1090-1153)

We then who are strong ought to bear with the scruples of the weak, and not to please ourselves. Let each of us please his neighbor for his good, leading to edification. For even Christ did not please Himself; but as it is written, "The reproaches of those who reproached You fell on Me." For whatever things were written before were written for our learning, that we through the patience and comfort of the Scriptures might have hope. Now may the God of patience and comfort grant you to be like-minded toward one another, according to Christ Jesus, that you may with one mind and one mouth glorify the God and Father of our Lord Jesus Christ. Therefore receive one another, just as Christ also received us, to the glory of God. Now I say that Jesus Christ has become a servant to the circumcision for the truth of God, to confirm the promises made to the fathers, and that the Gentiles might glorify God for His mercy, as it is written: "For this reason I will confess to You among the Gentiles, And sing to Your name." And again he says: "Rejoice, O Gentiles, with His people!" And again: "Praise the Lord, all you Gentiles! Laud Him, all you peoples!" And again, Isaiah says: "There shall be a root of Jesse; And He who shall rise to reign over the Gentiles, In Him the Gentiles shall hope." Now may the God of hope fill you with all joy and peace in believing, that you may abound in hope by the power of the Holy Spirit.

ROMANS 15:1-13 NKJV

STANDING FIRM

A LETTER TO CHRISTIANS

Every man shall give as he is able, according to the blessing
of the LORD thy God which he hath given thee.

DEUTERONOMY 16:17

Dear friends we must consecrate not only ourselves — body and soul — but all we have. Some of you may have children; perhaps you have an only child, and you dread the very idea of letting it go. Take care, take care; God deserves your confidence, your love, and your surrender. I plead with you; take your children and say to Jesus: "Anything Lord, that pleases Thee." Educate your children for Jesus. God help you to do it. He may not accept all of them, but He will accept of the will, and there will be a rich blessing in your soul for it. Then there is money. When I hear appeals for money from every Society; when I hear calculations as to what the Christians of England are spending on pleasure, and the small amount given for Missions, I say there is something terrible in it. God's children with so much wealth and comfort, and giving away so small a portion! God be praised for every exception! But there are many who give but very little, who never so give that it costs them something, and they feel it. Oh, friends! Our giving must be in proportion to God's giving. He gives you all. Let us take it up in our Consecration prayer: "Lord, take it all, every penny I possess. It is all Thine." Let us often say "It is all His." You may not know how much you ought to give. Give up all, put everything in His hands, and He will teach you if you will wait. ~ Andrew Murray (1828-1917)

CONCERN FOR OUR TIME

To everything there is a season,
A time for every purpose under heaven. . .
ECCLESIASTES 3:1 NKJV

God hath given to man a short time here upon earth, and yet upon this short time eternity depends: but so, that for every hour of our life (after we are persons capable of laws, and know good from evil) we must give account to the great Judge of men and angels. And this is it which our blessed Saviour told us, that we must account for every idle word; not meaning that every word which is not designed to edification, or is less prudent, shall be reckoned for a sin; but that the time which we spend in our idle talking and unprofitable discoursings; that time which might and ought to have been employed to spiritual and useful purposes — that is to be accounted for. For we must remember that we have a great work to do, many enemies to conquer, many evils to prevent, much danger to run through, many difficulties to be mastered, many necessities to serve, and much good to do; many children to provide for, or many friends to support, or many poor to relieve, or many diseases to cure; besides the needs of nature and of relation, our private and our public cares, and duties of the world, which necessity and the providence of God have adopted into the family of religion. ~ Jeremy Taylor (1613-1667)

DON'T LET TEMPTATIONS OVERPOWER YOU

. . .the Lord knows how to deliver the godly out of temptations. . .
—————— II Peter 2:9 NKJV ——————

If it should ever happen that through some of these temptations and your own weakness, you waver and perhaps fall into sin, and thus lose the way for a time, return as soon as possible to the right path by using such remedies as the Church ordains. Do not think of your past sins, for that will harm you and favour your enemies; but make haste to go on your way as if nothing happened. Think only of Jesus, and of your desire to gain His love, and nothing will harm you. Finally, when your enemies see that you are so determined that neither sickness, fancies, poverty, life, death, nor sins discourage you, but that you will continue to seek the love of Jesus and nothing else, by continuing your prayer and other spiritual works, they will grow enraged and will not spare you the most cruel abuse. They will make their most dangerous assault by bringing before you all your good deeds and virtues, showing that all men praise, love, and honour you for your sanctity. This they will do to make you vain and proud. But if you offer your life to Jesus you will consider all this flattery and falsehood as deadly poison to your soul, and will cast it from you. ~ Henry Suso (1296-1366)

A NEW BEGINNING

For God so loved the world, that He gave His only begotten Son, that whosoever believeth in Him should not perish, but have everlasting life.

JOHN 3:16 KJV

How glorious, then, is the blessing which every one receives that believes in the Lord Jesus. Not only does there come a change in his disposition and manner of life; he also receives from God out of heaven an entirely new life. He is born anew, born of God: he has passed from death into life. This new life is nothing less than Eternal Life. This does not mean, as many suppose, that our life shall now no more die, but shall endure into eternity. No: eternity life is nothing else than the very life of God, the life that He has had in Himself from eternity, and that has been visibly revealed in Christ. This life is now the portion of every child of God. This life is a life of inconceivable power. Whenever God gives life to a young plant or animal, that life has in itself the power of growth, whereby the plant or animal as of itself becomes large. Life is power. In the new life, that is, in your heart, there is the power of eternity. More certain than the healthful growth of any tree or animal is the growth and increase of the child of God, who in reality surrenders himself to the working of the new life. ~ Andrew Murray (1827-1917)

UNDERSTANDING GOD THROUGH OBEDIENCE

See, I have set before thee this day life and good, and death and evil;
In that I command thee this day to love the LORD thy God,
to walk in his ways, and to keep his commandments and his statutes
and his judgments, that thou mayest live and multiply:
and the LORD thy God shall bless thee in the land
whither thou goest to possess it.

DEUTERONOMY 30:15, 16 NKJV

God's revelations are sealed to us until they are opened to us by obedience. You will never get them open by philosophy or thinking. Immediately you obey, a flash of light comes. Let God's truth work in you by soaking in it, not by worrying into it. Obey God in the thing He is at present showing you, and instantly the next thing is opened up. We read tomes on the work of the Holy Spirit when ... five minutes of drastic obedience would make things clear as a sunbeam. We say, "I suppose I shall understand these things someday." You can understand them now: it is not study that does it, but obedience. The tiniest fragment of obedience, and heaven opens up and the profoundest truths of God are yours straight away. God will never reveal more truth about Himself till you obey what you know already. Beware of being wise and prudent. ~ Oswald Chambers (1874-1917)

TRUTH IS GOD'S WAY

"If you abide in My word, you are My disciples indeed."
——— JOHN 8:31 NKJV ———

The truth can neither be communicated nor be received without being as it were before the eyes of God, nor without God's help, nor without God being involved as the middle term, since he is the truth. It can therefore only be communicated by and received by "the single individual," which, for that matter, every single human being who lives could be: this is the determination of the truth in contrast to the abstract, the fantastical, impersonal, "the crowd" — "the public," which excludes God as the middle term (for the personal God cannot be the middle term in an impersonal relation), and also thereby the truth, for God is the truth and its middle term . . . It is clear that to love the neighbor is self-denial, that to love the crowd or to act as if one loved it, to make it the court of last resort for "the truth," that is the way to truly gain power, the way to all sorts of temporal and worldly advantage — yet it is untruth; for the crowd is untruth.

~ Søren Kierkegaard (1813-1855)

Now I myself am confident concerning you, my brethren, that you also are full of goodness, filled with all knowledge, able also to admonish one another. Nevertheless, brethren, I have written more boldly to you on some points, as reminding you, because of the grace given to me by God, that I might be a minister of Jesus Christ to the Gentiles, ministering the gospel of God, that the offering of the Gentiles might be acceptable, sanctified by the Holy Spirit. Therefore I have reason to glory in Christ Jesus in the things which pertain to God. For I will not dare to speak of any of those things which Christ has not accomplished through me, in word and deed, to make the Gentiles obedient—in mighty signs and wonders, by the power of the Spirit of God, so that from Jerusalem and round about to Illyricum I have fully preached the gospel of Christ. And so I have made it my aim to preach the gospel, not where Christ was named, lest I should build on another man's foundation, but as it is written: "To whom He was not announced, they shall see; And those who have not heard shall understand." For this reason I also have been much hindered from coming to you.

—— ROMANS 15:14-22 NKJV ——

STANDING FIRM

JESUS CHRIST HAS WON. . .

Finally, my brethren, be strong in the Lord,
and in the power of his might. Put on the whole armour of God,
that ye may be able to stand against the wiles of the devil.
———— EPHESIANS 6:10, 11 KJV ————

We are to "STAND," not struggle. "Having done all things, stand." The shield of FAITH is able to quench all the fiery darts of the evil one (Ephesians 6). "Faith does nothing; faith lets God do it all." the victory for us. "I live," says Paul, "yet not I, Christ LIVES IN ME." "Ye are of God," says John, "and have overcome them." How? Why? "Because greater is HE that is IN YOU, than he that is in the world" (1 John 4:4). . . . The secret of Victory is the Indwelling-Christ. Victory is in trusting, not in trying. "This is the Victory that overcometh the world"—and SIN— "even our faith" (1 John 5:4) . . . Yet all growth takes place without effort. "No man by taking thought can add one cubit to his stature," said our Lord. And this is true of our spiritual stature. ~ Unknown

AN ABUNDANCE OF LOVE

. . .He who is in you is greater than he who is in the world.
I JOHN 4:4 NKJV

Some souls, by virtue of the love that God gives them, are so cleansed that all creatures and everything they hear, or see, or feel by any of the senses, turns them to comfort and gladness; and the sensuality receives new savor and sweetness in all creatures. And just as previously the sensual appetites were carnal, vain, and corrupt, because of the pain of original sin, so now they are made spiritual and clean, without bitterness and biting of conscience. And this is the goodness of our Lord, that since the soul is punished in the sensuality, and the flesh shares the pain, that afterward the soul be comforted in the sensuality, and the flesh join in joy and comfort with the soul, not carnal, but spiritual, as it was a fellow in tribulation and pain. This is the freedom and the lordship, the dignity, and the worth that a man has over all creatures, which dignity he may so recover by grace here, that every creature appear to him as it is. And that occurs when by grace he sees, he hears, he feels only God in all creatures. In this way a soul is made spiritual in the sensuality by abundance of love, that is, in the nature of the soul. ~ Walter Hilton (-1396)

IMPORTANCE OF GOD'S LAW

Teach me to do thy will; for thou art my God . . .
——— PSALM 143:10 KJV ———

The Law is a mirror to show a person what he is like, a sinner who is guilty of death, and worthy of everlasting punishment. What is this bruising and beating by the hand of the Law to accomplish? This, that we may find the way to grace. The Law is an usher to lead the way to grace. God is the God of the humble, the miserable, the afflicted. It is His nature to exalt the humble, to comfort the sorrowing, to heal the broken-hearted, to justify the sinners, and to save the condemned. The fatuous idea that a person can be holy by himself denies God the pleasure of saving sinners. God must therefore first take the sledge-hammer of the Law in His fists and smash the beast of self-righteousness and its brood of self-confidence, self-wisdom, self-righteousness, and self-help. When the conscience has been thoroughly frightened by the Law it welcomes the Gospel of grace with its message of a Savior who came into the world, not to break the bruised reed, nor to quench the smoking flax, but to preach glad tidings to the poor, to heal the broken-hearted, and to grant forgiveness of sins to all the captives. ~ Martin Luther (1483-1546)

FAITHFUL FOLLOWERS

Write the vision And make it plain . . .

HABAKKUK 2:2 NKJV

Our supreme duty is that which we owe to God, and the next appertains to the soul. And yet these two are such loving correlates, that though every one of them is a duty of supreme consequence, and such as by no means we may presume to neglect or omit, yet cannot we possibly perform any one of them without the other. So that whosoever will serve God doth at the same time provide for his own soul; and he that is careful for his own soul doth at the same time serve God. So that the state of these two sovereign duties in man, is by a certain compendious dependency and co-intention rendered very easy, while the faithful performance of the one is a perfect consumation of both: for by the unspeakable tenderness and mercy of God, the good we do to our own souls is the most acceptable service and sacrifice that we can offer unto Him. ~ St. Eucherius of Lyons (-449)

THE BLESSING SECURED

. . .be filled with the Spirit. . .
EPHESIANS 5:18 KJV

What folly it would be for a man who had lost a lung and a half, and had hardly a quarter of a lung to do the work of two, to expect to be a strong man and to do hard work, and to live in any climate! And what folly for a man to expect to live — God has told him he cannot live — a full Christian life, unless he is full of the Holy Ghost! And what folly for a man who has only got a little drop of the river of the water of life to expect to live and to have power with God and man! Jesus wants us to come and to receive the fulfilment of the promise, "He that believeth in Me, streams of water shall flow out from him." Oh, begin to say, "If I am to live a right life, if I am in every part of my daily life and conduct to glorify my God, I must have the Holy Spirit — I must be filled with the Spirit." Are you going to say that? Talking for months and months won't help. Do submit to God, and as an act of submission say, "Lord, I confess it, I ought to be filled, I must be filled; help me!" And God will help you. ~ Andrew Murray (1828-1917)

REDEEMED, RESTORED, FORGIVEN

Redeemed, restored, forgiven, Through Jesus' precious blood,
Heirs of His home in heaven, Oh, praise our pardoning God!
Praise Him in tuneful measures Who gave His Son to die;
Praise Him whose sevenfold treasures Enrich and sanctify.
Once on the dreary mountain We wandered far and wide,
Far from the cleansing fountain, Far from the pierced side;
But Jesus sought and found us And washed our guilt away;
With cords of love He bound us To be His own for aye.
Dear Master, Thine the glory Of each recovered soul.
Ah! who can tell the story Of love that made us whole?
Not ours, not ours, the merit; Be thine alone the praise
And ours a thankful spirit To serve Thee all our days.
Now keep us, holy Savior, In Thy true love and fear
And grant us of Thy favor The grace to persevere
Till, in Thy new creation, Earth's time-long travail o'er,
We find our full salvation And praise Thee evermore.
~ Henry W. Baker (1821-1877)

But now no longer having a place in these parts, and having a great desire these many years to come to you, whenever I journey to Spain, I shall come to you. For I hope to see you on my journey, and to be helped on my way there by you, if first I may enjoy your company for a while. But now I am going to Jerusalem to minister to the saints. For it pleased those from Macedonia and Achaia to make a certain contribution for the poor among the saints who are in Jerusalem. It pleased them indeed, and they are their debtors. For if the Gentiles have been partakers of their spiritual things, their duty is also to minister to them in material things. Therefore, when I have performed this and have sealed to them this fruit, I shall go by way of you to Spain. But I know that when I come to you, I shall come in the fullness of the blessing of the gospel of Christ. Now I beg you, brethren, through the Lord Jesus Christ, and through the love of the Spirit, that you strive together with me in prayers to God for me, that I may be delivered from those in Judea who do not believe, and that my service for Jerusalem may be acceptable to the saints, that I may come to you with joy by the will of God, and may be refreshed together with you. Now the God of peace be with you all. Amen.

——————— ROMANS 15:23-33 NKJV ———————

SUFFERING

I will be glad and rejoice in thy mercy: for thou hast considered my trouble; thou hast known my soul in adversities . . .

PSALM 31:7 KJV

MEN who love God are so far from complaining of their sufferings, that their complaint and their suffering is rather because the suffering which God's will has assigned them is so small. All their blessedness is to suffer by God's will, and not to have suffered something, for this is the loss of suffering. This is why I said, Blessed are they who are willing to suffer for righteousness, not, Blessed are they who have suffered. All that a man bears for God's sake, God makes light and sweet for him. If all was right with you, your sufferings would no longer be suffering, but love and comfort. If God could have given to men anything more noble than suffering, He would have redeemed mankind with it: otherwise, you must say that my Father was my enemy, if he knew of anything nobler than suffering. True suffering is a mother of all the virtues. ~ William Ralph Inge (1860-1954)

TIME

*. . . neither shall your vine cast her fruit before the
time in the field, saith the LORD of hosts.*

—————— MALACHI 3:11 KJV ——————

It seems that most believers have difficulty in realizing and facing up to the inexorable fact that God does not hurry in His development of our Christian life. He is working from and for eternity! So many feel they are not making progress unless they are swiftly and constantly forging ahead. Now it is true that the new convert often begins and continues for some time at a fast rate. But this will not continue if there is to be healthy growth and ultimate maturity. God himself will modify the pace. This is important to see, since in most instances when seeming declension begins to set in, it is not, as so many think, a matter of backsliding. John Darby makes it plain that "it is God's way to set people aside after their first start, that self-confidence may die down. Thus Moses was forty years. On his first start he had to run away. Paul was three years also, after his first testimony. Not that God did not approve the first earnest testimony. We must get to know ourselves and that we have no strength. Thus we must learn, and then leaning on the Lord we can with more maturity, and more experientially, deal with souls." ~ Miles Stanford (1914-1999)

ABIDING COMFORTER

. . .give unto them beauty for ashes, the oil of joy for mourning,
the garment of praise for the spirit of heaviness;
that they might be called trees of righteousness,
the planting of the LORD, that he might be glorified.

ISAIAH 61:3 KJV

If I am walking along the street with a very disfiguring hole in the back of my dress . . . it is certainly a very great comfort to me to have a kind friend who will tell me of it. And similarly it is indeed a comfort to know that there is always abiding with me a divine, all seeing Comforter, who will reprove me for all my faults, and will not let me go on in a fatal unconsciousness of them . . . it is far more to a man's interest that he should see his own faults than that anyone else should see them, and a moment's thought will convince us that this is true, and will make us thankful for the Comforter who reveals them to us. I remember vividly the comfort it used to be to me, when I was young, to have a sister who always . . . kept me in order . . . I was always made comfortable, and not uncomfortable, by her presence. But when it chanced that I went anywhere alone, then I would indeed feel uncomfortable . . . The declaration is that He "comforts all our waste places;" and He does this by revealing them to us, and at the same time showing us how He can make our "wildernesses like Eden," and our "deserts like the garden of the Lord." ~ Hannah Whitall Smith (1832-1911)

CHRIST: THE HEAD OF THE CHURCH AND SOURCE OF ITS AUTHORITY

And there are differences of administrations, but the same Lord.

———— I CORINTHIANS 12:5 KJV ————

He rules the Church, not by force, but by His Word and Spirit. All human officers in the Church are clothed with the authority of Christ and must submit to the control of His Word . . . The power of the Church is spiritual, because it is given by the Holy Spirit, is a manifestation of the power of the Spirit, pertains exclusively to believers, and can be exercised only in a spiritual way. It is also a purely ministerial power, which is derived from Christ and is exercised in His name. God is a God of order, who desires that all things in the Church be done decently and in order. For that reason He made provision for the proper regulation of the affairs of the Church, and gave the Church power to carry the laws of Christ into effect. Colossians 1:18 "And He is the head of the body, the Church: who is the beginning, the firstborn from the dead; that in all things He might have the preeminence."
~ Louis Berkoff (1809-1833)

AM I A SOLDER OF THE CROSS

Watch ye, stand fast in the faith, quit you like men, be strong.
I CORINTHIANS 16:13 KJV

Am I a solder of the Cross, A foll'wer of the Lamb,
And shall I fear to own His cause Or blush to speak His name?
Must I be carried to the skies On flow'ry beds of ease
While others fought to win the prize And sailed thro' bloody seas?
Are there no foes for me to face? Must I not stem the flood?
Is this vile world a friend to grace To help me on to God?
Sure I must fight if I would reign; Increase my courage, Lord!
I'll bear the toil, endure the pain, Supported by Thy Word.
Thy saints in all this glorious war Shall conquer though they die;
They see the triumph from afar With faith's discerning eye.
When that illustrious Day shall rise And all Thine armies shine
In robes of victory through the skies, The glory shall be Thine.
~ Isaac Watts (1674-1748)

THE SOUL WINNER'S REWARD

The fruit of the righteous is a tree of life; and he that winneth souls is wise.
PROVERBS 11:30 KJV

It is far more pleasant to remember that there is a reward for bringing men to mercy, and that it is of a higher order than the premium for bringing men to justice; it is, moreover, much more within our reach, and that is a practical point worthy of our notice. We cannot all hunt down criminals, but we may all rescue the perishing. God be thanked that assassins and burglars are comparatively few, but sinners who need to be sought and saved swarm around us in every place. Here is scope for you all; and none need think himself shut out from the rewards which love bestows on all who do her service. At the mention of the word REWARD, some will prick up their ears, and mutter "legality." Yet the reward we speak of is not of debt, but of grace; and it is enjoyed, not with the proud conceit of merit, but with the grateful delight of humility . . . When we endeavor to lead men to God, we pursue a business far more profitable than the pearl fisher's diving or the diamond hunter's searching. No pursuit of mortal men is to be compared with that of soul winning. ~ Charles H. Spurgeon (1834-1892)

I commend to you Phoebe our sister, who is a servant of the church in Cenchrea, that you may receive her in the Lord in a manner worthy of the saints, and assist her in whatever business she has need of you; for indeed she has been a helper of many and of myself also. Greet Priscilla and Aquila, my fellow workers in Christ Jesus, who risked their own necks for my life, to whom not only I give thanks, but also all the churches of the Gentiles. Likewise greet the church that is in their house. Greet my beloved Epaenetus, who is the firstfruits of Achaia to Christ. Greet Mary, who labored much for us. Greet Andronicus and Junia, my countrymen and my fellow prisoners, who are of note among the apostles, who also were in Christ before me. Greet Amplias, my beloved in the Lord. Greet Urbanus, our fellow worker in Christ, and Stachys, my beloved. Greet Apelles, approved in Christ. Greet those who are of the household of Aristobulus. Greet Herodion, my countryman. Greet those who are of the household of Narcissus who are in the Lord. Greet Tryphena and Tryphosa, who have labored in the Lord. Greet the beloved Persis, who labored much in the Lord. Greet Rufus, chosen in the Lord, and his mother and mine. Greet Asyncritus, Phlegon, Hermas, Patrobas, Hermes, and the brethren who are with them. Greet Philologus and Julia, Nereus and his sister, and Olympas, and all the saints who are with them. Greet one another with a holy kiss. The churches of Christ greet you.

ROMANS 16:1-16 NKJV

STANDING FIRM

FALSE HOPE

For false Christs and false prophets shall rise and shall shew signs and wonders, to seduce, if it were possible, even the elect.
———— MARK 13:22 KJV ————

Utopias of historical progress cannot seduce those who believe in Christ. Utopias are the straws to which those cling who have no real hope; utopias are as unattractive as they are incredible, for those who know what real hope is. Utopias are not a consequence of true hope but a poor substitute for it and therefore a hindrance and not a help. The hope that is in Jesus Christ is different from all utopias of universal progress. It is based on the revelation of the crucified one. It is, therefore, not an uncertain speculation about the future but a certainty based upon what God has already revealed. One cannot believe in Jesus Christ without knowing for certain that God's victory over all powers of destruction, including death, is the end towards which the time process moves as its own end. ~ Emil Brunner (1889-1966)

WALK IN THE SPIRIT

... be filled with the Spirit ...

EPHESIANS 5:18 KJV

You will never be an overcomer until you are Spirit filled. The Bible says: "Walk in the Spirit and ye shall not fulfill the lust of the flesh" (Gal. 5:16). It is only as you are filled with the Holy Spirit that you are able to overcome your besetting sin. The Holy Spirit makes you a victorious Christian. Without His fullness you will be defeated, you will be a slave to sin. God wants to set you free. He wants to make you an overcomer. You cannot overcome yourself. Only the Holy Spirit within you can overcome. The Christian life is the outliving of the indwelling Christ. Only as He indwells in the fullness and power of the Holy Spirit will your outward life be the kind of a life it should be. Therefore, in order to have power over sin you must be filled with the Spirit. . .If you are going to be an effective witness you must be filled with the Spirit. Otherwise you will witness in the energy of the flesh and accomplish nothing. If you want your testimony to count for God, you must testify in the power of the Holy Ghost. ~ Oswald J. Smith (1889–1986)

THE SOLDIER, ATHLETE, AND FARMER

FROM II TIMOTHY 2:1-10

The soldier has the characteristics of endurance even in the face of difficulty. He ignores creature comforts and travels light. His only concern is to please and obey his Commander. He follows orders quickly. The athlete practices and submits to rigorous self-discipline. As his body cries out for rest, he beats it "into submission" in order to win. But just the training and striving are not enough to win. He must follow the rules. One step out of bounds and all is at naught. The farmer seems a less dramatic figure but his testing time is often the longest. It is only after committing his resources to death in the earth and long days of hard labor in the hot sun does he reap a harvest. He enjoys the fruit of his labor, but only after a long wait requiring patient faith. He has learned how to defer immediate gratification for long-range rewards of greater value. We need a Marine Corp: of Christians who mean business in the battle; Olympic class Christians who will not be stopped; 'plantation rancher' Christians who stick with the mighty crop. On the short term, it may appear foolish to serve the Lord at such a high level, but we will be the ones to make a difference when the weaklings, pampered, and lazy churchmen are forgotten. Recall Noah, who was feeling low as the religious crowd taunted him, but later, he was riding high! ~ John Hey (1939-)

THE WAY TO DIVINE KNOWLEDGE

According as his divine power hath given unto us all
things that pertain to life and godliness, through the
knowledge of him hath called us to glory and virtue . . .
——— II PETER 1:3 KJV ———

If Reason seems to have any Power against Religion, it is only where Religion is become a dead Form, has lost its true State, and is dwindled into Opinion; and when this is the Case, that Religion stands only as a well-grounded Opinion, then indeed it is always liable to be shaken; either by having its own Credibility lessened, or that of a contrary Opinion increased. But when Religion is that which it should be, not a Notion or Opinion, but a real Life growing up in God, then Reason has just as much power to stop its Course, as the barking Dog to stop the Course of the Moon. For true and genuine Religion is Nature, is Life, and the Working of Life; and therefore, where-ever it is, Reason has no more Power over it, than over the Roots that grow secretly in the Earth, or the Life that is working in the highest Heavens. If therefore you are afraid of Reason hurting your Religion, it is a Sign, that your Religion is not yet as it should be, is not a self-evident Growth of Nature and Life within you, but has much of mere Opinion in it.
~William Law (1686-1761)

GRACE OF GOD

. . .you heard and knew the grace of God in truth. . .
COLOSSIANS 1:6 NKJV

This grace of God is your strength, as it is your joy; and it is only by abiding in it that you can really live the life of the redeemed. Be strong, then, in this grace; draw your joy out of it; and beware how you turn to anything else for refreshment, or comfort, or holiness. Though a believing man, you are still a sinner; a sinner to the last; and, as such, nothing can suit you but the free love of God. Be strong in it. Remember that you are saved by believing, not by doubting. Be not then a doubter, but a believer. Draw continually on Christ and His fullness for this grace. If at any time you are beguiled away from it, return to it without delay; and betake yourself to it again just as you did at the first. To recover lost peace, go back to where you got it at first; begin your spiritual life all over again: get at once to the resting-place. Where sin has abounded, let grace much more abound. Do not go back to your feelings, or experiences, or evidences, in order to extract from them renewal of your lost peace. Go straight back to the free love of God. You found peace in it at first; you will find peace in it to the last. This was the beginning of your confidence; let it be both last and first.
~ F. Horatius Bonar (1808-1889)

THE MAJESTY OF GOD

I counsel thee to buy of me gold tried in the fire, that thou
mayest be rich; and white raiment that thou mayest be clothed,
and that the shame of thy nakedness do not appear;
and anoint thine eyes with eyesalve, that thou mayest see.

REVELATION 3:18 KJV

WHAT men stand most in need of, is the knowledge of God. They know, to be sure, by dint of reading, that history gives an account of a certain series of miracles and marked providences; they have reflected seriously on the corruption and instability of worldly things; they are even, perhaps, convinced that the reformation of their lives on certain principles of morality is desirable in order to their salvation; but the whole of the edifice is destitute of foundation; this pious and Christian exterior possesses no soul. The living principle which animates every true believer, God, the all and in all, the author and the sovereign of all, is wanting. ~Francois Fénélons (1651-1715)

Now I urge you, brethren, note those who cause divisions and offenses, contrary to the doctrine which you learned, and avoid them. For those who are such do not serve our Lord Jesus Christ, but their own belly, and by smooth words and flattering speech deceive the hearts of the simple. For your obedience has become known to all. Therefore I am glad on your behalf; but I want you to be wise in what is good, and simple concerning evil. And the God of peace will crush Satan under your feet shortly. The grace of our Lord Jesus Christ be with you. Amen. Timothy, my fellow worker, and Lucius, Jason, and Sosipater, my countrymen, greet you. I, Tertius, who wrote this epistle, greet you in the Lord. Gaius, my host and the host of the whole church, greets you. Erastus, the treasurer of the city, greets you, and Quartus, a brother. The grace of our Lord Jesus Christ be with you all. Amen. Now to Him who is able to establish you according to my gospel and the preaching of Jesus Christ, according to the revelation of the mystery kept secret since the world began but now has been made manifest, and by the prophetic Scriptures has been made known to all nations, according to the commandment of the everlasting God, for obedience to the faith—to God, alone wise, be glory through Jesus Christ forever. Amen.

ROMANS 16:17-27 NKJV

STANDING FIRM

THE PASSION OF CHRIST

And there followed him a great company of people,
and of women, which also bewailed and lamented him.
But Jesus turning unto them said, Daughters of Jerusalem,
weep not for me, but weep for yourselves, and for your children.
———— LUKE 23:27, 28 KJV ————

The passion of Jesus Christ, however sorrowful and ignominious it may appear to us, must nevertheless have been to Jesus Christ Himself an object of delight, since this God—man, by a wonderful secret of His wisdom and love, has willed that the mystery of it shall be continued and solemnly renewed in His Church until the final consummation of the world. For what is the Eucharist but a perpetual repetition of the Savior's passion, and what has the Savior supposed in instituting it, but that whatever passed at Calvary is not only represented but consummated on our altars? That is to say, that He is still performing the functions of the victim anew, and is every moment virtually sacrificed, as tho it were not sufficient that He should have suffered once; at least that His love, as powerful as it is free, has given to His adorable sufferings that character of perpetuity which they have in the Sacrament, and which renders them so salutary to us. Behold, Christians, what the love of God has devised. . .May He be our Savior in a blest eternity, where we shall be as much the sharer in His glory as we have been in His sufferings. ~ Louis Bourdaloue (1632-1704)

INWARD HUMILITY

The fear of the LORD is the instruction of wisdom;
and before honour is humility.

———— PROVERBS 15:33 KJV ————

O what a great Happiness is it for a Soul to be subdued and subject! what great Riches is it to be Poor! what a mighty honour to be despised! what a height is it to be beaten down! what a comfort is it to be afflicted! what a credit of knowledge is it to be reputed Ignorant! and finally, what a Happiness of Happinesses is it to be Crucified with Christ! This is that lot which the Apostle gloried in, "But God forbid that I should glory, save in the cross of our Lord Jesus Christ" Let others boast in their Riches, Dignities, Delights and Honours; but to us there is no higher honour, than to be denied, despised and crucified with Christ. But what a grief is this, that scarce is there one Soul which despises spiritual pleasures and is willing to be denied for Christ, imbracing his Cross with love, "For many are called, but few are chosen." (Matt. 22:14) says the Holy Ghost: many are they who are call'd to perfection, but few are they that arrive at it: because they are few who imbrace the Cross with patience, constancy, peace and resignation.

~ Miguel de Molinos (1628-1696)

STANDING FIRM

MAKING LIGHT OF CHRIST AND SALVATION: GOD FORBID!

But they made light of it, and went their ways...
———— MATTHEW 22:5 KJV ————

The things that we value do deeply affect us, and some motions will be in the heart according to our estimation of them. Oh sirs, if men made not light of these things, what working would there be in the hearts of all our hearers! What strange affections would it raise in them to hear of the matters of the world to come! How would their hearts melt before the power of the gospel! What sorrow would be wrought in the discovery of their sins! What astonishment at the consideration of their misery! What unspeakable joy at the glad tidings of salvation by the blood of Christ! What resolution would be raised in them upon the discovery of their duty! Oh, what hearers should we have, if it were not for this sin! Whereas now we are liker to weary them, or preach them asleep with matters of this unspeakable moment. We talk to them of Christ and salvation till we make their heads ache: little would one think by their careless carriage that they heard and regarded what we said, or tho we spoke at all to them. You that can not make light of a little sickness or want, or of natural death, no, not of a toothache, but groan as if you were undone; how will you then make light of the fury of the Lord, which will burn against the contemners of His grace! Doth it not behoove you beforehand to think of these things?

~ Richard Baxter (1615-1691)

A RIGHT HEART
PRODUCES RIGHT ACTIONS

I will behave myself wisely in a perfect way.
PSALM 101:2 KJV

It is indeed a most lamentable consequence of the practice of regarding religion as a compilation of statutes, and not as an internal principle, that it soon comes to be considered as being conversant about external actions rather than about habits of mind. This sentiment sometimes has even the hardiness to insinuate and maintain itself under the guise of extraordinary concern for practical religion; but it soon discovers the falsehood of this pretension, and betrays its real nature. The expedient, indeed, of attaining to superiority in practice by not wasting any of the attention on the internal principles from which alone practice can flow, is about as reasonable, and will answer about as well, as the economy of an architect who should account it mere prodigality to expend any of his materials in laying foundation, from an idea that they might be more usefully applied to the raising of the superstructure. We know what would be the fate of such an edifice. ~William Wilberforce (1759-1833)

SOWING THE TARES

Be not deceived; God is not mocked:
for whatsoever a man soweth,
that shall he also reap.

GALATIANS 6:7 KJV

When I was at the Paris Exhibition in 1867 I noticed there a little oil painting, only about a foot square, and the face was the most hideous I had ever seen. It was said to be about seven hundred years old. On the paper attached to the painting were the words, "Sowing the tares." The face looked more like a demon's than a man's, and as he sowed these tares, up came serpents and reptiles. They were crawling up on his body; and all around were woods with wolves and animals prowling in them. I have seen that picture many times since. Ah! The reaping time is coming. If you sow to the flesh you must reap corruption. If you sow to the wind you must reap the whirlwind. God wants you to come to him and receive salvation as a gift. You can decide your destiny today if you will. Heaven and hell are set before this audience, and you are called upon to choose. Which will you have? If you will take Christ He will receive you to his arms; if you reject him He will reject you. Now, my friends, will Christ ever be more willing to save you than He is now? Will He ever have more power than He has now? Why not make up your mind to be saved while mercy is offered to you?
~ Dwight L. Moody (1837-1899)

FREEDOM IN CHRIST

. . . the truth shall make you free. . .

JOHN 8:32 KJV

Christian freedom, in my opinion, consists of three parts. The first: that the consciences of believers, in seeking assurance of their justification before God, should rise above and advance beyond the law, forgetting all law righteousness... The second part, dependent upon the first, is that consciences observe the law, not as if constrained by the necessity of the law, but that freed from the law's yoke they willingly obey God's will... The third part of Christian freedom lies in this: regarding outward things that are of themselves "indifferent", we are not bound before God by any religious obligation preventing us from sometimes using them and other times not using them, indifferently... Accordingly, it is perversely interpreted both by those who allege it as an excuse for their desires that they may abuse God's good gifts to their own lust and by those who think that freedom does not exist unless it is used before men, and consequently, in using it have no regard for weaker brethren... Nothing is plainer than this rule: that we should use our freedom if it results in the edification of our neighbor, but if it does not help our neighbor, then we should forego it.

~ John Calvin (1509-1564)

CHALLENGE TO STAND FIRM

As we move into this new millennium, it appears that the issues we face as believers in the Lord Jesus Christ are ever changing and yet the challenge of the Apostle Paul rings as true today as ever. He exhorted the Christians in Corinth that in light of the resurrection of the Lord Jesus they are to stand firm, let nothing move them and always give themselves fully to the work of the Lord because they know their labor in the Lord is not in vain or empty. If there was ever a time in the history of the church for steadfastness, the need is today. We must be people of the Word of God, standing firm on its teachings, not being moved away from it by accusations of intolerance or political correctness. We need to be like people of old spending great amounts of time memorizing and meditating on the Scriptures, rather than captivated with reality television, situation comedies, and the endless number of sports extravaganzas. For our labor to not be empty or in vain, we need to do it by the Book. God's Word is clear and His expectations for us are understandable. The question is whether we will have the hunger for the Word created by the Holy Spirit or will we be satisfied to munch on the morsels of worldly and fleshly appetites. Will we cry out to God and ask Him to create an insatiable hunger to know Him and His Word? It is only by the sustaining work of the Holy Spirit using His Word that we can stand firm, not be moved, and give ourselves fully to the work of the Lord. May it be so in each of our lives. ~ David C. King (1943-)

PUBLIC DOMAIN

St. Thomas Aquinas (1225-1274) Born in Aquino, Italy and represents the pinnacle of the philosophical and theological school that flourished between 1100 and 1500 and attempted to reconcile faith with reason and the works of Aristotle with the scriptures. Received Th.M in Paris, France.

St. Augustine (345-440) A theologian of the early Christian church. Author of *The Confessions* and *The City of God*. St. Augustine, FL is named for him.

Henry W. Baker (1821-1877) Born at Belmont House, Vauxhall, Surrey, England. He attended Trinity College at Cambridge, was ordained in 1844, and became assistant curate at Great Hockesley, near Colchester, Essex. In 1851, he became Vicar of Monkland Priory Church in Herefordshire, England. He was editor-in-chief of the *Anglican Hymns Ancient and Modern*, and contributed hymns, tunes, and translations.

Raymond V. Banner (1937-) Graduated from Grace Bible Institute, Bob Jones University, and Dallas Seminary and lives in Mount Ayr, Iowa.

Richard Baxter (1615-1691) Was ordained in 1638 on the eve of the English Revolution. In 1640, the year the Long Parliament assembled, he agreed with those who wished to abolish a prelatical episcopacy. Baxter refused to conform to the Restoration church and suffered fines and imprisonment for his obstinacy. Despite the fact that he never occupied an important post, Baxter was an important leader during the Commonwealth and Restoration periods.

Louis Berkoff (1809-1833) Fundamentalist. Writer of Systematic Theology offered today in many seminaries.

F. Horatius Bonar (1808-1889) Born in Edinburgh. Member of the Free Church of Scotland. Ordained minister and pastored Chalmers Memorial Church in Edinburgh. Best known for his songs and poems.

Thomas Boston (1677-1732) Born in Duns, Berwickshire; read arts and divinity at Edinburgh; Ordained minister. An English Puritan.

William Booth (1829-1912) Founder of the Salvation Army. Born in Nottingham, England. He was converted to Christ through the efforts of a Methodist minister, and soon became interested in working with the outcasts and the poor people of Nottingham. He preached on the streets and made hundreds of hospital calls before he was 20 years of age. From 1850 to 1861 he served as a pastor in the Methodist Church, after which time he and his wife left the church and stepped out by faith in evangelistic work in East London.

Edward M. Bounds (1835-1913) Lawyer, Faithful Pastor, Army Chaplain, Devotional Writer, Beloved Husband-Father, Powerful Preacher and a Man of Fervent Prayer.

Louis Bourdaloue (1632-1704) Member of the Jesuit order; Professor of rhetoric and theology; Court Preacher in 1670; acquired fame as a Pulpit Orator unrivaled in his time.

Matthew Bridges (1800-1894) Hymn writer. The Friars, Maldon, Essex, England. Though raised as an Anglican, Bridges converted to Roman Catholicism in 1848. He lived in Quebec, Canada, for some years, but eventually returned to England.

Emil Brunner (1889-1966) Teacher Unsurpassed. Referred to as "divine-human encounter," or "man in revolt," or "the divine imperative."

John Bunyan (1628-1688) The most popular religious writer in the English language. He enjoyed peace and a cheerful confidence in the mercy of God.

Jeremiah Burroughs (1599-1646) Graduate of Emmanuel College, Cambridge, and the 'teacher' of an English congregation in Rotterdam. After his return from exile in 1641 he became 'Gospel preacher' to 'two of the greatest congregations in England, viz: Stepney and Cripplegate' (London). Belonged to the front rank of English puritan preachers and played a prominent part in the Westminster Assembly of divines.

John Calvin (1509-1564) French reformer and theologian. One of the most important figures of the Reformation. Studied the ideas of Luther and moved into the Protestant camp by 1533. On November 1 of that year, he delivered a speech in which he attacked the established church and called for reforms.

George Washington Carver (1860-1943) Educator, Agricultural/Food Scientist, Farmer. Born a slave. Managed to obtain a high school education. Admitted as the first black student of Simpson College, Indianola, Iowa. Attended Iowa Agricultural College (now Iowa State University) where, while working as the school janitor, he received a degree in agricultural science. Had a post at Tuskegee.

Oswald Chambers (1874-1917) Scottish Baptist minister converted under Spurgeon's ministry. He stressed availability to God.

Gilbert K. Chesterton (1874-1936) One of the finest writers of the 20th century. His book, The Everlasting Man, led atheist C.S. Lewis to become a Christian.

Saint Bernard of Clairvaux (1090-1153) One of the most commanding Church leaders and greatest spiritual masters of all times. Also a powerful propagator of the Cistercian reform.

Charles Coffin (1676-1749) Wrote "The Advent of Our King" and over 100 hymns. Principal of the college at Beauvais. 1718-Rector of the University of Paris. In 1727, he published some of his Latin poems, and in 1736, the bulk of his hymns appeared in the Paris Breviary and Hymni Sacri Auctore Carolo Coffin.

Fanny J. Crosby (1820-1915) Hymn writer whose sacred songs are sung wherever the English language is spoken.

A.C. Dixon (1854-1925) Wake Forest College and Southern Baptist Theological Seminary. In 1906, he accepted the pulpit of the Chicago Avenue Church (Moody Memorial Church) and he spent the war years ministering at Spurgeon's Tabernacle in London.

Henry Drummond (1851-1897) Born in Scotland, a gifted evangelist who assisted Dwight L. Moody during his revival campaigns. Theological writer, revivalist, explorer, geologist, ordained minister and a professor of theology.

George Duffield (1818-1888) Hymnologist. Graduated from Yale University and Union Theological Seminary. Ordained Presbyterian minister.

Johannes Eckhart (1260-1327) German Dominican philosopher.

Jonathan Edwards (1703-1758) One of the greatest preachers and churchmen in American history, was born in East Windsor. Entering Yale at the age of thirteen, Edwards graduated at the head of his class. Credited with bringing about the first Great Awakening of American history, beginning in 1734.

Francois Fenelons (1651-1715) French. Christian Counsel from a 300 year old writing.

Charles G. Finney (1792-1875) A master at presenting the intricacies of a Systematic Theology. A Voice from the Philadelphian Church Age.

John Flavel (1630-1691) Born at Bromsgrove in Worcestershire. Puritan theologian. English Presbyterian.

George Fox (1624-1691) Born in Fenny Drayton, Leicestershire. Founder of the Society of Friends (Quakers) University College, Oxford. Ordained minister. Leonard Ravenhill referred to Fox as "The Unshakable Shaker."

Theodorus J. Frelinghuysen (1691-1748) Born in West Friesland: After receiving a thorough classical education, he began the study of theology, was ordained to the ministry in the Reformed Dutch Church.

William Gurnall (1617-1679) Emanuel College, Pastor of the Church of Christ, Lavenham, Suffolk.

Jeanne Marie Vouvier de la Mothe Guyon (1647-1711) Born at Montargis. Madame Guyon was arrested in 1695 for teaching heresy and spent 6 years in prison.

Matthew Henry (1662-1714) Welsh-born, English nonconformist minister and Bible commentator. He is remembered for his practical and devotional multi-volume Exposition of the Old and New Testaments which is still published.

Dick Hillis (1913-) Founded OC International, an organization that places missionaries and workers throughout Asia.

Walter Hilton (-1396) English mystic. An innovator. Hilton urged holiness.

Charles Hodge (1797-1887) Taught at Princeton Seminary for nearly 60 years.

Thomas Hooker (1586-1647) Was born in July of 1586 in Marfield, Leicestershire, England. Educated at Queens College, Cambridge, and Emmanuel College, graduating with a BA in 1608 and an MA in 1611. Rector, lecturer, and minister. Cotton Mather called him "the Light of the Western Churches."

William Ralph Inge (1860-1954) Anglican Platonist author. Ordained Deacon. Educated at Eton College and King's College, Cambridge. Professor of divinity at Jesus College, Cambridge. In 1911, he was chosen to be the Dean of St. Paul's Cathedral in London. He was a columnist for 25 years for the *Evening Standard* and a trustee of London's National Portrait Gallery.

Samuel Johnson (1709-1784) Next only to William Shakespeare is perhaps the most quoted of English writers. Born in Lichfield, Staffordshire. He was deaf in the left ear, almost blind in the left eye, and dim of vision in the right eye. He responded to his disabilities by a fierce determination to be independent and to accept help and pity from no one.

St. John of the Cross (1542-1591) Mystical doctor and founder of the Discalced Carmelites.

Thomas Kelly (1769-1854) Well known conservative inspirational hymn writer.

Thomas à Kempis (1380-1471) born in Kempen in the duchy of Cleves in Germany. Educated by a religious order called the Brethren of the Common Life, and in due course joined the order, was ordained a priest, became sub-prior of his house (in the low Countries). Composed and compiled The Imitation of Christ.

Søren Kierkegaard (1813-1855) Danish existentialist philosopher. Born in Copenhagen. Profound and prolific writer in the Danish " golden age." Educated at a prestigious boys' school (Borgedydskolen), then attended Copenhagen University where he studied philosophy and theology.

Abraham Kuyper (1837-1920) Pastor, theologian, scholar, journalist, educator and statesman. Founded the Antirevolutionary Party, the first Dutch political party and the first Christian Democratic party in the world. Established the Free University, a Christian university established on Reformed principles. Elected to the Second Chamber of the Dutch Parliament and served as Prime Minister.

G.H. Lang (1874-1958) A Plymouth Brethren writer; a man of uncommon spirituality. His life was devoted to the study of God's Word.

Brother Lawrence (1610-1691) Born Nicholas Herman in Herimenil, Lorraine, a Duchy of France. Saved at age 18. Author of *The Practice of the Presence of God*.

C. S. Lewis (1898-1963) Anglican professor at both Oxford and Cambridge. He held to the orthoxdox Christian faith and remains perhaps the greatest of the recent apologists.

Abraham Lincoln (1809-1865) Hodgenville, Kentucky, little formal schooling. Self-educated, elected to the Illinois House of Representatives. Admitted to the bar in 1836. Became Vice-Presidential candidate for the (new) Republic Party in 1856 and was elected 16th President of the United States. Lincoln's slave emancipation principles led to the civil war between the North and the South in 1861.

David Livingstone (1813-1873) African Explorer. A curious combination of missionary, doctor, explorer, scientist and anti-slavery activist. Received a gold medal from the London Royal Geographical for being the first to cross the entire African Continent from west to east.

Martin Luther (1483-1546) Born in Eisleben. He attended school in Mansfeld, Magdeburg, Eisenach and Erfurt to become a lawyer. However, he decided to enter the Augustinian monastery in Erfurt. This decision culminated in the development of the Reformation of the Church.

St. Eucherius of Lyons (-449) Bishop of Lyons and ascetic author. Theologian.

George MacDonald (1824-1905) Scottish novelist and poet. Educated at university in Aberdeen, and Highbury College. A Congregational minister. Famous writer of youth and adult books.

Charles Henry Mackintosh (1820-1896) in business in Limerick, in 1844 he opened a school at Westport, undertaking the educational work with enthusiasm. He was active in the Irish Revival of 1859-1869.

Alexander Maclaren (1826-1919) Expository minister. Next to Spurgeon's, this Scottish preacher's sermons have been the most widely read of their time.

L.E. Maxwell (1895-1984) Founded Prairie Bible Institute in Three Hills, Alberta, Canada, in 1922. He was a professor, principal, and president and a prolific author.

Robert Murray McCheyne (1813-1843) His seven year ministry attracted great crowds.

F.B. Meyer (1847-1929) Baptist Ambassador for Keswick holiness spirituality. One of the most prominent English Baptist ministers.

Miguel de Molinos (1628-1696) Born in Muniesa, Spain. Spanish quietist. Ordained minister. In 1675, he published his *Spiritual Guide*, a small handbook teaching that Christian perfection is achieved by a mixture of contemplation.

G. Campbell Morgan (1898-1945) Perhaps the finest expository preacher of the first half of the 20th century. He began preaching at the age of 13.

Dwight L. Moody (1837-1899) Dispensational evangelist who was highly successful in Europe and America. Founder of the Moody Bible Institute.

George Muller (1805-1898) Prussian-born English evangelist and philanthropist. A man of faith and prayer, he established orphanages in Bristol and founded the Scriptural Knowledge Institution for Home and Abroad. Was a divinity student at the University of Halle which qualified him to preach in the Lutheran state church.

Andrew Murray (1828-1917) Born in a Dutch Reformed parsonage in Graaff Reinet, South Africa. It was here that his father, the Rev. Andrew Murray, Sr. was ministering to the Dutch settlers. Such men as David Livingstone and Robert Moffat frequently passed through their home on their way to the coast.

Watchman Nee (1903-1972) Born in Swatow, Fukien province, China in 1903. He was converted at the age of 17. Arrested and imprisoned for his faith by the Communists and died in prison in 1972.

John Henry Newman (1801-1890) Born in London, raised with bible religion, Newman experienced conversion at fifteen. He studied at Trinity College, Oxford, and ordained an Anglican priest, he became vicar of the university church, St. Mary the Virgin. Became leader of the Oxford Movement in England.

John Newton (1725-1807) After a reckless childhood and young adulthood, he was converted and studied Hebrew and Greek with Whitefield, Wesley, and the Nonconformists. He was eventually ordained, and became curate at Olney, Buckinghamshire, in 1764.

John Owen (1616-1683) Theologian. Was born of Puritan parents at Stadham in Oxfordshire. Admitted at age 12 to Queen's College, Oxford, where he took his B.A. and M.A.

Blaise Pascal (1623-1662) French theologian, mathematician, and philosopher.

Jessie Penn-Lewis (1861-1927) Helped launch the Keswick Convention that led to the great Welsh Revival, which was a key event in emerging Pentecostalism.

Edward Perronet (1726-1792) Moravian minister. He was one of the editors of the Brethren's German hymn book, published in 1566, to which he contributed many hymns.

Herbert Petrus (1530-1571) a Moravian minister, was ordained in 1562.

Folliott S. Pierpont (1835-1917) Born at Spa Villa, Bath, England, and was educated at Queen's College.

Arthur T. Pierson (1837-1911) Philadelphian Church Era. Preached over 13,000 sermons, wrote over fifty books and Bible lectures. Consulting editor for the *Scofield Reference Bible*, and was the author of the classic biography, *George Muller of Bristol*.

Leonard Ravenhill (1925-1994) Leonard Ravenhill was one of Britain's foremost outdoor evangelists of the 20th century.

Alan Redpath (1907-) Newcastle-upon-Tyne, United Kingdom. Accountant with Imperial Chemical Industries. In 1936, joined National Young Life Campaign until 1940 when he became pastor of Duke Street Baptist Church, Richmond, London, until 1953, when he came pastor of Moody Memorial Church in Chicago.

Samuel Rutherford (1600-1661) Scottish Presbyterian divine. Attended the University of Edinburgh and was Professor of Philosophy in that University. One of the Scots commissioned, appointed in 1643 to the Westminster Assembly.

John of Ruysbroeck (1293-1381) Flemish mystic with a religious education including considerable training in theology and philosophy.

J.C. Ryle (1816-1900) First bishop of Liverpool and the Anglican evangelical leader of the 19th century.

Philip Schaff (1819-1893) German-American theologian and church historian.

Cyriacus Schneegass (1546-1597) Born in Buffleben Germany. Graduated with an M.A. from the University of Jena. Pastor of the St. Blasius church at Friedrichroda. Also adjunct to the Superintendent of Weimar, and signed the Formula of Concord in 1579.

Joseph Scriven (1819-1886) Born at Ballymoney Lodge, Banbridge. His Baptismal entry is recorded in Seapatrick Parish Church, Banbridge. B.A. degree at Trinity College, Dublin. Cadet at the Military College, Addiscombe.

Dean Sherman (1945 -) Central Bible College, Spring Field, Missouri. Dean of College of Christian Ministries of the University of the Nations, Kailua-Kona, Hawaii. Founded YWAN in Australia, and helped found YWAM in New Zealand and Fiji. Married to Michelle; two grown married children serving the Lord in missions. One granddaughter.

A.B. Simpson (1844-1919) Founder of the Christian and Missionary Alliance and wrote 70 books on Christian living.

Hannah Whitall Smith (1832-1911) Arminian evangelical; wife of popular evangelist Robert Pearsall Smith. Taught the joy of Christ throughout a difficult life.

Oswald J. Smith (1889-1986) A Canadian pastor and evangelist.

Robert South (1638-1716) Born in the borough of Hackney, London, England, in 1638, South attracted wide attention by his vigorous mind and his clear, argumentative style in preaching.

Austin T. Sparks (1888-1971) London, England. Educated in both England and Scotland. At the age of 25 he was ordained as a pastor.

Charles Haddon Spurgeon (1834-1892) Born in Kelvedon, Essex. Became a Baptist pastor at the New Park Street Chapel and later the Metropolitan Tabernacle in London at age 20. In 1887, Spurgeon left the Baptist Union because no action was taken against people in the church charged with fundamental errors.

James Stalker (1848-1927) Scottish preacher. More widely known in America than any other Scottish preacher of his day. Spent twenty of his later years as a professor.

Miles Joseph Stanford (1914-1999) Writer of Christian materials. Outspoken proponent on the subjects of Dispensationalism and the Growth Truths of Romans 6-8.

James S. Stewart (1822-1894) Baptist minister. County Judge of Rowan County.

Henry Suso (1296-1366) German mystic. Theology student of Meister Eckhart in Cologne. Noted preacher in Switzerland and the area of the Upper Rhine.

Jeremy Taylor (1613-1667) Cambridge, England. Anglican bishop. Educated at Caius College in Cambridge and a fellow of All Souls College in Oxford; rector of Uppingham, Rutlandshire. He ran a school in Wales and served as chaplain to the Earl of Carberry at Golden Grove, Carmathenshire. Preached in Lisburn and Portmore. Bishop of Down and Connor in January and a member of the Irish Privy Council; entrusted with the diocese of Dromore; and was Vice Chancellor of the University of Dublin.

John Tillotson (1630-1694) Chaplain to Charles II and a prominant preacher of his age. Was appointed Archbiship of Canterbury 1691.

R.A. Torrey (1856-1928) Is to Bible exposition what C. S. Lewis is to Christian philosophy. Successor to D. L. Moody's ministry upon Moody's death.

A.W. Tozer (1897-1963) Arminian fundamentalist pastor in the Christian and Missionary Alliance, which grew out of the late-19th-century Holiness movement.

Thomas Traherne (1636-1674) Born in Hereford, England. English metaphysical poet and writer. Educated at the University of Oxford and ordained as an Anglican clergyman.

Henry Wace (1836-1924) Dean of Canterbury.

B.B. Warfield (1851-1921) Born in 'Grasmere' near Lexington, Kentucky. Surrendered to the ministry at age 21, entering Princeton Seminary for his training. Succeeded A.A. Hodge as a professor of Theology at Princeton, a post he occupied for over 33 years.

Anna Laetitia Waring (1823-1910) Born in Neith, Glamorganshire, Wales. Her most widely known hymns are: "Father, I know that all my life," "Go not far from me, O my Strength," and "My heart is resting, O my God."

Thomas Watson (1620-1686) One of the most popular preachers in London during the Puritan era.

Isaac Watts (1674-1748) Augustan; Southampton grammar school under John Pinhorne Academy at Stoke Newington: 1690; D.D., University of Edinburgh.

Charles Wesley (1707-1788) Westminster school: Christ Church, B.A. from Oxford, Christ Church, Oxford (M.A.) Ordained minister. Cofounder of Methodism and arguably the greatest hymn writer ever.

John Wesley (1703-1791) Anglican clergyman, evangelist, and cofounder of Methodism. Graduated from Oxford University and became a priest in the Church of England. Participated in a religious study group in Oxford organized by his brother Charles; its members being dubbed the "Methodists" for their emphasis on methodical study and devotion.

George Whitefield (1714-1770) Post Reformation. Born in Gloucester. Entered Pembroke College, Oxford at age 18. Member of a religious group known as the Holy Club or the Oxford Methodists that included John and Charles Wesley.

Smith Wigglesworth (1859-1947) In 1907, he received the baptism in the Holy Ghost, which changed his life forever. Smith Wigglesworth's ministry centered on salvation for the unconverted, healing for the sick, and a call to believers to be baptized in the Holy Ghost.

William Wilberforce (1759-1833) Hailed as a 'Renewer of Society,' was the conscience of Parliament. Educated at St John's College, Cambridge. Elected to the House of Commons from Hull and Yorkshire. Became an Evangelical Christian.

Biography Sketch and Permission given
by the following authors to J. Countryman to use quotes:

V. Gilbert Beers (1928-) lives in Elgin, Illinois. Author of more than 150 books and contributor to six study Bibles. AB, Wheaton College; MRE, M Div, Th.M, and ThD Northern Baptist Theological Seminary; Ph D, Northwestern University.

Joyce Carpenter (1931-) Raised in China to missionary parents, married and mother of four grown children all in the faith. Served with doctor husband as medical missionaries to Indonesia. Actively involved in church and community organizations. Bible teacher and public speaker. B.S. from Louisiana Baptist College.

Randy Cordell (1954-) Pastor of Lakeshore Christian Church, Nashville, TN. Graduate of Atlanta Christian College, studied at University of Georgia, West Georgia College, and currently enrolled in the Beeson Institute for Advanced Church Leadership.

Liz Curtis Higgs (1954-) Award-winning speaker; author of twenty books with more than two million copies in print. Lives with husband, Bill, and their two children in Louisville, Kentucky. "Excerpted from Unveiling Mary Magdalene by Liz Curtis Higgs, copyright 2001, published by WaterBrook Press."

John Hey (1939-) Served in Army in Vietnam. Married to Nora. Practices medicine in Greenwood, Mississippi. Helped fund and pastor Grace Bible Church. Active on several missionary and other Christian organizations. Four grown children all in the faith. Fellow, American Academy of Family Physicians. Diploma of the American Board of Family Practice.

David King (1943-) Emmaus Bible College Diploma; BS Trevecca Nazarene University; MS Vanderbilt University; Teacher/Administrator for over 30 years. Nashville, Tennessee.

Danny Lehmann (1954-) International teacher and speaker. Director of The Youth With A Mission base in Honolulu, Hawaii. Permission is granted to use quotes from *Before You Hit the Wall*, *Stoked*, and *Beautiful Feet* by Danny Lehmann. He and wife, Linda, have two grown sons, both serving the Lord, and one grandchild.

Martyn Lloyd-Jones (1899-1981) Minister of Westminster Chapel in London for 30 years, was one of the foremost preachers of his day. He wrote many books that have brought profound spiritual encouragement to millions around the world. His Crossway titles include the three-volume *Great Doctrines of the Bible series*, *The Cross*, and *Revival*. Special permission granted by Crossway Books to use quotes.

Robert McFarland (1939-) Director of Development, Covington Theological Seminary, Chattanooga, TN. Tennessee Temple University–Graduate of Theology; Covington Theological Seminary, Th.M. and Doctor of Ministry in Pastoral Studies.

Kenneth Mick (1938-) Graduated Columbia Bible College. Pastor and biblical counselor. Married to Betty and rejoices in five children and eighteen grandchildren. Currently pasturing Midway Baptist Church, Lewes, Delaware.

Jacquelyn Sheppard (1943-) Educator, Counselor and Bible Teacher, and international speaker. Minister's wife and mother of three missionary children.

STANDING FIRM

Glenn Sheppard (1943-) M. Div. Southern Seminary; B.A. Valdosta State University; Ordained Southern Baptist Minister. Pastor twenty-two years; Founding Director of the Office of Prayer for Spiritual Awakening for North American Mission Board of the Southern Baptist Convention; Founder and President of International Prayer Ministry; Founding member of American National Prayer Committee; Former Senior Associate for Prayer for Lausane Committee. Father of three grown children, all serving on foreign mission fields.

Permission given to use quotes by J. Countryman

Richard W. De Haan (1923-2002) Was President of RBC Ministries and teacher on RBC programs for 20 years. He was the son of RBC founder Dr. M. R. De Haan, and wrote a number of full-length books and study booklets for RBC. Richard went to be with the Lord in 2002. He leaves his wife, Marge, and four sons and 13 grandchildren.

Catherine Marshall (1914-1983) Born in Tennessee. Married Presbyterian minister and Chaplain of the U.S. Senate, Peter Marshall, who died of a heart attack in 1949. Mrs. Marshall wrote a biogrpahy of her late husband, *A Man Called Peter*, in 1951, a book which became extremely popular. She followed this early success with numerous devotional books and three novels, two of which, *Christy* and *Julie*, became bestsellers. Ten years after her first husband's death, Marshall remarried, this time to Leonard LeSourd, editor of *Guideposts*.

For additions, deletions, corrections, or clarifications
in future editions of this text, please contact Paul Shepherd,
Senior Acquisitions and Development Editor for Elm Hill Books.
Email *pshepherd@elmhillbooks.com*.